Contents

Conceived and directed by:
The Commonwealth Games Consortium Ltd
17 Abercromby Place,
EDINBURGH EH3 6LT
Telephone: 031-225 8686

General Editor: Peter Matthews
Assistant Editor: Stan Greenberg
Designer: Paul Mellows-Facer
Production Editor: Christopher Proudlove

Production by Norton Opax plc Group of Companies
Colour Separation by Lund Humphries Ltd
Typeset by Opax Publishing Ltd
Printed and Bound by Lund Humphries Ltd

Published for the Commonwealth Games Consortium by:
Opax Publishing Ltd
Opax House, Primrose Hill
Preston, Lancashire, England

The majority of colour illustrations, except where otherwise noted, are by:
**All-Sport Photographic Ltd,
All-Sport House, Greenlea Park, Prince George's Road, London SW19 2JD.**

Acknowledgements also to: Associated Sports Photography, The Photo Source, Syndication International Ltd, Photo Library International, Sporting Pictures UK, Colorsport, Peter Hicks, Jon Clift, Stan Greenberg, Robin Ward, The Scottish Tourist Board.

All proceeds from the sale of this book will go to the Commonwealth Games (Scotland) 1986.

BUCKINGHAM PALACE

The Commonwealth Games are unique. They are neither regional nor ethnic nor religious. Apart from the fact that all the participating countries are members of the Commonwealth, the great thing that most participants have in common is the ability to communicate with each other in the same language.

Teams from countries and territories of all sizes take part and the most enthusiastic ovations are always reserved for athletes from the smallest teams. Unlike so many international sporting events, the Commonwealth Games are more like a family festival.

I have attended every Commonwealth Games since 1954 and I can predict with confidence that all competitors, officials and spectators will thoroughly enjoy the experience.

Edinburgh has had previous experience of organising the Games and if the success of the IXth Games in 1970 is any criterion, the 1986 Games have every chance of being a major triumph.

Philip

President
Commonwealth Games Federation

GORDON'S
DRY GIN
IMPORTED
FROM ENGLAND

Distillers
The Athletics Sponsor of the XIII Commonwealth Games

Even before the start of the XIII Commonwealth Games a record has been created in that for the second time Edinburgh has been selected as the Host City and Scotland the country in which the Games will take place.

The term 'Friendly Games' was invented in 1970 because of the spirit of goodwill which was engendered at that time.

Another record will be the number of countries who have accepted the invitation and the number of competitors who will take part. The 1986 Commonwealth Games will be the biggest ever.

As Chairman of the Organising Committee, I am particularly pleased that this is the case as it proves that the voluntary association of Commonwealth nations is not only increasing in number but in their desire to meet and get to know each other better.

Although we will all enjoy the sporting competition, the overriding purpose is to break down barriers and meet together as a united Commonwealth of Nations.

Ken Borthwick

KENNETH W. BORTHWICK, C.B.E., D.L., O.St.J., J.P.
Chairman
XIII Commonwealth Games Organising Committee

XIII COMMONWEALTH GAMES
SCOTLAND 1986
BHS

As Lord Provost of the City of Edinburgh I extend to all those attending the XIII Commonwealth Games, whether as a competitor, an official or like myself a simple spectator, a truly warm and Scottish welcome. Edinburgh is delighted to see you and we hope that your stay in the City will be a happy one.

Edinburgh, the capital City of Scotland has particularly fond memories of the occasion in 1970 when the City last hosted these Games. I am confident that once again we will be able to capture that spirit which makes the Commonwealth Games 'The Friendly Games'.

The people of Edinburgh take you to their hearts and I feel sure that when the time comes to leave us you will take home with you happy memories of your visit.

To the competitors, the stars of the Games, may I wish them all good luck and every success. Win or lose, the great thing is to take part.

John McKay

Lord Provost

The Rt. Hon.
Dr. John McKay

British
TELECOM
THE POWER
BEHIND THE GAMES
XIII COMMONWEALTH
GAMES SCOTLAND 1986

Introduction

In 1970 Edinburgh was proud to stage Scotland's greatest ever sporting festival. Sixteen years on it again welcomes sportsmen and women from six continents to take part in the XIII Commonwealth Games.

Major international sporting events grow ever larger and more sophisticated. Games such as these rely on the use of scientific techniques in timing, measuring and recording. Equipment, from running shoes to rifles, has had the benefit of years of research. The athletes' preparations are carefully planned in line with physiological and psychological studies.

The ability to take part in sport has spread far and wide, so that more competitors from more countries come to the Games. Their performances are followed with keen interest, reported and broadcast by scores of journalists and commentators. So these Games are much bigger, even than those of 1970, and are a far cry from the so much simpler and smaller affair that was the first in this series, at Hamilton in Canada in 1930.

A common thread that runs through the Games is that of their friendly atmosphere. Of course the athletes compete with intensity, and of the thousands that enter only a few can be winners. Nonetheless these Games, perhaps above all international gatherings, retain the spirit of good-natured rivalry. Visitors to and citizens of Edinburgh will surely share this spirit in 1986.

The promotion of such an event is an increasingly costly affair, so especial gratitude is due to those organisations who have helped sponsor, taken advertising space or devoted resources to the success of the Games.

This book presents a guide to what's on, where and when for spectators at the venues or the millions more watching on television or listening on the radio all over the Commonwealth. Our experts point to what and who to look out for. The history of the Games is summarised, by Games and by sport, a complete list of past medallists is given, and some great champions outline what the Games have meant to them.

For sportsmen and women these Games provide a four-yearly goal in their pursuit of sporting excellence. Joining them in this celebration, the Organising Committee and the hundreds of helpers and officials of the various sports are devoting their time and skills to making this the best of all Games. We wish them all - competitors, officials, reporters, spectators - joy and success.

And when these Games are over, thoughts and aspirations will turn to Auckland, New Zealand, the site of the XIV Commonwealth Games in 1990.

Peter Matthews

Unmistakably, The Scotch House.

sh
THE
SCOTCH
HOUSE

The Nations of the Commonwealth Games

Fifty eight nations are affiliated to the Commonwealth Games Federation and are thus eligible to compete at the Games. These are the nations with their official three-letter abbreviations (as used in this book). Where a nation competed under a former name, that name is shown in the right-hand column.

		First CG Appearance	Former Name
ANT	Antigua	1966	
AUS	Australia	1930	
BAH	Bahamas	1954	
BAN	Bangladesh	1978	
BAR	Barbados	1954	
BER	Bermuda	1930	
BIZ	Belize	1962	British Honduras 1962-6
BOT	Botswana	1974	
BRU	Brunei	—	
CAN	Canada	1930	
CAY	Cayman Islands	1978	
CKI	Cook Islands	1974	
CYP	Cyprus	1978	
ENG	England	1930	
FAL	Falkland Islands	1982	
FIJ	Fiji	1938	
GAM	The Gambia	1970	
GHA	Ghana	1954	Gold Coast 1954
GIB	Gibralter	1958	
GRN	Grenada	1970	
GUE	Guernsey	1970	
GUY	Guyana	1930	British Guiana 1930-62
HGK	Hong Kong	1934	
IND	India	1934	
IOM	Isle of Man	1958	
JAM	Jamaica	1934	
JER	Jersey	1958	
KEN	Kenya	1954	
LES	Lesotho	1974	
MAL	Malaysia	1966	Malaya 1950-1962*
MAW	Malawi	1970	
MLT	Malta	1958	
MRI	Mauritius	1958	

		First CG Appearance	Former Name
NGR	Nigeria	1950	
NGU	Papua New Guinea	1962	
IRE	Ireland	1930	
NIR	Northern Ireland	1930	Ireland in 1930
NZL	New Zealand	1930	
SCO	Scotland	1930	
SEY	Seychelles	—	
SHE	St Helena	1982	
SIN	Singapore	1950	
SKI	St Kitts	1978	
SLE	Sierra Leone	1958	
SLU	St Lucia	1962	
SOL	Solomon Islands	1982	
SRI	Sri Lanka	1938	Ceylon 1938-70
SVI	St Vincent	1958	
SWZ	Swaziland	1970	
TAN	Tanzania	1962	Tanganyika 1962
TON	Tonga	1974	
TRI	Trinidad & Tobago	1934	
TUC	Turks & Caicos	1978	
UGA	Uganda	1954	
VAN	Vanuatu	1982	
WAL	Wales	1930	
WSA	Western Samoa	1974	
ZAM	Zambia	1954	Northern Rhodesia 1954
ZIM	Zimbabwe	1934	Southern Rhodesia 1934-62

Former participating nations

ADE	Aden	1962-66	
DOM	Dominica	1958	
NWF	Newfoundland	1930-34	(now part of Canada)
PAK	Pakistan	1954-70	
SAF	South Africa	1930-58	

* Constituent parts of Malaysia: Malaya 1950-62, Sabah (North Borneo) 1958-62 and Sarawak 1958-62 competed prior to formation of Malaysia.

Nations to have competed at all Games:
Australia, Canada, England, New Zealand, Scotland and Wales.
Guyana (formerly British Guiana) and Northern Ireland have competed at all Games but one.

Welcome to Edinburgh

The City of Edinburgh District Council welcomes visitors to the XIII Commonwealth Games.

The Council has played a major role in bringing this important sporting gathering of nations to Scotland and has supplied the facilities to match the high standards required in sport today.

To our many friends from home and abroad we urge you to look at Edinburgh's other attractions – our museums, our galleries, our beautiful parks and gardens. For more information about what our great capital city has to offer visit our Tourist Information Centre at Waverley Market, 3 Princes Street.

Enjoy your stay with us and haste ye back.

Commonwealth Games Medals by Nation

* No longer member of the Commonwealth
** Ireland in 1930
*** See list on page 13 for former names

Rank	Nation	Gold	Silver	Bronze	Total
1	England	321	286	277	884
2	Australia	305	274	233	812
3	Canada	201	226	233	660
4	New Zealand	69	91	120	280
5	Scotland	48	55	81	184
6	South Africa*	60	44	47	151
7	Wales	16	31	36	83
8	Kenya	29	16	30	75
9	India	24	28	20	72
10	Jamaica	18	14	16	48
11	Nigeria	14	12	19	45
	Northern Ireland**	12	13	20	45
13	Pakistan*	20	13	10	43
14	Ghana***	12	14	12	38
15	Uganda	6	13	11	30
16	Trinidad & Tobago	7	11	11	29
17	Malaysia***	8	8	9	25
	Zambia***	2	10	13	25
19	Zimbabwe***	3	5	13	21
20	Guyana***	2	5	5	12
21	Bahamas	3	6	2	11
22	Tanzania	3	4	3	10
23	Fiji	2	2	5	9
24	Singapore	4	1	3	8
25	Barbados	1	3	2	6
26	Hong Kong	4	1	-	5
	Sri Lanka***	2	2	1	5
	Western Samoa	-	1	4	5
29	Isle of Man	1	-	3	4
30	Papua-New Guinea	-	2	1	3
31	St. Vincent	1	-	1	2
	Bermuda	-	1	1	2
	Guernsey	-	1	1	2
	Swaziland	-	-	2	2
35	Gambia	-	-	1	1
	Jersey	-	-	1	1
	Malawi***	-	-	1	1
Total		1198	1193	1248	3639

Edinburgh in 1986

The Commonwealth comes home

by Alwyn James

In a very real sense, the great influx of participants and observers from all corners of the earth can be seen as a home-coming. The Commonwealth's roots lie in the now discredited idea of Empire, a complex globe-trotting frenzy in which Scots led the way.

An acknowledgement of the unique contribution made by the Scots has come in recent years from a most unexpected source - a US television programme - and in deference to the good Presbyterian habit of using a quotation as the launch-pad for every worthwhile sermon, it even starts with some memorable words: "To seek out new worlds and new civilisations . . . to boldly go where no man has gone before . . .". There cannot be many people in the English-speaking world who have got through the 1970s and 1980s without coming across the language's most celebrated split infinitive introducing *Star Trek*, that long-running peep into the future through the log-books of the Star Ship Enterprise.

We are shown that in those distant days the nations have become internations, that the harmonious team manning, or rather personning, the space-ship, has

Robin Ward

Edinburgh is ideally situated for travel in search of the Scottish countryside. Here, the snow-capped Ochill Hills seem a stone's throw across the River Forth from the city centre.

The medieval townscape of Edinburgh's Royal Mile.

been culled from all segments of this globe of ours. There is the black and voluptuous Uhura, the reliable and Slavonic Chekhov, the thoughtful and Oriental Sulu and, in case we have left out nations as yet unknown, there is the all-purpose Spock, offspring of a terrestrial mother and extra-terrestrial father.

So far, so good, but when we come to look at the key people running the ship, more than a touch of racialism creeps in. The ship's leader, a man of thought and action, is one James T. Kirk, about as Scottish a name as one could produce. On a long journey to strange and unpredicted environments, the man of medicine is no less important, and here we have moved from the Lowlands of Scotland to the Highlands with the name of McCoy. Coincidence perhaps, so we progress to the next officer - the Chief Engineer, Montgomerie Scott, usually called Scottie and occasionally to be seen sporting an interesting tartan plaid during formal dinners.

There could, of course, be a simple explanation for the clutch of Caledonians running this ship of the future - the author may have been a Scot, the programme may be subsidised by the Scottish Tourist Board, the names may have been picked out of an old New York telephone directory.

I would like to believe that the Scottish names are a hangover from that astonishing period from about 1790 to 1910 (although don't take either of those dates as rigid) when Scots tackled almost every aspect of human venture in which they were able 'to seek out new worlds . . . to boldly go where no man had gone before,' and achieved fame in virtually all of them. A nation that numbered around 1.3 million at that first date and had reached only 2.3 million by the end, led the world in a handful of activities, notably those represented by Kirk, Scottie and McCoy, namely exploration, soldiering, medicine, engineering and invention, but also including a few not represented aboard USS Enterprise, such as literature, economics, philosophy, politics and sport.

I, by good fortune rather than inspiration, recently came across a very graphic measure of the Scottish international contribution by looking at the wide range of individual Scots who have been honoured on the postage stamps of the world. In a very real sense, this measures the links between Scotland and the dozens of countries who have made a trek from as little as a couple of hundred miles to as great as 12,000 miles to be represented at these Commonwealth Games.

The Scots honoured on postage stamps (appropriately enough, the sticky perforated labels were invented by a Dundonian named James Chalmers) include the first man to cross North America from Atlantic to Pacific (Alexander MacKenzie), the man to do the same

Robin Ward

Argyll and Sutherland Highlanders in full regalia evoke Scotland's soldiering traditions.

'down under', crossing Australia from south to north (John McDouall Stuart), the first Premier of Canada (John A. MacDonald), the greatest land explorer (David Livingstone) and the most successful polar explorer (James Clark Ross). In all, more than 65 Scots have been honoured on the stamps of in excess of 150 countries - a truly worldwide acknowledgement of the Scottish contribution in medicine (the conquerors of malaria, tuberculosis and infection); in soldiering (the liberator of Chile, Peru and Brazil); in administration (including Australia's most humanitarian Scot, Lachlan Macquarie); in industry and engineering. In return, the countries of the Commonwealth gave opportunities to individual Scots which could never have been achieved in the restricted confines of their homeland. Andrew Fisher would have remained a coal miner

Robin Ward

Edinburgh Castle, floodlit at night, looms mysteriously above the Grassmarket.

had he stayed in Scotland; he went to Australia to become Prime Minister.

It is, therefore, particularly appropriate that these Commonwealth Games should be hosted here in Edinburgh. The capital city is perhaps unique in Europe in maintaining today very much the same appearance that it would have had in those years when Scots left their homeland to set up new lodgings in the lands of the Commonwealth. It is an unusually rewarding city to walk around. The fact that a couple of centuries ago, political power moved south to London, has meant that the city has survived without the great centralisation stresses of business and industry. You will not find here the great tower blocks of most modern capitals, but rather a fabric of older architecture, updated certainly, but without any loss of character.

Walk down the Royal Mile, that thin, centuries-old link between the castle and the Palace of Holyroodhouse, and you will find yourself transported back to medieval Scotland as far as the scale and relationship of buildings is concerned. A street without equal, a street which would need more than a few hours to get to know. Here, in the congested alleyways, so many of the exciting deeds of Scottish history took place. Pop down one or two of these and get a feel for Scottish history - the close where the *Encyclopaedia Britannica* first saw the light of day, the close where schoolboy pranks centuries ago resulted in the shooting dead of a sheriff out to quell some juvenile high spirits; the close where the body-snatchers of Edinburgh performed their dark deeds.

And when you have got to know something of the Old Town, do what Edinburgh man did 200 years ago - cross over by the Mound or the North Bridge to the gracious architecture of the New Town, set up as an overspill in the latter years of the 18th century and today representing perhaps the peak of British domestic architecture, with its elegant homes and rigid geometry. In particular, call in at Charlotte Square and see the Georgian house lovingly reconstructed to give something of the flavour of those days.

As befits a capital city, Edinburgh houses many of the national institutions of Scotland which are well worth a visit: the National Museum in Chambers Street is fascinating but on a scale that is not overpowering; the National Art Galleries - there are three of them - representing Scotland's finest collections of paintings and sculptures; and don't miss the castle, a museum in itself, and a very real part of the scenery. With a short walk you can almost forget that you are talking about a capital city and

Robin Ward

Preparing to fire the One o'clock Gun, a daily ritual at Edinburgh Castle

Robin Ward

The Burrell Collection, amassed by a Glasgow shipowner, is one of the great personal artistic collections of our time.

enter the Queen's Park, with the towering Arthur's Seat providing a mountainous landscape which few, if any, capital cities can boast.

Visitors to the last Commonwealth Games will see a greater change, perhaps, in the eating facilities in Edinburgh than in any other aspect of the city. Here, to the traditional Scottish restaurants and inns, have been added the cooking skills of the Indians, the Pakistanis and the Chinese, not to mention in recent years an effusion of restaurants from the Middle East. North America has not been left out, and you will find some very passable copies of the traditional Transatlantic eating houses. Edinburgh can even boast an Armenian restaurant, with the eminently forgettable name, 'The Armenian Aghtamar Lake Van Monastery in Exile'!

Do not feel that you are in any way restricted to Edinburgh. It may be the host city for these Commonwealth Games, but it is within easy access of other parts of Scotland, each with their own delights to offer. Travel to Glasgow, Scotland's first city, and at one time the proud holder of the title, Second City of the Empire. To Glasgow the world came for its ships, its locomotives and its engineering. Today, this great Victorian city is regaining something of its former dignity and challenging Edinburgh for the title of arts centre of Scotland. Glasgow is the home of the Scottish Opera, Scottish Theatre Ballet and Scottish National Orchestra as well as one of the great magnets for visitors to the Commonwealth Games, the Burrell Collection. The last-named, in a specially created building which itself received praise galore, is one of the great personal artistic collections of our time, built up by Sir William Burrell. Within a year of opening, the Burrell Collection had ousted Edinburgh Castle from its position as the great tourist attraction of Scotland.

Only a few dozen miles away from Edinburgh - 45 minutes by train - Glasgow should be seen by anyone spending a reasonable amount of time in Scotland.

Edinburgh is also ideally situated for travel to the north or south in search of the Scottish countryside. To the south, the rolling hills of the Borders shelter a very real feature of Scottish life - here the small independent communities produce the world's finest cloth, softest cashmere and most rugged rugby players. To the north of Edinburgh, no less easily accessible, lie the Highlands, and by car or train, a visit to the north will certainly add another dimension to any visit to Scotland. Here is perhaps the prototype of the international image of uninhabited glens, misty bens and mysterious lochs. Don't miss them.

Robin Ward

Glencoe in the heart of the Scottish Highlands

The Games Venues

by Sandy Sutherland

When the 1986 Commonwealth Games take place in Edinburgh, history will be made, for it will be the first time that the Games have returned to a host city - and the venues still ring with the memories of a memorable Games in 1970, the Games which coined the nick-name 'The Friendly Games'.

Meadowbank
Athletics and Badminton

Nowhere will this be more marked than at Meadowbank where none of us present on those halcyon, though rather damp, July days will ever forget the thrill of seeing Lachie Stewart nip past the great Ron Clarke to steal the 10000 metres gold, or Ian Stewart and Ian McCafferty in an epic duel with the Kenyan Kip Keino for the 5000 metres gold, which resulted in a glorious one-two for Scotland on the final day. The noise of that 30,000 crowd was ear-splitting and a full Meadowbank is still the finest athletics stadium in Britain. It is also the home of a football team, Meadowbank Thistle.

Normally the capacity is only 15,000 but for the 1970 Games extra temporary seating was erected, which more than doubled that. A similar exercise will be undertaken in 1986 providing a total capacity of 22,500 plus 42 executive hospitality chalets with a bird's eye view of events.

Rosemary Stirling (800 metres) and Rosemary Payne (discus) are two more Scottish gold medallists whose shadows may well linger at the scene of their triumphs. But there was tragedy too in 1970, such as the fall of New Zealander Sylvia Potts, a few feet from the line in the 1500 metres, and Australian Kerry O'Brien on the penultimate lap of the steeplechase.

Perhaps one day their ghosts will return to haunt a stadium which was the scene of so much happiness, the smiles of the Queen and the Royal Family matching those of the competitors who thronged round in an unforgettable closing ceremony.

Meadowbank has known other triumphs since its heady beginnings. The 1973 European Cup finals were staged there and two world records set - in the women's discus and javelin - and the track surface has been both repaired and relaid since.

A new electronic scoreboard will adorn the arena in 1986. And Ron Hill will no doubt be watching closely as the runners retrace the route he took Eastwards from Meadowbank to Longniddry and back on his way to the marathon gold.

Meadowbank will stage indoor events as well as on the track, and the opening and closing ceremonies. It is also the start and finish of the 30 kilometre road walk to Prestonpans and back.

Syndication International Ltd.

The Opening Ceremony of the 1970 Commonwealth Games at the Meadowbank Stadium.

Badminton, which since 1970 has added a team competition as well as the individual events, will occupy both the main indoor arena, hall one, which houses 2,300 spectators and the adjacent hall two, capacity 800.

International basketball, volleyball and even indoor cricket are just some of the big events which go on there. And judo, which is included in the Games for the first time, although only as a demonstration sport.

Scottish Tourist Board

The Commonwealth Pool

The Velodrome
Cycling

Without doubt the cycling venue has been the problem child of the Games organisation, as indeed it was in 1970. Scotland's weather does not easily lend itself to the staging of track cycling outdoors and the wooden track erected in 1970 (and not intended as a permanent structure) had deteriorated badly. After much debate and many different plans, including the possibility of a covered velodrome, the City of Edinburgh District Council agreed to renovate and refurbish the old velodrome on the same site with a completely new track of Afzelia, an extremely tough wood noted for its water-resistant properties, at a total cost of £435,000.

The 250 metre banked track is one of only two world championship standard tracks in Britain and specialist contractor Ron Webb has predicted a life of at least 30 years. But, as in 1970, when rain disrupted the programme, the organisers will be praying for dry weather. The velodrome is situated in the Meadowbank complex and will be well served by both bus and rail, being close to the new British Rail Meadowbank halt.

The Queen's Park was used for the road race in 1970 but, since then, the road has been narrowed considerably so a switch was required. The new Edinburgh by-pass was chosen and, with its magnificent back-drop of the Pentlands, will prove a popular and scenic venue. The dual-carriageway runs from Wester Hailes to Hill-End where a loop section of single carriageway will also be included.

The Commonwealth Pool
Swimming and Diving

The Royal Commonwealth Pool is the second major venue to be still available in 1986. As its name suggests, it too owes its origin to 1970 and, like Meadowbank, it is not only a fine monument to the past but a constantly and heavily used facility by today's citizens of Edinburgh.

There is room for over 2,000 spectators in the imposing surroundings but seats will still be scarce for the main swimming finals. One problem has been the depth of the eight-lane 50 metre pool for, since it was built, breaststroke swimmers in particular have started with a dive which requires rather more water.

One Olympic connection there, will be the electronic scoreboard which was bought from the Los Angeles organising committee after the 1984 Olympics.

Although this is not renowned as a 'fast' pool there was one world record in 1970 from 16-year-old Australian Karen Moras in the 800 metres freestyle and Karen also won the 200 and 400 freestyle.

Ingliston
Boxing

Boxing is one of the sports which will have a new venue this time, the Exhibition Hall at Ingliston. Better known as the showground for the Royal Highland Show, Ingliston is the property of the Royal Highland and Agricultural Society, and has in its grounds a motor racing circuit.

Capable of housing 5,000 spectators, the hall has already been the venue for major darts and indoor soccer six-a-side tournaments and the building was also designed to include a full 200 metres indoor athletics track, a capability so far neglected by that sport.

Immediately adjacent to Edinburgh Airport and to one of the largest outdoor markets in Scotland, the Ingliston Exhibition hall is situated some 25 minutes from Edinburgh city centre, the extra spectator capacity being crucial in the decision to move away from the originally intended central venue at the Usher Hall.

Balgreen
Lawn Bowls

Edinburgh District Council's Balgreen rinks will again be the sward for the 1986 bowling events. Adjacent to Murrayfield, the home of Scottish rugby, Balgreen is also handily situated for the famous Edinburgh zoo.

Temporary terraced seating will be erected to bring the spectator accommodation up to 3,000. This will ring with shouts if the Scottish medal contenders, who this time include the ladies, can emulate Alex McIntosh and his four in their silver medal success of 1970, on the same green.

Playhouse
Weightlifting and Wrestling

'Wham', 'Heavy Metal' and 'Nutcracker' have other connotations at the weightlifting and wrestling venue than one might normally expect, for the Playhouse Theatre in Edinburgh, which provides the stage for these two most theatrical of sports, is more accustomed these days to pop concerts or Scottish ballet.

Perfectly situated on Leith Walk, within walking distance of Princes Street, Waverley Station and St. Andrew's Square bus station, the privately-owned Playhouse can accommodate up to 3,000 spectators and will give those events a suitably 'grand' back-drop.

The Royal Highland and Agricultural Society of Scotland

Ingliston Hall during the Scottish Agricultural Winter Fair

Strathclyde Regional Council

Aerial view of Strathclyde Park

Kippen to Musselburgh
Shooting

The sound of gun-fire will crackle across the Scottish countryside next July from as far apart as Carnoustie in Angus to Kippen in Stirlingshire to Musselburgh in East Lothian.

Barry Buddon, an army range near the famous championship golf course at Carnoustie, is the venue for the full bore rifle competition and that is 73 miles from the Games village which will necessitate the shooters and officials staying there for five days.

Kippen, near Stirling, the location for the clay pigeon (skeet and Olympic trench) shooting, is 47 miles from the village. Visitors could take in the 'Bonnie Banks of Loch Lomond' or Stirling Castle depending on whether they take the 'high road' or the 'low road'.

Edinburgh University's splendid new Pleasance gymnasium, with its double games hall, will host the air-weapons contest and competitors will be able to walk there comfortably from the village.

The last shooting venue to be settled was that for small bore rifle and pistol. These will be staged at the Ash Lagoons, an area of reclaimed land between Musselburgh and Prestonpans. And England beware! It was near here that Sir John Cope came a cropper in the Battle of Prestonpans during the 1745 Jacobite Rebellion.

Strathclyde Country Park
Rowing

The whole of Scotland, and not just Edinburgh, is involved in the Games. The most notable example of this is Strathclyde Country Park, located on the banks of the Clyde between Motherwell and Hamilton, the venue for the rowing events.

Strathclyde Regional Council, responsible for the Park, have undertaken a major development programme to bring the purpose-built, six-lane rowing course up to world class standard. The Park was reclaimed from some 1,600 acres of land ravished by the worst effects of the coal and steel industries of Lanarkshire, and in the past ten years there has been a near miraculous transformation involving the diversion of the River Clyde, the construction of a huge man-made loch (complete with beaches) and the creation of extensive leisure and sports facilities.

The largest single capital investment (£650,000) for these Games is that for the two new control towers, which have been built incorporating the latest computer timing equipment. The finishing tower is connected to the loch-side by a new causeway, and for the Games a 2,500 seat grandstand has been constructed.

Apart from the rowing and other water sports facilities, the Park has pitches for many team sports, and throughout the year it hosts events as diverse as horse shows, hill climbs, caravan exhibitions and firework displays. In complete contrast, large areas are nature reserves with over 130 species of birds observed. The other unusual attractions for visitors are the Duke of Hamilton's Mausoleum which stands 120 feet high and is famous for its 15-second echo in the Chapel, and the remains of a Roman bath-house from the Antonine period.

Within easy reach of over half of Scotland's population, Strathclyde Country Park will ensure that 'The Friendly Games' are given a warm welcome in the West of Scotland.

YOU CAN BE SURE OF SHELL

EVE KIRK

ATHLETES PREFER SHELL

Yesterday and today
You can be sure of Shell

Lorry Poster Eve Kirk 1934

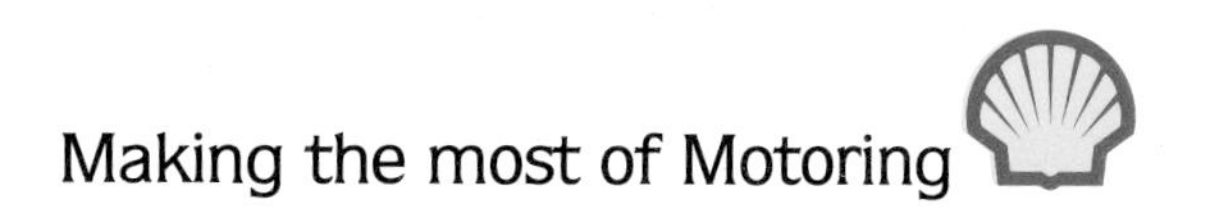
Making the most of Motoring

Quote from the note of guidance drawn up by the original representative meeting which decided on the first Games of 1930:-"It will be designed on the Olympic model, both in general construction and in its stern definition of the amateur. But the Games will be very different, free from both the excessive stimulus and babel of the international stadium. They should be merrier and less stern, and will substitute the stimulus of a novel adventure for the pressure of international rivalry."

Commonwealth History

A survey of all Games from 1930 to 1982

by Stan Greenberg

The original concept of an 'Empire Games' was first mooted in the summer of 1891 by J. Astley Cooper, an Englishman, in a magazine article in the *Greater Britain*. He suggested a United English Festival in Industry, Culture and Sport. The latter, he suggested, should consist of running, rowing and cricket. The historian J.A. Froude, in a letter to *The Times* in early October praised the idea and even suggested that the Americans would be interested in taking part.

On 30 October 1891 Cooper answered him in what has become a landmark letter on the subject, also to *The Times*. The term 'Pan-Britannic Festival' caught on and a number of further letters to the newspaper over the next two years elicited support from the Premier of New Zealand, the former Mayor of Adelaide and others. The last item on the subject was a report in March 1895 stating that the outcome of the Pan-Britannic movement in South Africa was the formation of a South African Amateur Athletic Association. Nothing more seems to have happened on the subject until, following the 1908 Olympic Games in London, Richard Coombes of Australia suggested a sports meeting restricted to competitors from the British Empire. Possibly as an outcome of his suggestion such a meeting was arranged as part of the 1911 Festival of Empire held in London to celebrate the Coronation of King George V. Nine events were held: five of athletics, two of swimming and one each of boxing and wrestling. Incidentally the manager of the Australasian team (comprising Australia and New Zealand) was the aforementioned Richard Coombes.

In 1920 a combined team from the British Empire met the United States in a post-Olympic athletics meeting which began a four-yearly series of such matches. The Empire Games concept was stimulated, not least in Canada, and in 1924 Norton Crow, the retiring secretary of the Canadian AAU, reiterated the idea which was well received. It was another Canadian, M.M. 'Bobby' Robinson, who finally made it happen. Robinson was a sports reporter for the Hamilton *Spectator*, as well as the manager of the Canadian track and field team for the 1928 Olympic Games in Amsterdam. At the instigation of Dr. J. Howard Crocker, President of the Canadian AAU, he sounded out the managers of the other Empire teams at Amsterdam to elicit support for an Empire Games at Hamilton. His efforts received a boost at a meeting in London where the third British Empire v USA match was held after the Olympics. At that meeting it was agreed that Hamilton should host such a Games in 1930 which "should be merrier and less stern" than the Olympics, substituting the "stimulus of novel adventure for the pressure of international rivalry". No solely team sports were to be allowed, but team events such as relays and team fencing have been included over the years.

In January 1930 Robinson visited London with the proposal that the Home countries should all send separate teams, unlike the Olympic practice of a single combined British team. King George V agreed to become the patron of the Games. So almost exactly 39 years after Astley Cooper's article his dream became a reality.

Plus ça change, plus c'est la même chose
(The more things change, the more they are the same.)

The following quote from *The Times* editorial of 25 August 1930, on the success of the England team at Hamilton, might appear to be as applicable now as then: "Englishmen will probably never be convinced that hurling missiles of various designs, however great the skill required, is equivalent to running once, or twice, or four times round a track. But since a system of differential scoring is not likely to be adopted within two years, they would do well to cultivate throwing disci, putting shot, and hopping, stepping and jumping before they go to Los Angeles for the next Olympic Games."

Hamilton
Canada
16-23 August 1930

Due primarily to the enthusiasm and persistence of M.M.'Bobby' Robinson, a Canadian newspaperman and official, the first British Empire Games were held in his home town of Hamilton, Ontario. Just months before it had seemed that the concept would not get off the ground, and it was only in January of 1930 that Robinson had got agreement that Britain should send four separate teams.

The world depression was beginning to hit hard, but the City of Hamilton financially assisted teams, especially those from Australia, New Zealand and South Africa, which had to travel a long way. At that time, and until the next Games to be held in Canada in 1954, teams invariably travelled by boat. Some 120 British competitors sailed in the 'Empress of Canada' and the 'Duchess of Atholl'. The latter, with the bulk of the party, arrived, due to fog, with only two days to spare. In all about 400 competitors from 11 countries took part in six sports. Women could only compete in swimming events, and the few female competitors were housed in a hotel. The male competitors were housed in dormitories of the Prince of Wales School, next to the stadium.

The Opening Ceremony attracted 20,000 spectators in fine weather to see the formal opening of the Games by Viscount Willingdon, the Governor-General, in the presence of the Canadian Prime Minister, Mr. R.B. Bennett. The competitor's oath was taken by Canada's great athlete, Percy Williams, the Olympic sprint champion. He later won a dramatic 100 yards final after pulling a muscle some distance from the finishing line. In his heat he set an Empire record of 9.6 seconds.

At the Opening Ceremony the teams were led into the arena by a Highlander, carrying the Union Jack, particularly fitting as Hamilton's population of 150,000 included a very high proportion of residents of Scottish descent. Therefore it was no surprise that the victory of Scotland's Duncan McLeod Wright in the marathon later in the week, met with great popular approval from the home crowd.

The very first event of the Games, held on the grass track of the stadium soon after the inauguration ceremonies, was a heat of the 440 yards hurdles won by Lord Burghley of England. He later won the final, one of his three gold medals. However, the first Games title went to a Canadian, Gordon Smallacombe, who won the triple jump (or hop, step and jump as it was named then).

The stadium was the scene of much drama during the week, apart from the Williams incident. Indeed, a perfect example of the spirit of these Games occured in the 100 yards heats, when Alan Elliott of New Zealand was disqualifed, properly so, for two false starts. The crowd, mainly Canadian, was so vociferous in his favour that the referee reinstated him. However, he failed to make the final. One of the closest track races ever seen at the Games came about in the 3 miles when England's Stan Tomlin beat Australia's Alex Hillhouse by just 0.2 seconds. Hillhouse later won another silver medal in his debut in the 2 miles steeplechase, despite coming a cropper at the water jump.

In the six miles John Savidan of New Zealand, who had walked in the parade only 3 hours earlier, was the victim of an error by the lap counting official and ended his finishing spurt only to find that there was still 440 yards to go. Happily he was able to hang on to his lead.

Boxing

The nearest to a triple crown of titles was achieved by South African Lawrie Stevens, who only won a silver medal in the 1930 Commonwealth Games at featherweight, but then took the 1932 Olympic lightweight title and followed that four years later by winning the world professional lightweight championship.

Symbol

The official symbol of the Games was adopted in July 1952. It is a gold crown inside a gold link chain, all on a dark blue background with the letters CG below the crown (originally the letters were BE and CG).

Lord Burghley, later the Marquess of Exeter and President of the International Olympic Committee, on his way to victory in the Olympic 400m hurdles in 1928. In Hamilton he won triple Commonwealth gold.

Interestingly, in the high jump one of the Canadian competitors, Duncan MacNaughton was disqualified for using an illegal technique. Two years later he won the Olympic title in Los Angeles. The javelin was won by Stan Lay of New Zealand, with a distance that was not beaten at the Games for a record 24 year period.

An unusual 'visitor' to the Games was the airship R-100 which passed over the stadium during the week.

The most prolific winner at Hamilton was Joyce Cooper of England who won four swimming golds of which three were in individual events. In the freestyle relay her English team-mates included her sister Doreen. They were the first siblings to win gold medals at the same Games. Miss Cooper had actually been born in Ceylon, and there were to be many instances in the future Games of competitors born in one member of the Empire representing another, a situation often encouraged and only rarely causing acrimony. The youngest gold medal winner at Hamilton was also an English swimmer, Celia Wolstenholme who was aged 15 years 90 days when she won the 200 yards breaststroke. The youngest male champion was Canada's George Burleigh, aged 16 when a member of the victorious freestyle relay. The outstanding men in the pool were Noel Ryan of Australia who won two freestyle gold medals and the host country's Alfie Phillips who won both diving titles. Some confusion still remains as to the winner of a bronze medal in those diving events, for while that in the springboard went to Canada's Arthur Stott, there is confusion over the highboard event. The Canadian report lists Stott but it was probably won by Arthur 'Terry' Scott of England.

One of the most popular sports was rowing, which was often plagued by high winds. An estimated 70,000 people lined the banks of Hamilton Bay on Lake Ontario to watch the final of the single sculls, won by the almost legendary oarsman Bobby Pearce of Australia.

At Hamilton a committee was set up to draft a constitution for an Empire Sports Federation. New Zealand and South Africa both requested the honour of hosting the next Games in 1934, with South Africa the selection.

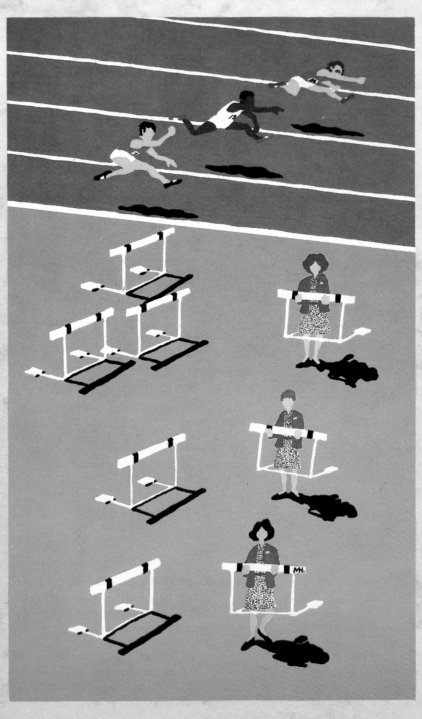

London England

4-11 August 1934

During the Olympic Games of 1932 in Los Angeles the British Empire Games Federation had been formed. One of its first actions was to transfer the 1934 Games from South Africa to England, mainly due to fears about the attitude of white South Africans to black sportsmen from other Empire countries. Another 'political' problem arose with the replacing of Ireland by a team from Northern Ireland only.

At the White City Stadium, London, on 4 August, exactly 20 years to the day after Britain and the Empire had entered World War I, the Games were declared open by Sir George Truscott, Deputy Lord Mayor of London in front of 50,000 spectators. Some 6,000 pigeons were released and the oath of allegiance was taken by Robert 'Bonzo' Howland, who later won a silver medal in the shot.

Some 500 competitors from 16 countries took part in six sports, with cycling replacing the rowing that had been held in Hamilton four years before. The Australians had taken 37 days, by boat, to reach England, and this 'tyranny of travel' was to bedevil teams for another 20 years.

The athletic events were badly affected by poor weather and the cinder track was often waterlogged. This held the standard of performance down to a generally lower level than that at Hamilton. Nevertheless there were some excellent performers on view including England's Arthur Sweeney who won three gold medals, and his team-mate Eileen Hiscock who went one better by adding a silver to her three golds. One of the most unusual doubles in track and field history was achieved by Gladys Lunn of England. She won the javelin on the opening day and followed that two days later with the gold medal at 880 yards. This latter event was not held again in the Games for 28 years, due mainly to outdated official intransigence towards women's running. The men's 880 yards was won by one of Canada's greatest Olympians, Phil Edwards, who in London was running in the colours of his native British Guiana. The marathon was won by his Olympic colleague Harold Webster, a Canadian born in England, who was at least eight years older than his stated age of 32.

When the band played 'There's a long long trail a-winding'

At the other end of the age scale was another Canadian, Sam Richardson, who won the long jump when 16 years 263 days old, to become the youngest ever male Commonwealth track and field champion.

A light hearted incident came as the marathon runners left the stadium on their 26-mile-plus journey, when the band began to play the popular wartime song "There's a long long trail a-winding". Due to traffic problems the race could not be started from Windsor Castle as had the 1908 Olympic race. Watching the runners with interest, no doubt, was Jack Holden who had been placed fourth in the six miles and was to triumph in the 1950 marathon, 16 years later.

In the mile Jack Lovelock of New Zealand beat England's Sydney Wooderson on the only major championship occasion that these two great runners were to meet. South Africa's Hendrik Hart retained both his shot and discus titles and improved his medal in the javelin from a bronze to a silver. The only other athlete to win two gold medals was England's Godfrey Rampling in the 440 yards individual race and the mile relay. His daughter Charlotte was to become the well-known film actress.

The most prolific winner at these Games was Phyllis Dewar, the Canadian swimming champion, who won two individual and two relay gold medals in the newly opened Empire Pool, Wembley,

Jack Lovelock of New Zealand won the Commonwealth 1 mile title in 1934. He went on to win the Olympic 1500m in a world record time of 3:47.8 at Berlin in 1936, after which he was interviewed at the first-ever televised Games.

which had accommodation for 6,000 spectators. Her countryman George Burleigh was the best male swimmer with three golds, while Australia's Noel Ryan retained both the titles he had won at Hamilton, at 440 yards and 1500 yards freestyle. Another first for the Games came in the pool when Bob and Irene Pirie of Canada became the first brother and sister to win gold medals. The youngest competitors at the Games were also in the swimming events with 13 year old Margaret Gomm of England in the 200 yards breaststroke, and 14 year old Molly Ryde of South Africa winning a silver medal in the freestyle relay.

The House of Lords retained its interest in the Games with Lord David Douglas-Hamilton winning a bronze boxing medal for Scotland. His team-mate and fellow bronze medallist Archie Dudgeon, a 21 stone wrestler, was the heaviest man ever to compete in the Games.

Sydney Australia

5-12 February 1938

Australia's wrestling hero, Dick Garrard, won his second Commonwealth gold medal at Sydney. He went on to win again in 1950.

The Games at Sydney, held in conjunction with the 150th anniversary of European settlement in Australia, at Farm Cove near Sydney, were out of season for most of the other major countries.

The Opening Ceremony was performed by Lord Wakehurst, the Governor of New South Wales, at the Sydney Cricket Ground before 40,000 spectators. The oath was taken by cyclist Edgar 'Duncan' Gray. He later failed in his attempt to defend his time trial title, but won the sprint gold medal. A total of 466 competitors, of whom 88 were women, from 15 countries were entered for seven sports, rowing having been re-admitted. The teams from Britain were away from home for four months due to the long sea voyages to and from Australia.

The track and field events were held on a grass track, almost 'D' shaped, which proved very fast and springy. The star of the Games was the host country's Decima Norman, who won five gold medals (100 and 220 yards, long jump and two relays) a total never bettered by a woman in any sport at a single Games. Almost as famous was her mascot - a black swan doll named Wah-hoo. By comparison the most gold medals won by a male sportsman at Sydney was three by Canada's hurdler John Loaring, although his team-mate Bob Pirie won two gold and three silver medals in the swimming pool.

On the running track there was a certain amount of criticism of some of the judging, most particularly in the men's 440 yards race in which England's Bill Roberts was awarded first place over Canada's Bill Fritz, although many present considered that the Canadian was a foot in front. A newspaper photograph of the finish appeared to uphold that view. Controversy came too in the 120 yards hurdles in which Tom Lavery's outstanding win in 14.0 seconds was disallowed as an Empire record on the evidence of a fluttering handkerchief - there were no wind gauges in those days.

Cyril Holmes, the English Rugby Union international, could not quite match his predecessor Arthur Sweeney in the sprints, for he won a silver in the relay to add to his 100 yards/220 yards gold medals. A New Zealander, Cecil Matthews, by winning both the 3 miles and the 6 miles events, achieved the only distance running track double in the Games to date.

As always some of the champions were quite unheralded. Perhaps none more so than Canada's Harold Brown. He was not originally chosen for the Canadian team, although his brother Wallace was. His home town paid for him to go as well and he rewarded their faith by winning the long jump. The mile was won by Jim Alford who thus gained the first Games gold medal for Wales - although it must be noted that the 1930 winner of the same event, for England, was another Welshman, Reg Thomas. Other than the wins of Holmes and Roberts the only other gold medal won by England in athletics was the women's high jump by Dorothy Odam. Sixteen years later she was still good enough to win a silver medal.

In the swimming pool Phyllis Dewar of Canada added another gold medal, in the relay, to the four she had won in London. Her team-mate, Bob Pirie, was otherwise the star of the pool with five medals as the Australian and English swimmers swept nearly all before them. The only non-Australian diving victory went in the highboard to England's Doug Tomalin, competing in his third Games.

In wrestling Dick Garrard, the hometown hero, retained his 1934 Lightweight title, as he was to do again in 1950.

Overall the home team won 65 medals, by far the highest total gained by any country. Some of the competitors later achieved prominence in other fields. Among them were: Margaret Dovey (AUS) a finalist in the 220 yards breaststroke, who married Gough Whitlam, Prime Minister of Australia in the 1970s; three-time bronze medal sprinter Ted Best (AUS) who became Lord Mayor of Melbourne; Gordon Freeth (AUS), the winner of a gold medal in the coxed fours, who was later knighted and became Australian High Commissioner in London. Eric Coy of Canada, the discus champion, turned to a very different sport and was North American Snowshoe racing champion for seven years.

Montreal, Canada was selected as the venue for the Games of 1942. However, due to the outbreak of World War II they were not held, but interestingly they would have been on the same site as was later selected for the 1976 Olympic Games.

Games venues and dates

			Countries	Sports	Men	Women	Total
I British Empire Games	Hamilton, Canada	16-23 August 1930	11	6	-	-	400
II British Empire Games	London, England	4-11 August 1934	16	6	-	-	500
III British Empire Games	Sydney, Australia	5-12 February 1938	15	7	378	88	466
IV British Empire Games	Auckland, New Zealand	4-11 February 1950	12	9	495	95	590
V British Empire & Commonwealth Games	Vancouver, Canada	30 July-7 August 1954	24	9	568	94	662
VI British Empire & Commonwealth Games	Cardiff, Wales	18-26 July 1958	35	9	967	163	1130
VII British Empire & Commonwealth Games	Perth, Australia	22 November-1 December 1962	35	9	727	136	863
VIII British Empire & Commonwealth Games	Kingston, Jamaica	4-13 August 1966	34	9	894	196	1050
IX British Commonwealth Games	Edinburgh, Scotland	16-25 July 1970	42	9	1095	288	1383
X British Commonwealth Games	Christchurch, New Zealand	24 January-2 February 1974	38	9	977	299	1276
XI Commonwealth Games	Edmonton, Canada	3-12 August 1978	46	10	1149	326	1475
XII Commonwealth Games	Brisbane, Australia	30 September-9 October 1982	46	10	1176	407	1583
XIII Commonwealth Games	Edinburgh, Scotland	24 July-2 August 1986					
XIV Commonwealth Games	Auckland, New Zealand	3-13 February 1990 (Provisional)					

Auckland New Zealand

4-11 February 1950

After a gap of 12 years caused by World War II, the Games of 1950 were awarded to Auckland at a meeting of the British Empire Games Federation held in London soon after the 1948 Olympics. There had been intense rivalry between Christchurch and Auckland for the honour, but the latter prevailed. Once again the teams from Britain were involved in a trip of over three months in all, the sea voyage alone occupying some five weeks each way.

The Games were opened officially at Eden Park by Sir Bernard Freyberg VC, Governor-General of New Zealand, in front of 40,000 spectators. The oath was taken by veteran javelin thrower Stan Lay, on behalf of the 590 competitors, of which 95 were women. There were 12 countries represented and the sports now numbered nine with the inclusion of fencing and weightlifting. Water polo was also added to the swimming programme but only two teams competed and it was dropped thereafter. Black Africa was represented for the first time, by a team from Nigeria. Their first medal was a silver in the men's high jump.

The athletics events were held on a grass track which proved to be excellent, but this was the last time that Games athletics was held on such a surface. That high jump competition was won by the reigning Olympic champion, Jack Winter of Australia, using the old-fashioned scissors technique, probably the last major title won by a man using that style.

The youngest winner was Joan Harrison of South Africa, at 440 yards freestyle, aged 14 years 73 days, at that time the youngest ever champion. Australian sprinter Marjorie Jackson won a total of four gold medals while her team-mate Shirley Strickland amassed three gold and two silver medals. The

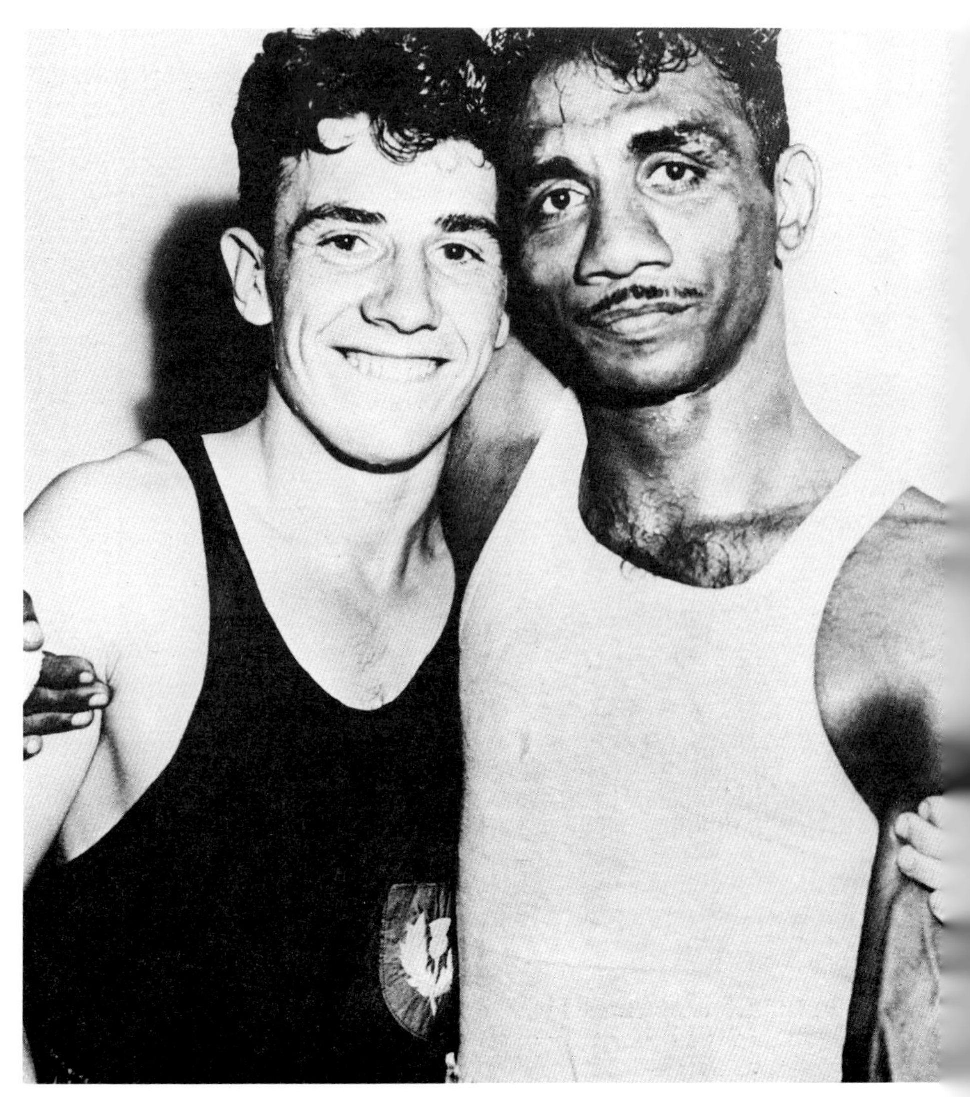

most golds won by a male sportsman at these Games was three by sprinter John Treloar, also of Australia. In fact Australia's domination of the Games at Auckland was to be greater than that of any country at any Games. They won a total of 80 medals, of which 34 were gold, compared to the next highest, 48 and 19 by England.

However, it should be noted that the Australians did not gain a single medal in any running event over 440 yards. Apart from Stan Lay and 42-year-old marathon winner Jack Holden, a number of other veterans competed, including the former Dorothy Odam, now Tyler, who retained her high jump title, and England's Don Finlay, who narrowly failed to add a bronze medal to the gold he had won in 1934. Evidence of the emergence of some of the smaller Commonwealth countries came with victories in the 440 yards hurdles by Ceylon's Duncan White, and in the shot by one of the most popular competitors at Auckland, Maitaka Tuicacakau of Fiji.

Although the Australian sprinters stole the limelight in the women's events there was a notable debut to a distinguished international career in the long jump, in which New Zealand's future Olympic champion Yvette Williams won her first major title.

There was a very strange coincidence in the men's 100 yards final, when Canada's Don Pettie was disqualified for two false starts. (In 1930, in Canada, New Zealand's Alan Elliott had similarly been disqualified). Like Elliott, Pettie was reinstated by the Jury of Appeal, with the agreement of the other finalists, and he won a bronze medal. The largest crowd of the Games - some 40,000 - turned out for the final day of athletics, although ironically this was the only time umbrellas were required.

In the swimming pool Marjorie McQuade of Australia won three gold medals, which was matched by team-mate Judy-Joy Davies. In women's diving, England's Edna Child achieved the first double win by a female diver in the Games.

Surprisingly, no male swimmer won more than one gold medal, a situation that has never happened again in Commonwealth Games swimming. Four swimmers and two divers did win a gold and a silver. The divers were Peter Heatly of Scotland, who was to win two more golds and a bronze in the next two Games, and George Athans of Canada, winner of the springboard title. His son, George Athans junior, was twice world champion at water skiing in the 1970s.

In cycling the great Russell Mockridge won two golds and a silver as only England stopped a clean sweep by the Australians. In fencing the reverse was true as the Australian épée team was triumphant. In that team was a young Allan Jay, later a stalwart of future England fencing teams. In rowing Australia's Olympic sculling champion Mervyn Wood easily won his speciality and then won again in the double sculls event.

Auckland was the last of what may be termed the 'old-fashioned' Games. In future most competitors would travel by air, be timed electronically, and perform before enormous audiences, courtesy of television.

(Above) The Olympic pool, New Market, Auckland, where the Empire Games swimming events were held. (Left) Good friends, Hugh Riley (left) the Scottish winner of the Empire flyweight title, and K. Edwin, of Ceylon, the runner up.

Vancouver
Canada
30 July - 7 August 1954

For the first time most of the 662 competitors, of which 94 were women, travelled to the Games by air. Representing a record 24 countries they were entered for the same nine sports as in Auckland.

The Games were opened by Field Marshal Earl Alexander of Tunis (former Governor-General of Canada) in the presence of Prince Philip and 25,000 spectators at the newly-built Empire Stadium. The oath was taken by Bill Parnell who had won the mile for Canada in 1950. These Games will always be remembered for two dramatic races. The new cinder track, the first used at the Games since 1934, was the scene of the 'Miracle Mile' between Roger Bannister and John Landy in which both of them clocked under four minutes for the distance.

On the same day, the last of the meeting, held in near 30°C (90°F) temperatures, there was the horror of the finish of the marathon when Jim Peters appeared in the stadium some $3\frac{1}{2}$ miles in front of the next runner, but was severely affected by heat exhaustion. After collapsing on 11 or 12 occasions he was finally carried off the track only 200 yards short of the finish line, and rushed to hospital. Though he recovered he never ran again. The eventual winner, Joe McGhee of Scotland, also collapsed three times but finished - only six of the original 16 starters did so. Other athletics performances were completely overshadowed by the above two events, but there was much else to enthuse about.

Marjorie Jackson, Australia's sprint queen, won another three gold medals to bring her total from two Games to seven, a record for the sport, while her Antipodean neighbour, Yvette Williams of New Zealand also won three golds in the unusual combination of long jump, shot and discus. In the high jump the ever-green Dorothy Odam-Tyler took the silver medal 16 years after winning the gold in Sydney. In the men's events England's distance runners took all six medals in the 3 and 6 miles, as well as another clean sweep in the 880 yards. English athletes also won half of the eight field event titles, a remarkable performance considering that they had only won a total of three such events in the previous four Games.

The University of British Columbia's new 526,000 gallon swimming pool proved to be exceptionally fast and only the 220 yards breaststroke record (set in 1938 when the

Record Breakers

Since 1954 every winner of the Commonwealth Games 1500m/1 mile title at athletics has also broken world records, either before or after gaining the gold medal. Roger Bannister (2), Herb Elliott (4), Peter Snell (6), Kip Keino (2), Filbert Bayi (2), David Moorcroft(1) and Steve Cram (4) - a total of 21 in all.
The 1982 10000 metres final was won by Gidamis Shahanga of Tanzania. This was very unusual as he had won the marathon in 1978, and though Dave Power of Australia had taken both the races in the same Games (1958), never has a marathon winner reduced his distance at a later Games and been successful. The Brisbane race is remembered for another, more bizarre, reason. Two runners from the Cayman Islands, the total Games team, were lapped repeatedly during the race causing considerable difficulties for the other competitors, while a light plane flew over the stadium towing a banner exhorting them to greater efforts. David Bonn eventually finished in a time of 41min 21.50 sec, over 13 minutes behind the winner.

Marjorie Jackson off to a fine start, in the first heat of the 100 yards in 1954. On the left is Anne Pashley of England, who was fourth in the final. She later became a star of the opera.

butterfly technique was allowable) was unbroken. The outstanding competitor was Australia's Jon Henricks who won three gold medals, while two other men and three women won two golds each.

The youngest winner at the Games was Natalie Myburgh of South Africa in the freestyle relay, when only 77 days past her 14th birthday. At the other end of the age scale was Australia's veteran oarsman Mervyn Wood, who won two gold medals on the same day, aged 37 years 96 days.

The site of the rowing events, on the Vedder Canal some 50 miles from the city, was the subject of some criticism, as an adverse current badly penalised some stations more than others.

There had also been suggestions that the new 250 metres cedar cycling track with its 45 degree banking would not be conducive to fast times, but that was soon dispelled. There was serious disagreement in the 1000 metres sprint series which led to the disqualification of the strong favourite, Lionel Cox of Australia, in the final. No silver medal was awarded, and Cox's compatriot Dick Ploog did not take part in the third place deciding heat. However, two days later Ploog, only 17 years of age, tied for the 1000 metres time trial title. The lawn bowling competitions were remarkable for the absence of many of the best Home countries competitors, so that entries from Hong Kong and Southern Rhodesia were given an opportunity to make their mark. In fencing England's stranglehold on the men's individual titles was finally broken by Ivan Lund of Australia winning the épée gold medal. The weightlifting was of a high standard, none more so than in the heavyweight division in which two men surpassed totals of 1,000 lbs for their lifts, only the second time in history that two men had surpassed that total in the same competition. The winner, Canada's Doug Hepburn, a 21 stone giant, had been born with a club-foot condition, but the subsequent operation was only a partial success and left him with a weak ankle. The degree to which he overcame this can be gauged by the fact that he had won the world title the year before his Games victory. In the wrestling contests Australia's Dick Garrard, now 45 years old and competing in his fourth Games, won a bronze medal, while the heavyweight title went to England's Ken Richmond.

At Vancouver the Games moved into another era, with the introduction of photo-finish equipment and other electronic aids for the judges, and its first ever television coverage.

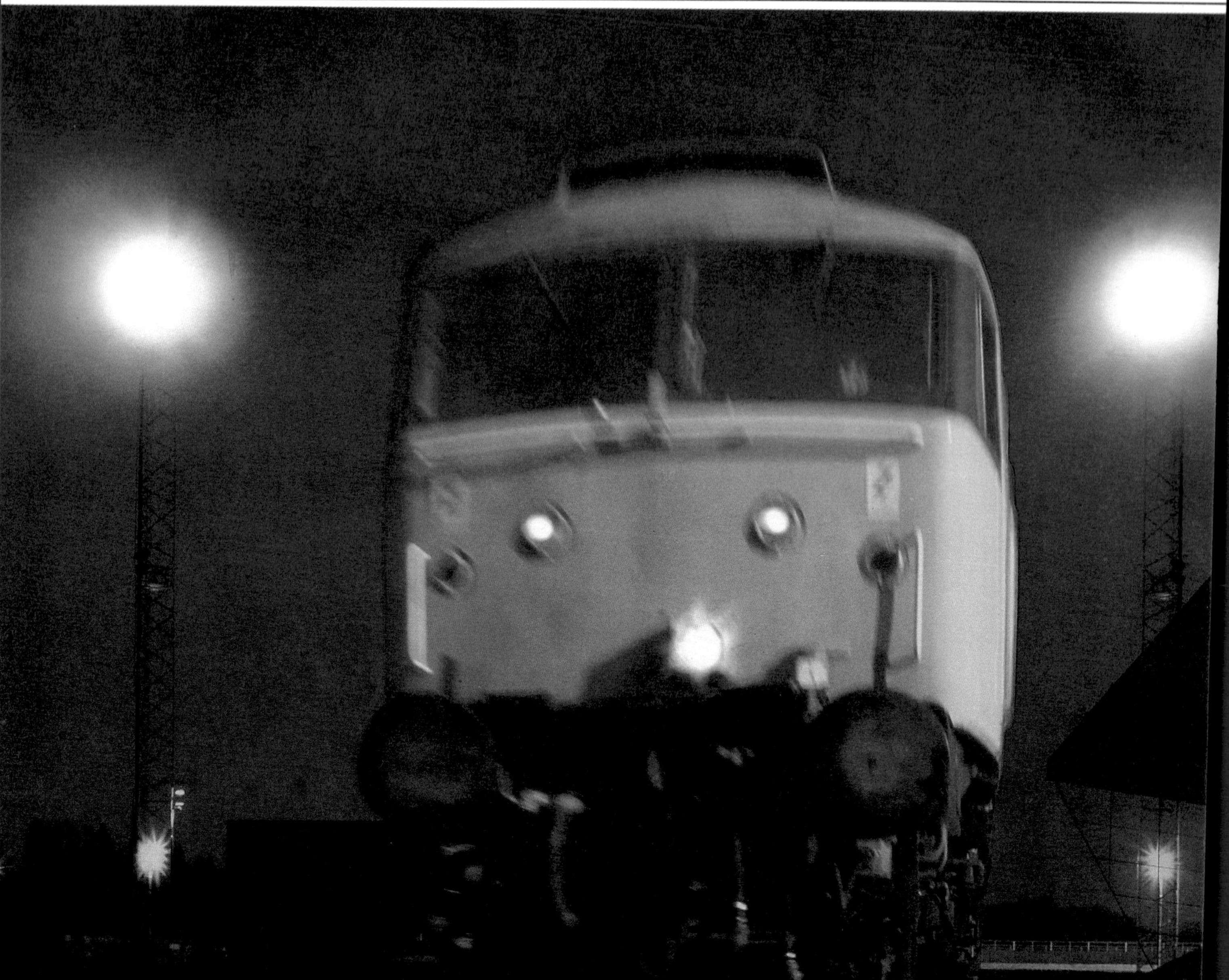

(Right) Dave Power, double distance triumph.
(Below left) A record four medals for Jamaican hurdler Keith Gardner.

Cardiff Wales

18-26 July 1958

Copying the Olympic tradition, a relay of runners was organised to carry a message from the Queen at Buckingham Palace to Cardiff Arms Park, the famous Rugby Union venue, where the opening ceremony was conducted in front of 30,000 people. A record 1,130 competitors, of which 163 were women, representing 35 countries participated in nine sports. The Games were opened by Prince Philip and the oath was taken by swimmer John Brockway.

Initially, crowds in the main stadium remained small, despite generally excellent weather, but gradually the excitement of the Games took hold and later tickets were difficult to obtain.

Standards were high and in athletics three world records were set, in the women's javelin, women's 4 x 110 yards relay and the men's 440 yards hurdles. The javelin record went to Anna Pazera, a Pole who had defected to Australia during the 1956 Olympic Games. She threw more than 20 feet (6.10m) further than her previous best. She was aided no doubt by an unusual wind in the stadium which many present considered gave Edward Sampson a 'wind-aided' English Native record at 440 yards in the early rounds of that event. A highly unusual situation occured in the 120 yards hurdles final when Jacobus Swart of South Africa fell just before the finishing line, and actually crossed that line backwards. After originally being placed last by the judges, it was later established from the photo-finish picture that he had, in fact, finished in second place. The event was won by defending champion Keith Gardner of Jamaica, who scored a unique double for the Games by also winning the 100 yards sprint. A silver medal in the 220 yards and a bronze in the 4 x 440 yards relay were added during Gardner's hectic but profitable week. In 1954 Marlene Matthews-Willard of Australia had broken down in her 100 yards heat, but she more than made amends this time by winning both the 100 and the 220 yards titles and gaining a silver medal in the relay. Val Sloper of New Zealand began her remarkable Games career by winning the shot, while silver medals in the long jump and 220 yards respectively went to future Olympic greats Mary Bignal and Betty Cuthbert. Gert Potgieter's record in the 440 yards hurdles was a magnificent performance, intrinsically superior to the 400 metres mark held by America's Glenn Davis. However, most attention on the track went to two Australian runners, Herb Elliott and Dave Power. Elliott became the first of only two men to win the 880 yards/mile double, and Power won a unique 6 miles/marathon couplet. Field event performances showed signs of moving nearer to world standards, although some remained pitifully low.

In the swimming pool there was no lack of class performances as the 2,300 capacity crowds saw a tremendous spree of record breaking with 27 improvements to Games records and 11 to world marks. The Australians swept nearly all before them with only a few of the Home countries swimmers, especially the English girls, gainsaying them. The most successful swimmers were John Devitt and his team-mate John Konrads, who each won three gold medals. With his sister Ilsa, the youngest winner at the Games when taking the 440 yards freestyle aged 14 years 136 days, the Latvian-born

Konrads became the first brother and sister to win gold medals at the Games. John himself was the youngest male champion in Cardiff, winning a relay gold aged 16 years 59 days. The most successful female competitor at the Games was Australia's Olympic champion swimmer Dawn Fraser with two golds and two silver medals.

Two particular wins which brought the predominantly British crowd to its feet were Scotland's Ian Black's victory in the 220 yards butterfly, after valiantly gaining a silver behind Konrads in the 440 yards freestyle, and England's Judy Grinham's world record swim in the 110 yards backstroke.

The opening ceremony at the Maindy Stadium, Cardiff, a much smaller affair than the extravaganzas of the 1980s.

There was a surprise double by Charmian Welsh of England in the women's diving while Scotland's Peter Heatly won back the highboard title that he had first taken in 1950.

Spectators at beautiful Lake Padarn, in North Wales, witnessed the swansong of the amazing Mervyn Wood, who, aged 41 years 83 days, won a double sculls silver medal in his third Games. The Canadian eight, built around the 1956 Olympic coxless fours gold medallists, won easily. In fencing, the English competitors swept all before them with Bill Hoskyns winning three gold medals. Olympic champion Gillian Sheen won the women's foil with the 1950 and 1954 titlist Mary Glen-Haig in third place. Some marvellous old gentlemen appeared in the bowls events, not least the 63 year old Percy Baker who gained a silver medal for England in the singles. Boxing honours went to South Africa with four gold medals, a silver and two bronzes. For the first time the principle of two bronze medallists was introduced. One of the most popular winners was Melbourne Olympic champion, Dick McTaggart of Scotland, who is the only man to win both such titles. In weightlifting, Barbados won its first gold medal through the good offices of a London bus conductor, Blair Blenman, who took the middle-weight title, narrowly on bodyweight, for his native island.

Despite a recently introduced clause in the Constitution of the British Empire and Commonwealth Games Federation, to the effect that no discrimination against a country or person on the grounds of race, colour, religion or politics, be permitted, South Africa fielded a team that was totally white. This resulted in many scenes of protest. Two years later South Africa left the Commonwealth.

It had been intended that Queen Elizabeth would attend the closing ceremony, but she was not well. However, a recording was played over the loudspeakers in which, to great cheers, she announced her intention to invest Prince Charles with the title of Prince of Wales.

Perth Australia

22 November - 1 December 1962

Many of the visitors to Perth were coming from wintry conditions back home and therefore tended to overdo the sunbathing in the intense heat of Western Australia's sun, for which they suffered accordingly. Temperatures were high throughout the Games, although at times relief was brought by excessive winds which often seriously affected the standard of performances, particularly at athletics and rowing.

The Games were officially opened by Prince Philip, the Duke of Edinburgh, in the presence of the Prime Minister of Australia, Robert Menzies, at Perry Lakes Stadium, and 50,000 spectators watched the oath taken by veteran fencer Ivan Lund, who would win the épée gold medal in his fourth Games. A total of 863 competitors, including 136 women, from a record-equalling 35 countries were entered for the same nine sports as had been contested in the previous three Games. Included in those countries were three one-man teams, from Barbados, British Guiana and St. Lucia, but there was one major omission: South Africa had declared itself a Republic the year before and had withdrawn from the Commonwealth.

The Games had actually begun prior to the official opening with the lawn bowls getting underway three days earlier. England's David Bryant began his unprecedented series of gold medals here. The first gold medal of the Games was won, surprisingly, by New Zealand's Melody Coleman in the women's foil, although it would not be unfair to suggest that her success was partially due to the effects of the excessive heat on some of the competitors. This can be borne out by the fact that the first four places went to Antipodean competitors, in an event traditionally dominated by the English. Over on the Canning River there was criticism of the small entry list, only five countries being represented, but the rowing events were keenly contested and one notable feature was that three different sets of brothers gained silver medals, the Lawrences and Watkinsons of New Zealand and the Lukes of Wales.

Peter Snell.

In the main stadium the strong winds at times created havoc with expected performance levels but competition was intense, no more so than in the men's sprints, both won by Seraphino Antao of Kenya. The bronze medal in the 100 yards was reallocated 48 hours after the presentation ceremony when it was returned by Gary Holdsworth and given to Mike Cleary (both AUS), not the result of a protest but on the track referee's recommendation for a further viewing of the photo-finish. Former mile champion Herb Elliott was on hand, reporting for a newspaper, to see his heir-apparent Peter Snell win the 880 yards/mile double, the latter in a suprisingly mediocre time, although he had run for New Zealand's 4 x 440 yards relay team earlier in the day. The six miles, run in 39°C (103°F) temperature and described as "less a race than a fight for survival", was won by the remarkable 19 year old Canadian Bruce Kidd, who later gained a bronze in the 3 miles. This event contained some of the greatest names in the sport and was won by the defending champion, the New Zealander with the withered arm, Murray Halberg. There were grave misgivings about the marathon scheduled for 3.40 pm but happily the temperature had dropped considerably, although

Anita Lonsbrough added three gold medals at Perth to the two she had won in 1958.

still very warm, and there was some rain which helped cool the runners. The winner, Brian Kilby emulated his English predecessor Jack Holden, the 1950 champion, by also winning the European title in the same year.

The most prolific medal winner in athletics was England's female sprinter Dorothy Hyman, with two golds and a silver. George Kerr of Jamaica, Pam Kilborn of Australia and Val Young of New Zealand also won two gold medals each. Future Olympic champion Lynn Davies was only fourth in the long jump, but just three-quarters of an inch off the silver medal, while in sixth place in the 80m hurdles was Ann Packer, who went on to win the 1964 Olympic 800 metres title.

Early criticism of the new Beatty Park swimming pool proved to be totally unfounded as record after record was smashed. Australian supremacy was only halted now and again by English or Canadian swimmers. Australia won over half of all swimming medals available, with the Scots-born Murray Rose taking four golds for them. England's Anita Lonsbrough was the most successful female swimmer with three golds and a silver. There was controversy in one of her victories, the 110 yards breaststroke, when the judges were divided as to whether she had beaten Vivien Haddon of New Zealand who had touched under water. The English girl was finally given the gold medal although it was reported that the automatic timing device, then not used officially, had given Haddon the faster time. The youngest champion at the Games was Linda Ludgrove who won the 110 yards backstroke for England aged 15 years 80 days, while the youngest male was Australia's Ian O'Brien. He won the men's 110 yards breaststroke when some six months older than Ludgrove. Pakistan won seven of the eight finals in wrestling, with the eighth man taking a silver medal.

There was a bad shortage of qualified officials in the boxing, which was exacerbated by the protest made at the inclusion of a South African as a judge and referee. In a compromise ruling he was retained but did not officiate in bouts containing African boxers. Some team managers were recruited to help as ringside officials, but there were some strange decisions, not least that which gave Clement Quartey victory over Olympic champion Dick McTaggart. The Ghanaian gave the best comment on the decision by promptly fainting in the ring.

The venue for 1966 was decided when Kingston beat Edinburgh by 17 votes to 16 after Salisbury, Rhodesia had withdrawn.

Medallists at épée and sabre, Ivan Lund (left) of Australia and Benedek Simo (right) of Canada, in action during the men's team foil fencing.

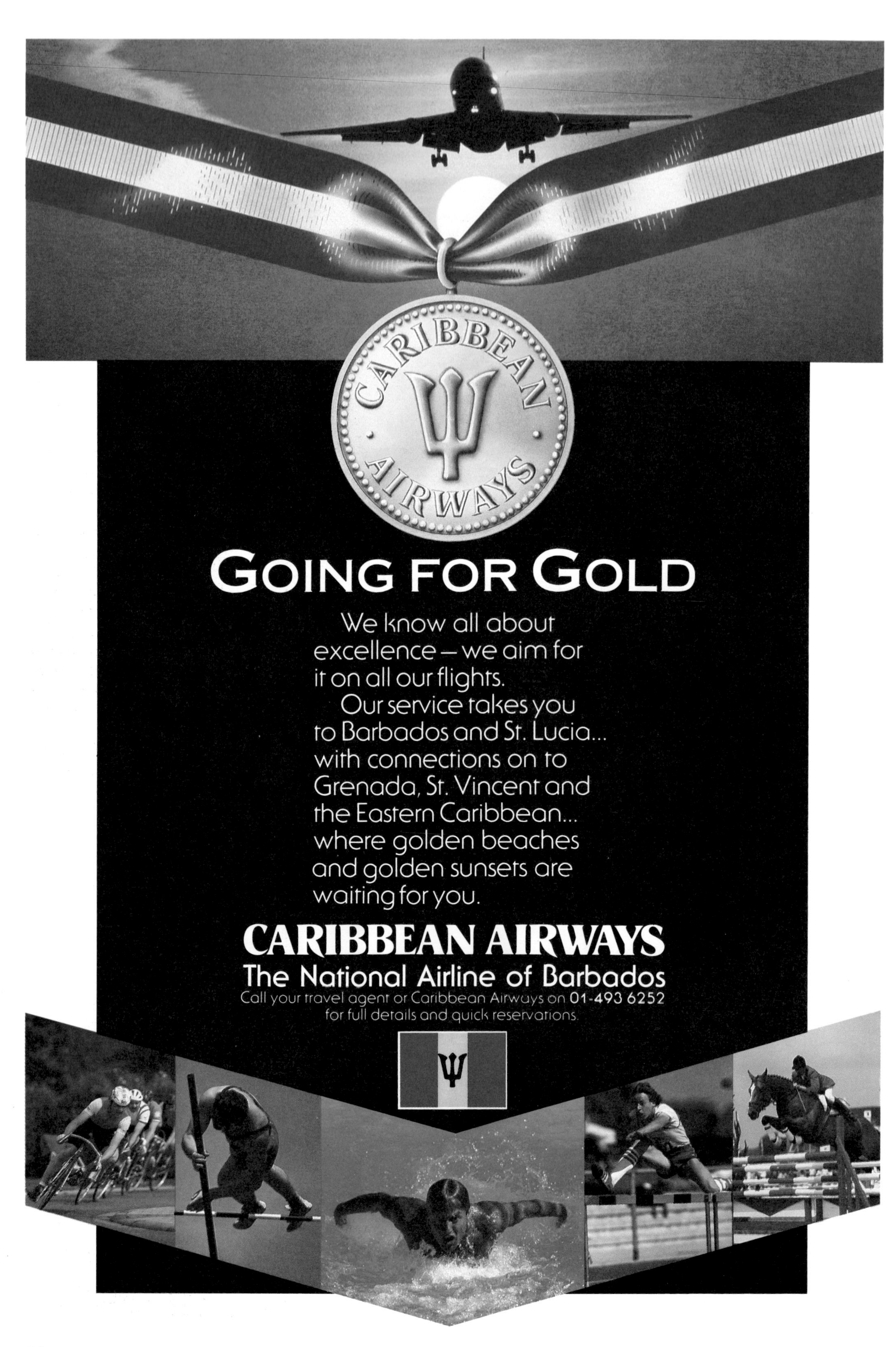
CARIBBEAN
AIRWAYS
GOING FOR GOLD
We know all about
excellence – we aim for
it on all our flights.
Our service takes you
to Barbados and St. Lucia...
with connections on to
Grenada, St. Vincent and
the Eastern Caribbean...
where golden beaches
and golden sunsets are
waiting for you.
CARIBBEAN AIRWAYS
The National Airline of Barbados
Call your travel agent or Caribbean Airways on 01-493 6252
for full details and quick reservations.

Kingston Jamaica

4-13 August 1966

Jamaica became the first Caribbean nation, and indeed the smallest country, to have been selected to host the Games. Rowing and lawn bowls were not held as there were no facilities for those sports in Jamaica, and badminton and shooting made up the nine sports for which there were 1,050 competitors, including 196 women, from 34 countries.

Innovations included eight lanes at both the running track and the swimming pool. Another newcomer to the Games was the Canadian flag - this was the first time that the new Maple Leaf flag was flown at an international sports meeting.

The opening was performed by Prince Philip, before 40,000 people in the new National Stadium at Independence Park, at 9.45 pm due to the excessive heat and humidity experienced in August in Jamaica. For the same reason some of the athletics events were re-scheduled for the mornings, the marathon beginning at 5.30 am, although the temperature had risen to 29°C (85°F) by the end of the race. One of the many little mishaps occurred then, when Scotland's Jim Alder, leading by 50 yards, was misdirected on entering the stadium precincts and finally reached the track to find himself some 30 yards behind Bill Adcocks of England. Happily he was able to regain the lead and win. There were a number of other 'hiccups' in the organisation, such as in the shooting when initially everything was ready to start except that there was no ammunition.

The National Stadium, Kingston as viewed from the top of the diving tower.

Another bizarre happening came in the boxing when Oxford Rugby Blue John Coker of Sierra Leone was disqualified from the competition because there were no gloves big enough for his oversize hands, which had unusually long thumbs.

But with good humour all round most competitors - housed in excellent accommodation at the University of the West Indies - settled down to their competitions. One strange complaint, in the hot and humid conditions prevalent, was that from an Aden athlete who complained that he felt cold.

Fifteen world records were broken in the swimming pool, while in athletics the standards, though not quite that good, were very high. Harry Jerome of Canada finally won the gold medal that had eluded him in previous Commonwealth and Olympic sprint competitions, holding Tom Robinson of the Bahamas back to his third consecutive 100 yards silver medal.

The Kenyans were practically unbeatable on the track from 880

Hugh Porter, individual pursuit champion.

yards upwards, with Kip Keino taking the 1 mile/3 miles double. In the former he smashed the field, leading for all but the first 100 yards. In the latter he had a truly magnificent race with Ron Clarke of Australia. Other African victories went to Ghana, the 220 yards and sprint relay, and Nigeria, the triple jump, while Violet Odogwu of Nigeria became the first black African woman to win a Games medal when she took the bronze in the long jump. Most medals in athletics were won by triple gold medallist Diane Burge of Australia in the sprints, and Val Young of New Zealand repeated her shot/discus double from Perth. Three other athletes, pole vaulter Trevor Bickle (AUS), hammer thrower Howard Payne (ENG) and hurdler Pam Kilborn (AUS) retained their titles.

The swimming pool frothed with the power of the Australian men who won ten of the thirteen swimming events, but their women were strangely subdued, only taking one gold medal. All four diving events went to England, with Brian Phelps successfully defending his titles at both springboard and highboard. The women's highboard title was only won by two-hundredths of a point, one of the closest ever finishes in a major championship.

Peter Reynolds of Australia won four golds and would have had a fifth had his winning team in the 4 x 110 yards medley relay not been disqualified for an illegal change. A new women's record medal haul was made by Canada's 'Mighty Mouse' Elaine Tanner, with four golds and three silvers. Winning the first of her titles when aged 15 years 164 days, she became the youngest champion at Kingston. Another outstanding swimmer was Ralph Hutton of Canada, who won one gold, five silver and two bronze medals for a record total of eight medals at one Games. Typical of the competitiveness of the Australians was the attempt on the world record by the disqualified medley relay team after the swimming programme was finished. Despite the water temperature being some ten degrees higher than the maximum recommended by the international swimming authorities, the Australians smashed the world mark with a time actually faster than that they had unavailingly clocked in the Games final.

The first gold medal of the Games was won by little Precious McKenzie

Ron Clarke.

whose British naturalisation had been rushed through to enable him to take part in Kingston for England.

In cycling, England's Hugh Porter won the individual pursuit title to add to the family collection; he is married to swimmer Anita Lonsbrough. Introduced for the first time at Kingston, shooting provided competitors of a very high standard, such as the small bore rifle gold medallist Gil Boa of Canada, a former winner of the Queen's Prize at Bisley and the 1954 world champion. The winner of the free pistol, Charles Sexton of England, was, at just a month short of his 60th birthday, the oldest champion at the Games. At the weightlifting competition the usual order of contests was changed so that the middleweight class should be last. In this was Louis Martin, who though competing for England was born in Jamaica. There was a moment of high drama when some confusion arose when he asked for a weight increase in pounds and it was taken by officials to be kilograms. The resulting lift was disastrous, but the mistake was realised and rectified and Jamaica was happy.

By the end of a highly successful Games a then record 22 countries had won at least one medal.

At Kingston a conference decided that the word 'Empire' would be dropped from the title of the Games. Henceforth they would be known as The British Commonwealth Games.

Edinburgh Scotland

16-25 July 1970

Tragedy for Sylvia Potts of New Zealand as she falls at the finish of the 1500m, won by Rita Ridley from Joan Page (now Allison).

The first Games to be held in Scotland were a great success, fully living up to the 'Friendly Games' label. Even the rain, all too frequent, could not dampen the spirits of all concerned.

Prince Philip, the Duke of Edinburgh, officially opened the Games in front of a capacity crowd of 30,000 spectators at the opening ceremony staged at Meadowbank Stadium with great aplomb. From traditional highland dancing to the split second fly past by the RAF, all was handled with great warmth of spirit and splendid organisation. The oath on behalf of the athletes was taken by the Scottish high jumper Crawford Fairbrother.

There were a record 1,383 competitors, including 288 women, at the Games from a record 42 countries. The nine sports scheduled were the same as at Kingston, except that shooting was replaced by lawn bowls. For the first time athletics and swimming events were staged at metric distances.

The stadium in the £2.4 million Meadowbank complex proved first-class, although the prevailing East-West winds along the parallel Firth of Forth swept along the home straight at up to nearly ten metres per second on occasion. These helped the sprinters to very fast times, but adversely affected performances around the track.

A new standard in organisation was reached in Edinburgh and spectators and athletes alike much appreciated the excellent announcing over the stadium public address system. There was much to enthuse about at the athletics. Two young sprinters, at the start of what were to prove to be marvellous careers, Don Quarrie of Jamaica and Raelene Boyle of Australia, won three gold medals each. Kenya's four gold medals were confined to the shorter distances as the Home Countries' distance runners, led by Ian and Lachie Stewart of Scotland, dominated the longer races. Howard Payne won his third consecutive hammer title on the same day that his wife Rosemary won the discus, he for England and she for the host country. That day was also David Hemery's 26th birthday and his successful defence of the high hurdles title was greeted by a rendering of "Happy Birthday to You" from the presentation band. Another family double came with the victories of John (400 metres hurdles) and Sheila (long jump) Sherwood, both of England. The 5000 metres, won by Ian Stewart, was considered by those present as one of the greatest ever races at that distance, while Ron Hill's marathon win was in a time only beaten once

Lachie Stewart with the Scots mascot after his 10000m triumph.

The Queen's coach circles the track of the Meadowbank Stadium at the closing ceremony.

in history at that time. In the women's events Pam Kilborn of Australia won her third consecutive hurdles title, and then won another gold in the relay to take her medal haul to six golds in three Games. Fiji won its first athletics medal for 20 years when a total unknown, Saimoni Tamani, won the 400 metres bronze, improving his best time by over two and a half seconds. There were some dramatic moments too, as when Sylvia Potts of New Zealand fell within some two strides of winning the 1500 metres, and finally finished in ninth place. World record holder Kerry O'Brien (AUS) fell into the water jump with a lap to go in the steeplechase and was out of the race, as his unheralded team-mate, Tony Manning, took the gold medal. The only world record broken on the track was by 17 year old Marilyn Neufville in the women's 400 metres with 51.02 seconds. She was the centre of a

David Hemery.

Louis Martin.

rare controversial incident between members of the Commonwealth when prior to the Games she was persuaded to compete for Jamaica, where she was born, and not for England which had nurtured her running ability thus far.

At the pool the Australians were back to their winning ways, taking 20 gold, 10 silver and 12 bronze medals. Their main opposition came from the Canadians. Mike Wenden, Lynn 'Pokey' Watson and Denise Langford all won four golds and a silver for Australia, and Langford was the youngest champion at Edinburgh when taking her first title aged 14 years 199 days. Diving doubles were won by Don Wagstaff (AUS) and Beverley Boys (CAN).

The youngest male champion, wrestler Ved Prakash, was nearly refused permission to compete, although he had contested the world championships just before the Games. The problem was that he was reported to be only 12 years of age. In fact his passport indicated that he was six months short of his 15th birthday when he took the light-flyweight title. Lesley Allardice of England was even younger, just 13, when she won a bronze medal in the 4 x 100 metres freestyle relay. By contrast, Scotland's David Pearson was 37 days short of his 64th birthday when he won a silver medal in the bowls fours event.

African boxers won eight of the eleven titles with Philip Waruinge of Kenya, who had won the Val Barker style prize at the Mexico Olympic Games, successfully defending his featherweight gold medal. Bill Hoskyns of England won a fencing title (épée) for a record third time as the sport bowed out of the Commonwealth Games. Another to win a title for the third Games in a row was weightlifter Louis Martin.

Cycling was bedevilled by strong winds and rain, but Jocelyn Lovell of Canada gave a preview of what he was to achieve eight years later by winning a complete set of medals at Edinburgh.

In all, competitors from 27 countries won medals, far and away the greatest dispersion in the history of the Games.

Christchurch New Zealand

24 January - 2 February 1974

The tenth British Commonwealth Games were meant to be 'The Friendly Games' and such they proved to be. Although one of the smallest cities to host the occasion, Christchurch, with a population of about 170,000, made every possible effort to make the Games memorable for its ambience as well as for performance. In this they were successful, even though there were several problems in the months leading up to the opening ceremony. Not least was the threatened boycott by African countries because of the proposed Springbok tour of New Zealand scheduled for 1973. After much public debate on the subject the tour was cancelled at the request of the New Zealand Prime Minister, Norman Kirk, and the African withdrawal was averted. Christchurch also had financial troubles due to unforeseen extra expense, but people around the country rallied to its aid, and the money was raised in time.

The official opening was performed by Prince Philip, Duke of Edinburgh in front of 35,000 spectators at Queen Elizabeth II stadium. Hammer thrower Warwick Nicholl took the oath on behalf of the 1,276 competitors, including 299 women, representing 38 countries. There were nine sports as usual, but shooting had replaced fencing. The sportsmen and women were housed at the University of Canterbury's campus at Ilam.

The Maori ceremonial display at the opening ceremony.

Filbert Bayi on his way to victory at 1500m.

The atmosphere of these Games can best be illustrated by the decathlon medal ceremony when the losing competitors were invited to line up behind the medallists so that they too could receive the plaudits of the crowd. The weather for most of the period was excellent and performances reflected this.

Possibly the outstanding performer of the Games was Tanzania's Filbert Bayi, who won the 1500 metres title, leading from gun to tape to set a new world record of 3:32.16 from John Walker of New Zealand and Ben Jipcho, who led Kenya in its finest showing ever with his own two gold medals in the 5000 metres and 3000 metres steeplechase. African athletes in all won eight golds, five silvers and 12 bronze medals in the men's events with their women adding another gold, a silver and four bronze. Nigeria's Modupe Oshikoya became the most successful black African female athlete by winning a set of medals from the long jump, pentathlon and hurdles. The pentathlon was won by Olympic champion Mary Peters of Northern Ireland, making her last appearance as an athlete. Another veteran to taste victory was the host country's Robin Tait, in his fourth Games, who won the discus with a superlative personal and Commonwealth record on his third

The 10000m was a rough race, with David Bedford (leading) much troubled by jostling from the Kenyans Richard Juma and Paul Mose. Bedford finished fourth as Richard Tayler of New Zealand, who had stayed clear of the trouble, stormed through to win from England's David Black.

Jenny Turrall, gold at the age of 13.

throw. He then withdrew from the competition much to the chagrin of New Zealand television which had missed his great throw. Jamaica's Don Quarrie and Australia's Raelene Boyle repeated their sprint doubles from Edinburgh, but Boyle also won a gold in the relay.

Sporting history was made in the New Zealand team by the selection of Colleen Mills (400 metres), daughter Donna (high jump) and son Philip (110m hurdles). Unfortunately, father Les Mills (1966 discus champion) was not selected or they would have set a record unlikely ever to be beaten at a major championship.

The swimming pool was part of the main Queen Elizabeth II complex, on the other side of the main stand. It hosted the usual quota of top class performances, headed by Scotland's David Wilkie who won two individual gold medals within a few hours, and Australia's 'grand old man' (actually aged 24) Mike Wenden, who took his total of medals from three Games to a record 13 (nine gold, three silver, one bronze).

Jenny Turrall of Australia became the youngest gold medallist at any Commonwealth Games when she won the 400 metres freestyle aged 13 years 262 days. She had won a silver medal in the relay six days earlier. The oldest champion at Christchurch was David Baldwin, a member of the victorious New Zealand fours in bowls, aged 53 years 49 days. Scotland's aptly named William Scott won a bronze medal in the same event three months past his 64th birthday. In the new Games sport of shooting, Yvonne Gowland, an Australian mother of two children, won the small bore rifle event, while the rapid fire pistol contest went to the Reverend Bill Hare, who had only just made the Canadian team.

Middleweight boxer Frankie Lucas failed to be selected for the England team, so he represented his native St. Vincent, and won the gold medal.

At a meeting of the Games Federation in Christchurch it was decided to delete the word 'British' from the titles of the governing body and the Games themselves; they now became The Commonwealth Games Federation and the Commonwealth Games respectively.

These Games, which had opened with the Maori ceremonial challenge to the Duke of Edinburgh, ended with a joyous intermingling of competitors and officials from all countries at the closing ceremony of what had truly been 'The Friendly Games'.

Golden Moments

Until 1982 British male swimmers had only won two of the possible 52 gold medals for freestyle events in the Games since 1930. Both of those were won in 1938 by England's Bob Leivers (1650 yards) and the 880 yards relay team, which included Leivers. At Brisbane Andrew Astbury, also of England, doubled that figure by winning both the 200m and 400m freestyle events. Similarly, Britain's women had only won three of a possible 39 gold medals in such events, all by England in 1930. At Brisbane they equalled that figure with another three golds, with June Croft matching Joyce Cooper from 1930 by winning the 100m and 200m and helping her team-mates to victory in the relay. By a strange coincidence they had the same initials, 'J.C.'

Edmonton
Canada
3-12 August 1978

These were the first Games to be officially opened by the Queen, which she did before a capacity crowd of 42,000 in blazing sunshine at the new £21 million Commonwealth Stadium. It had a rather unusual shape due to the fact that it had been built with its future as a Canadian Football venue in mind. Queen Elizabeth read out the message that had been carried in relay from Buckingham Palace, where she had given it to Filbert Bayi of Tanzania, to Edmonton, where it was delivered by the final runner, Canadian pentathlete Diane Jones-Konihowski. The oath on behalf of the competitors was taken by the 1974 diving gold medallist Beverley Boys. A record 46 countries sent 1,149 male and 326 female competitors, who took part in a record 10 sports, as gymnastics had been added to the programme.

Two men were the stars of these Games. In athletics England's Daley Thompson began his collection of international championship medals by winning the decathlon with a Commonwealth record score of 8,467 points, over 800 points ahead of the second placed man. During that competition he also set a Games record for the long jump by clearing 8.11m (26ft 7¼in), which exceeded the individual event record. At the swimming pool, Canada's Graham Smith set a new individual record for a single Games celebration by winning six gold medals. He is a member of a remarkable swimming family: brother George won two gold and two silver medals in 1970; sisters Susan (two silvers and a bronze) and Sandra (finalist in two events) also competed at Edinburgh; sister Becky won a gold and two silver medals in 1974 and a silver and a bronze at Edmonton. Other highlights in swimming were the three gold medals by Carol Klimpel of Canada and Ron McKeon of Australia, while Tracey Wickham set two of only three world records broken throughout the Games on the way to gaining two golds, two silvers and a bronze.

The fears of some, voiced prior to the Games, that the altitude of Edmonton, albeit only 667m (2,100ft), would affect sea-level competitors, appeared to be realised as the East African runners dominated the distance events. Only England's Brendan Foster was able to stop them, in the 10000 metres, and by adding this gold to his silver in 1974 and his bronze in 1970, he not only made up the set, but also uniquely became a medallist at 1500m, 5000m and 10000m in Commonwealth Games competition. However, he commented afterwards on the effects of the altitude on his time. A major surprise occurred in the marathon when a complete unknown entered the stadium first, to beat two fancied Canadians. Gidamis Shahanga caused consternation among television and radio reporters, most of whom had never heard of him before. Indeed many of the Tanzanian team management were not too sure who he was. Elsewhere, multi-world record holder Henry Rono of Kenya, matched his countryman Ben Jipcho's feat of 1974 by winning the 5000 metres and steeplechase events with consummate ease.

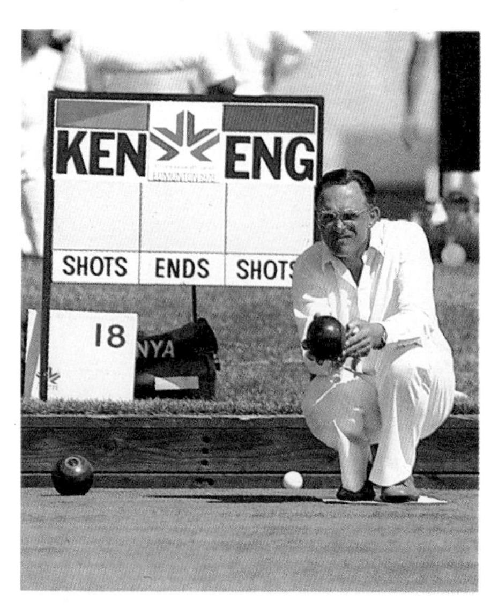

The greatest bowler in Games history - David Bryant lines up with care. At Edmonton, at the age of 46, he won his fourth successive singles title.

Raelene Boyle (silver) and Don Quarrie (gold) both added to their medal collections, but only in the 100 metres, both being injured and withdrawing from other events. In women's athletics, this was the first time that both Games sprint titles had not been won by the same athlete. British sprinters regained some of their lost prestige as England's Sonia Lannaman won the

The 'unknown' marathon victor, Gidamis Shahanga of Tanzania.

Raelene Boyle.

100 metres and took silver at 200, while Scotland's Allan Wells reversed the process; both of them added relay gold medals to their respective tallies. Eight years after her brother Ian's 5000 metres triumph, Mary Stewart, representing England, won the 1500 metres gold medal, while Judy Peckham of Australia added the 800 metres title to her husband Laurie's two gold high jump medals from 1966 and 1970. In the women's 3000 metres race, twin sisters Paula Fudge and Ann Ford (née Yeoman) created a little bit of history by winning the gold and bronze medals respectively. Incidentally, Raelene Boyle's older brother Ron won a bronze medal in the tandem cycling at the velodrome, where the host country's Jocelyn Lovell became the first cyclist ever to win three golds at a single Games.

Heat was an ever present problem for some competitors, not least on the badminton courts where temperatures of nearly 32°C (90°F) were recorded. The boxers also suffered, and this might account for the difficulty encountered by Northern Ireland's Barry McGuigan in beating his opponent from Papua New Guinea in the final of the bantamweight contest. In bowls, although the ever-present David Bryant won his fourth singles title, England's pairs had an early shock defeat, also by representatives of Papua New Guinea. An even smaller, although more populous, part of the Commonwealth caused some surprises when Hong Kong won both the pairs and fours titles. Just missing a medal in the Northern Irish fours team was one of the youngest ever bowlers in Games history, Michael Dunlop, only ten days past his 18th birthday. At the other extreme, in the same event for Wales, was John Thomson who won a bronze medal at 57 years of age.

Brisbane Australia

30 September - 9 October 1982

Excellent facilities and first class organisation highlighted the X11th Games at Brisbane, as Australia set out to prove itself to the world as a major sporting power. At times the excessive jingoism of some of the spectators almost marred an otherwise pleasant occasion, and the intense rivalry between the Australian and Canadian swimmers did finally overstep the bounds of good sportsmanship and behaviour, but once again the Games provided top-class entertainment.

The Games were opened by the Duke of Edinburgh in the newly constructed 58,000-seat Queen Elizabeth II stadium, which was packed for the occasion. He read the message from the Queen which had been brought to Australia by 1938 Games star Decima Hamilton (née Norman) and which had then travelled by baton relay some 16,000 km around Australia. Very strong winds barely affected the lavish opening ceremony, which incorporated 6,000 schoolchildren, 5,000 pigeons, 50,000 balloons and a 13m (40ft) mechanical model of the Games kangaroo mascot, Matilda. The oath was taken by swimmer Tracey Wickham, who was later in the week presented with her 400m freestyle gold medal by the Queen. The unseasonable cold spell, some 8-10 degrees less than expected, did not deter the 1,176 male and 407 female competitors from 46 countries who were present.

The biggest cheer of the day at the opening ceremony was reserved for the two-man team, both shooters, from the Falkland Islands.

Christina Boxer.

The change in the weather may have exacerbated the influenza outbreak which struck later in the week and which seriously affected some competitors. Also, due to the strength of the wind, a planned nine-man parachute drop into the stadium had to be cancelled.

Brisbane was awarded the Games in July 1976 when its only rival, Birmingham, withdrew its application, and many new facilities were built for the ten sports involved. There was one change in sports, as archery replaced gymnastics. At the Chandler Sports Complex, which comprised the aquatic centre, sports hall, theatre and a velodrome, many records were set. The previously mentioned tense relations, between the Canadians and the Australians, were intensified by the Canadians wearing T-shirts depicting a kangaroo being strangled by a beaver. However, the first gold medal at swimming was won by June Croft, one of nine won by English swimmers and divers. All the other winners were from the two major powers, although their rivalry caused a series of disqualifications to their relay teams which resulted in much bad feeling, culminating in extremely churlish behaviour by the Canadian team after the last event of the swimming programme, watched by the Queen. The actual design of the pool eliminated any washback or wave action from the sides and was thus conducive to fast times. Australians Neil Brooks and Lisa Curry won three gold medals each, but were surpassed by June Croft who added a silver to her three golds.

Chris Snode of England retained both his diving titles, but there were new champions in the women's events. The gold medal in women's highboard went to Jenny Donnett of Australia, whose mother, Barbara McAulay won the 1954 springboard

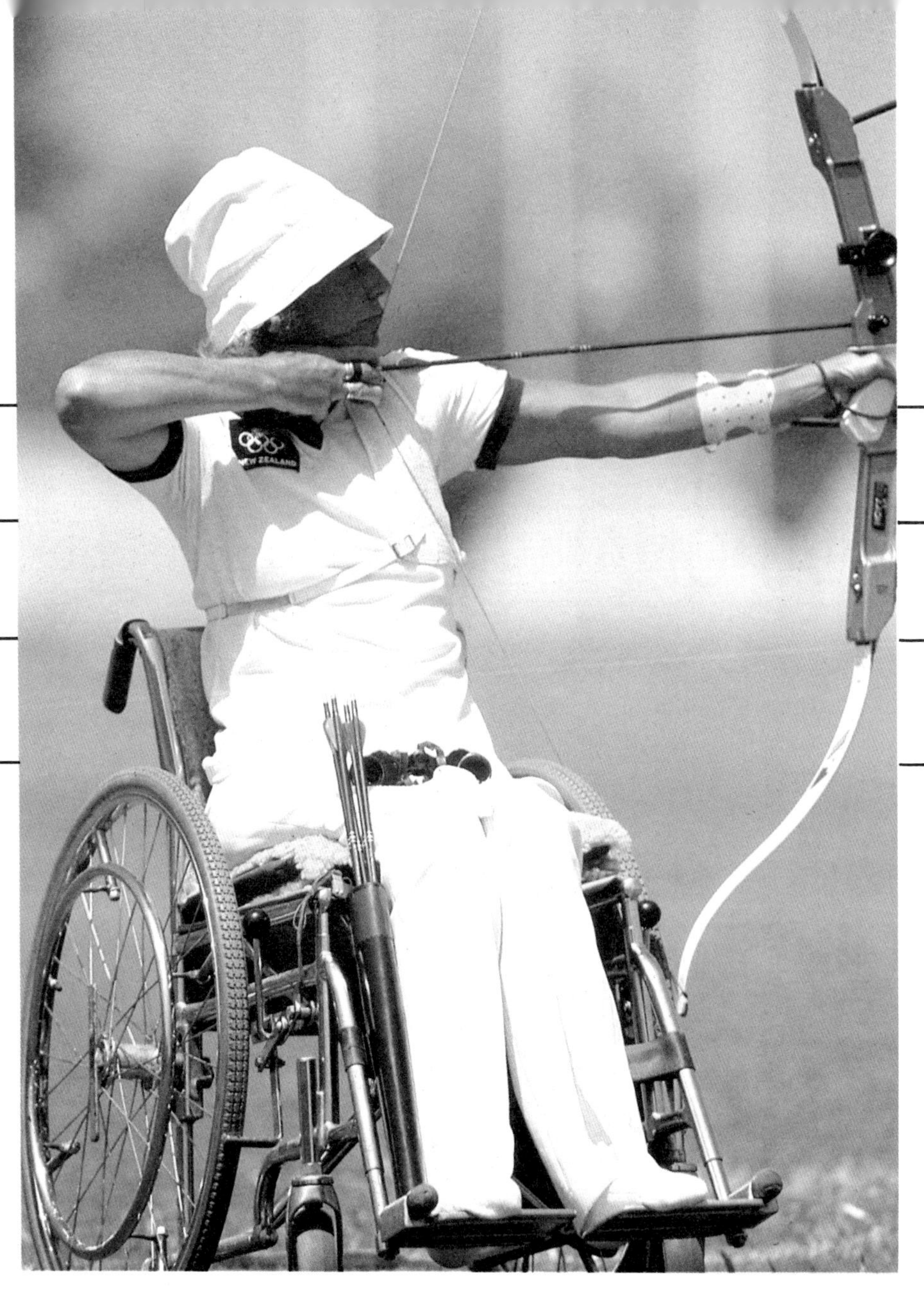

Neroli Fairhall, the remarkable New Zealand archer. A paraplegic since the age of 25 in 1969, but a Commonwealth champion in 1982.

(Above) Tracey Wickham retired after maintaining Australia's great women's swimming tradition, with gold medals at 400m and 800m freestyle.

title, and whose aunt, Irene Donnett, had won the springboard in 1938.

In athletics, both Don Quarrie and Raelene Boyle were attending their fourth Games. Quarrie, injured, could only reach the semi-final of the 100 metres, but Boyle notched up a record eighth and ninth medals with a gold in the 400 metres and a silver in the 4 x 400 metres relay. Also in that relay was 1978 200m gold medallist Denise Robertson-Boyd, whose husband Ray won the pole vault in Brisbane. The men's 200 metres resulted in a first at a major championships when Scotland's Allan Wells, defending champion and winner of the 100m title earlier, and England's Mike McFarlane were adjudged to have tied for the gold medal. Wells proved the most successful man in athletics when he also gained a bronze medal in the sprint relay, but was surpassed by Canada's Angella Taylor who won a total of two golds, a silver and a bronze. There were 17 Games records in the stadium, but the pride of place must go to Keith Connor of England in the triple jump in which he cleared a distance, albeit wind-assisted, only once surpassed in history, to win a tremendous contest with Australia's Ken Lorraway.

Shooting events had been increased since the last Games from six events to 20, and Malcolm Cooper of England gained two gold, three silver and a bronze medal as the most successful marksman. He was later to add an Olympic gold in 1984 to become the only man to achieve a Commonwealth/Olympic shooting double. The winner of the full bore rifle, Arthur Clarke (SCO), was only two months short of his 60th birthday, while the bronze medallist in the same event, Charles Trotter of Guernsey was also 59 years of age.

One of the most remarkable champions in these, or any other Games, was New Zealand's Neroli Fairhall, a paraplegic, who won the women's archery title from her wheelchair. At 38 she was more than twice the age of the runner-up, Janet Yates of Northern Ireland.

Two demonstration sports had been arranged, as allowed, during the Games. Hong Kong beat Australia at table tennis, and local team Richmond beat its rival Carlton at Australian Rules football.

The Games concluded with the Queen and Prince Philip taking an unscheduled lap around the track in their open car, cheered by the massed ranks of the athletes and officials who proceeded to celebrate, in their own uninhibited way, a memorable ten days of sport.

SCHEDULE OF EVENTS

THURSDAY - JULY 24

Opening Ceremony

The opening ceremony - Meadowbank 1970.

The 13th Commonwealth Games begins on the afternoon of Thursday, 24 July at Meadowbank Stadium with the official opening of the Games by HRH Prince Philip

The ceremony, always a magnificent spectacle at major Games, will be produced and presented by the host broadcaster, the BBC. Prior to the traditional and colourful march past of the competing teams, there will be a dance extravaganza by some 6,500 Scottish schoolchildren. In a tradition dating back to 1958, Her Majesty the Queen has earlier handed over a specially-designed baton, containing a message from her. The baton is run in relay to the Games city, and this Queen's relay is climaxed by the entry into the Stadium of the final runner, a past Scottish medallist, whose identity is kept secret until this moment. Prince Philip will read the message and then declare the Games open. The ceremony closes with the exchange of flags, the firing of a salute of guns, the release of balloons and finally the oath is taken by a representative of the Scottish team, who pronounces on behalf of all the assembled competitors:

"We declare that we will take part in the Commonwealth Games of 1986 in the spirit of true sportsmanship, recognising the rules that govern them and desirous of participating in them for the honour of our Commonwealth and the glory of sport."

FRIDAY JULY 25

BADMINTON
Meadowbank Sports Centre

1400	Team event	- 6 matches
1900	Team event	- 6 matches

BOWLS
Balgreen Bowling Centre

0900	Men	Singles, Pairs
	Women	Singles, Pairs
1330	Men	Pairs
	Women	Pairs, Fours
1800	Men	Singles, Fours
	Women	Fours

BOXING
Ingliston Show Ground

1930	Preliminary bouts

CYCLING

1100	100km Road Team Time Trial

ROWING
Strathclyde Country Park

1100	Women	Coxless Pairs heats
1130	Men	Eights heats
1200	Women	Double Sculls heats
1230	Men	Lightweight Sculls heats
1300	Men	Single Sculls heats
1330	Women	Eights heats
1400	Men	Lightweight Coxless Fours heats
1600	Women	Coxless Pairs repêchage

Synchronised swimming is included at the Games for the first time in 1986. The Canadians Sharon Hambrook and Kelly Kryczka won the silver medals at the duet when this event was introduced to the Olympic Games at Los Angeles in 1984.

1630	Men	Eights repêchage
1700	Women	Double Sculls repêchage
1730	Men	Lightweight Sculls repêchage
1800	Men	Single Sculls repêchage
1830	Women	Eights repêchage
1900	Men	Lightweight Coxless Fours repêchage

SHOOTING
Musselburgh

0930	Rapid Fire Pistol Pairs
1400	Free Pistol Pairs

Kippen

1100	Olympic Trench Pairs

Pleasance, Edinburgh University

1030	Air Rifle pairs

SWIMMING
Royal Commonwealth Pool

1000	Women	100m Freestyle heats
	Men	100m Breaststroke heats
	Women	400m Individual Medley heats
	Men	400m Freestyle heats
	Women	4 x 200m Freestyle Relay heats
1300	Women	Synchronised Swimming Figures
1830	Women	100m Freestyle final
	Men	100m Breaststroke final
	Women	400m Individual Medley final
	Men	400m Freestyle final
	Women	4 x 200m Freestyle Relay final
2115	Women	Synchronised Swimming Solo preliminaries

WEIGHTLIFTING
Playhouse Theatre

1400	52kg class
1930	56kg class

SATURDAY JULY 26

ATHLETICS
Meadowbank Stadium

0900	Men	Hammer qualifying
1000	Women	Heptathlon 100m Hurdles
1025	Men	100m first round
1030	Women	Discus qualifying
1045	Women	Heptathlon High Jump
1110	Women	400m heats
1135	Men	400m first round
1220	Men	110m Hurdles heats
1300	Men	Hammer final
1400	Women	100m heats
1415	Women	Heptathlon Shot
1435	Men	3000m Steeplechase final
1510	Men	100m second round
1600	Men	110m Hurdles semi-finals
1620	Women	Heptathlon 200m
1640	Women	400m semi-finals
1700	Men	400m second round
1735	Women	3000m heats
1810	Men	10000m final

BADMINTON
Meadowbank Sports Centre

1400	Team event - 6 matches
1900	Team event - 6 matches

BOWLS
Balgreen Bowling Centre

0900	Men	Singles, Fours
	Women	Singles, Pairs
1330	Men	Pairs
	Women	Singles, Pairs, Fours
1800	Men	Singles, Pairs, Fours
	Women	Fours

BOXING
Ingliston Show Ground

1400	Preliminary bouts
1930	Preliminary bouts

Two British athletes who won Commonwealth silver medals in 1982 will hope to go one better this time. (Bottom left) Martin Girvan of Northern Ireland in the hammer. (Top left) Judy Simpson, England's talented heptathlete, who could also qualify for the Games at 100m hurdles or high jump.

Canadian medley swimmer Alex Baumann already has two Commonwealth and two Olympic gold medals in his collection.

CYCLING
Meadowbank Velodrome

1900		1000m Individual Time Trial

ROWING
Strathclyde Country Park

1100	Women	Coxless Pairs final
1130	Men	Eights final
1200	Women	Double Sculls final
1230	Men	Lightweight Sculls final
1300	Men	Single Sculls final
1330	Women	Eights final
1400	Men	Lightweight Coxless Fours final

SHOOTING
Musselburgh

0930		Small Bore Rifle Prone Pairs
1130		Rapid Fire Pistol Pairs

Kippen

1100		Skeet Pairs

SWIMMING
Royal Commonwealth Pool

1000	Men	100m Butterfly heats
	Women	200m Individual Medley heats
	Men	400m Individual Medley heats
	Women	200m Breaststroke heats
	Men	4 x 200m Freestyle Relay heats
1300	Women	Synchronised Swimming Figures
1830	Men	100m Butterfly final
	Women	200m Individual Medley final
	Men	400m Individual Medley final
	Women	200m Breaststroke final
	Men	4 x 200m Freestyle Relay final
2115	Women	Synchronised Swimming Duet preliminaries

WEIGHTLIFTING
Playhouse Theatre

1400		60kg class
1930		67.5kg class

SUNDAY

JULY 27

Kenyans have won the last three steeplechase titles, and have strong candidates for 1986 in Julius Kariuki, Julius Korir and Joshua Kipkemboi. Their run started in 1974 and this picture shows Evans Mogaka (third) leading Ben Jipcho, who went on to win. John Davies (top of the picture) of Wales was second.

ATHLETICS
Meadowbank Stadium

1000	Men	Decathlon 100m
	Women	Shot qualifying
1030	Women	400m Hurdles heats
1045	Men	Decathlon Long Jump
1105	Men	400m Hurdles heats
1215	Women	Heptathlon Long Jump
1230	Men	400m semi-finals
1235	Men	Decathlon Shot
1355	Women	Heptathlon Javelin
1400	Men	110m Hurdles final
1415	Women	100m semi-finals
1435	Men	Decathlon High Jump
1440	Men	100m semi-finals
1500	Men	3000m Steeplechase final
1520	Women	400m final
1532	Men	400m final
1555	Women	Discus final
1600	Women	Heptathlon 800m
1625	Women	100m final
1635	Men	100m final
1700	Women	3000m final
1735	Men	Decathlon 400m

BADMINTON
Meadowbank Sports Centre

1000	Team event - 2 play-offs
1400	Team event - 2 play-offs
1900	Team event - 2 play-offs

Sarah Hardcastle won the 1984 Olympic silver medal at 400m freestyle, and will surely be the favourite for this event in Edinburgh.

BOWLS
Balgreen Bowling Centre

0900	Men	Singles, Fours
	Women	Singles, Fours
1330	Men	Pairs
	Women	Singles, Pairs
1800	Men	Singles, Pairs, Fours
	Women	Pairs

BOXING
Ingliston Show Ground

1400	Preliminary bouts
1930	Preliminary bouts

CANOEING
DEMONSTRATION SPORT
Strathclyde Country Park

1000	1000m events
1400	500m events

CYCLING
Meadowbank Velodrome

1430	Sprint heats
	4000m Individual Pursuit heats
1900	Sprint repêchage
	4000m Individual Pursuit quarter-finals

SHOOTING
Musselburgh

0930	Small Bore Rifle 3 Positions Pairs

Pleasance, Edinburgh University

1200	Air Pistol Pairs

SWIMMING
Royal Commonwealth Pool

1000	Women	400m Freestyle heats
	Men	100m Freestyle heats
	Women	100m Backstroke heats
	Men	200m Backstroke heats
	Women	4 x 100m Freestyle Relay heats
1300	Women	Highboard Diving
	Men	Springboard Diving
1830	Women	400m Freestyle final
	Men	100m Freestyle final
	Women	100m Backstroke final
	Men	200m Backstroke final
	Women	4 x 100m Freestyle Relay final
2115	Women	Synchronised Swimming Solo final

WEIGHTLIFTING
Playhouse Theatre

1400	75kg class
1930	82.5kg class

A LONG-RUNNING SUCCESS.
G-RMSS
S
Royal Mail
:Datapost
In 1635 King Charles I opened up his courier service to his countrymen, and the Royal Mail became a right for all. Since then, the rest of the world has looked to The British Post Office as a model for ideas and innovation. We were the first in the world to introduce the postage stamp, a scheduled airmail service and more recently a public international facsimile service.
Today in the UK, the Royal Mail operates a complex nationwide network, delivering 42 million letters and parcels every working day to 23 million addresses.
That involves 27,000 vehicles, 4,000 trains daily and a fleet of aircraft. Its worldwide services cover virtually all countries in the world efficiently, economically.
In the midst of all our plans and giant operations, we have not forgotten what we stand for. We are still, and always will be, a uniquely personal business.
The Royal Mail is proud to support the Queen's Relay and is delighted that the baton is entrusted to our Datapost Service on its journey around Great Britain and to the Isle of Man and the Channel Islands. It is the kind of responsibility we have never taken lightly, from that very first day back in 1635.
The Post Office
In business to serve you

Sporting Pictures (UK) Lt

MONDAY JULY 28

Men's coxless fours

ATHLETICS
Meadowbank Stadium

0915	Men	Decathlon 110m Hurdles
1000	Men	High Jump qualifying
	Men	Decathlon Discus
1125	Men	Decathlon Pole Vault
1130	Men	800m heats
1145	Women	Javelin qualifying
1200	Women	200m heats
1235	Men	200m 1st round
1400	Women	400m Hurdles semi-finals
1405	Women	Shot final
1425	Men	400m Hurdles semi-finals
1450	Women	800m semi-finals
1500	Men	Decathlon Javelin
1510	Men	800m semi-finals
1530	Women	200m semi-finals
1555	Men	200m 2nd round
1630	Men	Decathlon 1500m
1700	Women	400m Hurdles final
1715	Men	400m Hurdles final
1725	Women	10000m final
1820	Men	5000m heats

BOWLS
Balgreen Bowling Centre

0900	Men	Singles, Fours
	Women	Singles, Pairs
1330	Men	Pairs
	Women	Singles, Pairs, Fours
1800	Men	Singles, Pairs, Fours
	Women	Fours

The second day of the decathlon. The day's events start at 9.15 a.m. with the 110m hurdles. Daley Thompson bids for an unprecedented hat trick of titles.

BOXING
Ingliston Show Ground

1400	Preliminary bouts
1930	Preliminary bouts

CYCLING
Meadowbank Velodrome

1900	Sprint quarter and semi-finals 4000m Individual Pursuit semi-finals and final

JUDO
DEMONSTRATION SPORT
Meadowbank Sports Centre

0900		Various weights

ROWING
Strathclyde Country Park

1030	Women	Coxed Fours heats
1100	Men	Coxless Fours heats
1130	Women	Lightweight Sculls heats
1200	Men	Double Sculls heats
1230	Men	Coxless Pairs heats
1300	Women	Single Sculls heats
1330	Women	Lightweight Coxless Fours heats
1400	Men	Coxed Fours heats
1545	Women	Coxed Fours repêchage
1615	Men	Coxless Fours repêchage
1645	Women	Lightweight Sculls repêchage
1715	Men	Double Sculls repêchage
1745	Men	Coxless Pairs repêchage
1815	Women	Single Sculls repêchage
1845	Women	Lightweight Coxless Fours repêchage
1915	Men	Coxed Fours repêchage

SHOOTING
Barry Buddon

1030		Full Bore Rifle Pairs

Musselburgh

1030		Centre Fire Pistol Pairs

Kippen

1100		Olympic Trench Individual 1st 100

Australia's Debbie Flintoff defends her title at 400m hurdles. She had a fine 1985 season with three Commonwealth records at the event.

SWIMMING
Royal Commonwealth Pool

1000	Women	800m Freestyle heats
	Men	200m Freestyle heats
	Women	100m Butterfly heats
	Men	200m Breaststroke heats
	Women	100m Breaststroke heats
	Men	4 x 100m Freestyle Relay heats
1300	Women	Highboard Diving
	Men	Springboard Diving
1830	Men	200m Freestyle final
	Women	100m Butterfly final
	Men	200m Breaststroke final
	Women	100m Breaststroke final
	Men	4 x 100m Freestyle Relay final
2115	Women	Synchronised Swimming Duet final

WEIGHTLIFTING
Playhouse Theatre

1400		90kg class
1930		100kg class

TUESDAY
JULY 29

Associated Sports Photography

The weightlifting events reach their climax with the two heaviest classes. Can anyone match the prestige accorded to Louis Martin, the greatest name in Commonwealth lifting, who proudly displays the gold medal he won in Edinburgh 16 years ago?

BADMINTON
Meadowbank Sports Centre

1030	Women	Singles rounds 1 & 2
1400	Men	Singles rounds 1 & 2
1800	Women	Doubles rounds 1 & 2
1930	Men	Doubles round 1

BOWLS
Balgreen Bowling Centre

0900	Men	Singles, Pairs
	Women	Singles, Fours
1330	Men	Pairs
	Women	Singles, Pairs
1800	Men	Singles, Fours
	Women	Pairs, Fours

BOXING
Ingliston Show Ground

1930		Preliminary bouts

CYCLING
Meadowbank Velodrome

1430		Sprint final
1900		4000m Team Pursuit heats and quarter-finals

Jon Sieben was a surprise Olympic champion in 1984 at 200m butterfly. It would be no surprise if he were to win in Edinburgh.

ROWING
Strathclyde Country Park

1100	Women	Coxed Fours final
1130	Men	Coxless Fours final
1200	Women	Lightweight Sculls final
1230	Men	Double Sculls final
1300	Men	Coxless Pairs final
1330	Women	Single Sculls final
1400	Women	Lightweight Coxless Fours final
1430	Men	Coxed Fours final

SHOOTING
Musselburgh

0930	Rapid Fire Pistol Individual 1st 30 Small Bore Rifle Prone Individual

Kippen

1100	Olympic Trench final

SWIMMING
Royal Commonwealth Pool

1000	Women	200m Freestyle heats
	Men	200m Butterfly heats
	Men	100m Backstroke heats
	Men	1500m Freestyle heats
	Women	4 x 100m Medley heats
1300	Women	Springboard Diving
	Men	Highboard Diving
1830	Women	200m Freestyle final
	Men	200m Butterfly final
	Women	800m Freestyle final
	Men	100m Backstroke final
	Women	4 x 100m Medley final

WEIGHTLIFTING
Playhouse Theatre

1400	110kg class
1930	110+kg class

WEDNESDAY
JULY 30

Mike Tredgett, England's most capped Badminton player.

BADMINTON
Meadowbank Sports Centre

1400	Men	Singles rounds 3 & 4
1430	Women	Singles rounds 3 & 4
1600	Men	Doubles rounds 2 & 3
1700	Women	Doubles round 3
1830	Mixed	Doubles round 1

BOWLS
Balgreen Bowling Centre

0900	Men	Singles, Fours
	Women	Singles, Pairs
1330	Men	Pairs
	Women	Singles, Pairs, Fours
1800	Men	Singles, Pairs, Fours
	Women	Fours

BOXING
Ingliston Show Ground

1400	Semi-finals
1930	Semi-finals

CYCLING
Meadowbank Velodrome

1430	4000m Team Pursuit semi-finals
1900	10 Miles heats

SHOOTING
Barry Buddon

1030	Full Bore Rifle Individual stages 1 & 2

Musselburgh

0930	Rapid Fire Pistol Individual final
1400	Free Pistol Individual

Pleasance, Edinburgh University

1030	Air Rifle Individual

SWIMMING
Royal Commonwealth Pool

1000	Men	200m Individual Medley heats
	Women	200m Butterfly heats
	Women	200m Backstroke heats
	Men	4 x 100m Medley heats
1300	Women	Springboard Diving
	Men	Highboard Diving
1830	Men	200m Individual Medley final
	Women	200m Butterfly final
	Men	1500m Freestyle final
	Women	200m Backstroke final
	Men	4 x 100m Medley final

WRESTLING
Playhouse Theatre

1800	First rounds

(Right) Sammy Koskei, 800m challenger.
(Below) Fatima Whitbread.

THURSDAY JULY 31

ATHLETICS
Meadowbank Stadium

0930	Men	Long Jump qualifying
1100	Women	High Jump qualifying
1130	Men	Pole Vault qualifying
	Men	30km Walk
1145	Men	Discus qualifying
1200	Women	Long Jump qualifying
1400	Men	Long Jump final
1430	Women	100m Hurdles heats
1435	Men	High Jump final
1455	Men	200m semi-finals
1515	Women	800m final
1530	Men	800m final
1535	Women	Javelin final
1600	Women	200m final
1625	Men	5000m final
1705	Men	200m final

BADMINTON
Meadowbank Sports Centre

1400	Mixed Doubles rounds 2, 3 & 4
1800	All events semi-finals

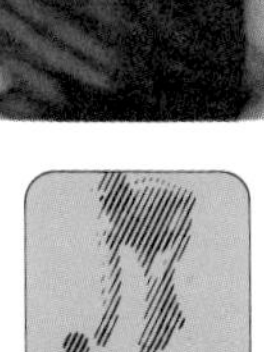

BOWLS
Balgreen Bowling Centre

0900	Men	Singles, Fours
	Women	Singles, Fours
1330	Men	Pairs
	Women	Singles, Pairs
1800	Men	Singles, Pairs, Fours
	Women	Pairs

CYCLING
Meadowbank Velodrome

1900	4000m Team Pursuit final
	10 Miles final

SHOOTING
Barry Buddon

1030 Full Bore Rifle Individual final

Musselburgh

0930 Small Bore Rifle 3 positions Individual

Kippen

1100 Skeet Individual 1st 100

Pleasance, Edinburgh University

1200 Air Pistol Individual

WRESTLING
Playhouse Theatre

1800 Second rounds

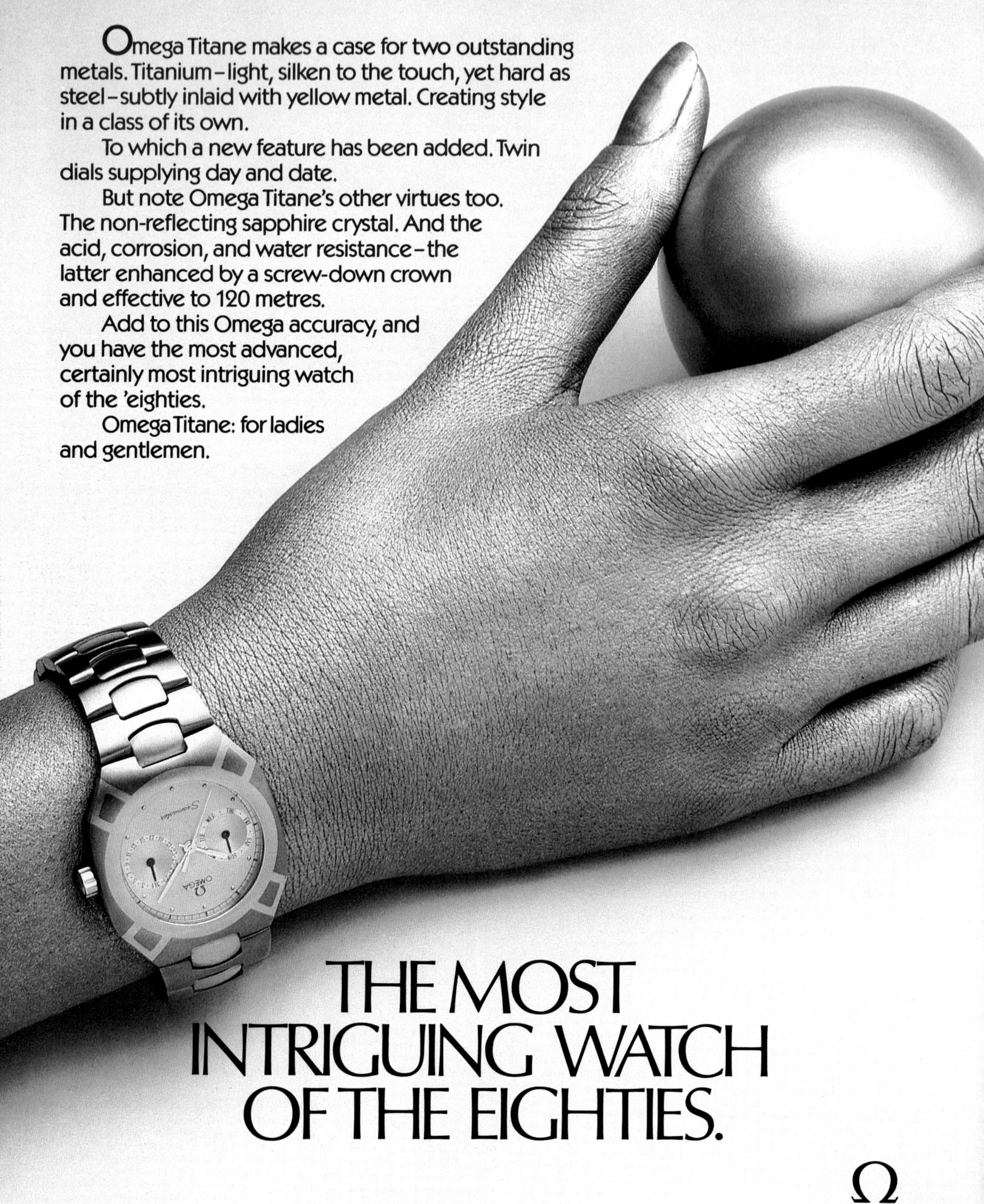
Omega Titane makes a case for two outstanding metals. Titanium – light, silken to the touch, yet hard as steel – subtly inlaid with yellow metal. Creating style in a class of its own.
To which a new feature has been added. Twin dials supplying day and date.
But note Omega Titane's other virtues too. The non-reflecting sapphire crystal. And the acid, corrosion, and water resistance – the latter enhanced by a screw-down crown and effective to 120 metres.
Add to this Omega accuracy, and you have the most advanced, certainly most intriguing watch of the 'eighties.
Omega Titane: for ladies and gentlemen.
OMEGA
THE MOST INTRIGUING WATCH OF THE EIGHTIES.
Ω
OMEGA
Titane
For further information contact your Omega Agent or telephone 0703 611612.
Official timekeepers of the XIII Commonwealth Games Scotland 1986.

The women's marathon is included for the first time in Games history. England's Veronique Marot set a British record at New York in 1985.

FRIDAY AUGUST 1

ATHLETICS
Meadowbank Stadium

1030	Men	Javelin qualifying
1100	Men	Marathon
1115	Men	Triple Jump qualifying
1130	Women	Marathon
1200	Men	Shot qualifying
1300	Men	Pole Vault final
1400	Women	Long Jump final
1440	Women	4 x 100m Relay heats
1445	Women	High Jump final
1502	Men	4 x 100m Relay heats
1525	Women	1500m heats
1540	Men	Discus final
1555	Men	1500m heats
1635	Women	100m Hurdles final
1650	Women	4 x 400m Relay heats
1730	Men	4 x 400m Relay heats

BADMINTON
Meadowbank Sports Centre

1400	All events play-offs for bronze medals
1830	All events finals

BOWLS
Balgreen Bowling Centre

0900	Men	Singles
	Women	Pairs
1300	Men	Fours
	Women	Fours
1700	Men	Pairs
	Women	Singles

BOXING
Ingliston Show Ground

1830	Finals

SHOOTING
Musselburgh

1030	Centre Fire Pistol Individual

Kippen

1100	Skeet Individual final

WRESTLING
Playhouse Theatre

1000	Third and fourth rounds
1900	Finals

We fly more people to more countries than any other airline.

(Below left) Phil Brown snatches second place for the British 4 x 400m relay team in Los Angeles from Innocent Egbunike of Nigeria. The two may clash again in Edinburgh in the last event of the Games. (Below right) Closing ceremony at Brisbane in 1982.

SATURDAY AUGUST 2

Associated Sports Photography

ATHLETICS
Meadowbank Stadium

1230	Men	Javelin final
1245	Men	Triple Jump final
1300	Women	1500m final
1305	Men	Shot final
1320	Women	4 x 100m Relay final
1345	Men	4 x 100m Relay final
1355	Men	1500m final
1435	Women	4 x 400m Relay final
1505	Men	4 x 400m Relay final

CYCLING

0800	100 Miles Road Race

CLOSING CEREMONY

Immediately after the last session of athletics has been completed at Meadowbank Stadium, the closing ceremony begins. It is a time for pageantry and a joyous send-off to the Games, but it is also tinged with sadness as another great occasion comes to an end, and the sportsmen and women, officials and spectators disperse to their homes around the globe. The Games will be closed by HM The Queen as Head of the Commonwealth. The flag of the Commonwealth Games Federation is entrusted to the safe keeping of the Lord Provost of Edinburgh, who is asked to deliver it to the next host city of the Commonwealth Games. And so we look forward to the Games at Auckland, New Zealand in 1990.

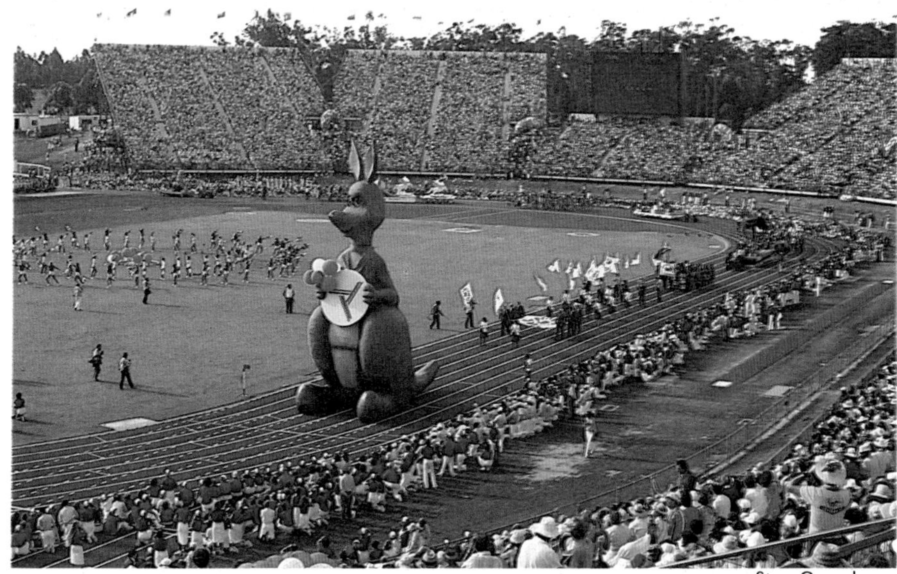

Stan Greenberg

Athletics Preview

by Peter Matthews

Associated Sports Photography

Shirley Strong, the defending champion from 1982 at 100m hurdles, and again the leading contender provided that she can shake off the effects of two Achilles tendon operations in 1985.

Seb Coe beats Steve Cram in the 1984 Olympic 1500m final. These two great athletes may clash at Edinburgh at 800m and 1500m.

Associated Sports Photography

An analysis of medal prospects for a major Games, written before the occasion, is fraught with difficulties. So much can happen as the athletes build up to such an event. They can get injured or become ill; indeed at any given time all too high a proportion of top athletes are out of racing action. Consider, for instance, the problems that have beset England's wonderful trio of Coe, Cram and Ovett. One should perhaps not be too surprised by such incidence of injury, for top athletes push themselves to the limit, and sometimes over it. However, medical supervision and facilities are not always adequate to cope with the needs of such finely-tuned bodies. Then again, unknowns can emerge and those one might have forgotten or written off can rekindle their desire and prepare single-mindedly and effectively for their target. So now all over the Commonwealth men and women are working, and have worked for an appreciable time, towards that day when just a few of them will fully achieve their ambitions and triumph in this particular great event, the Commonwealth Games in Edinburgh.

Amongst the successful athletes will be those whom few would include on lists of medal candidates prepared months in advance, or even on the day of competition, but then such unpredictability is one of the great joys of following sport. However, few gain success without long and hard preparation, even if their potential has not been apparent to keen observers. I can certainly suggest many names to look out for who have shown likely form.

Undoubtedly the bulk of the track and field medals in Edinburgh will be won by athletes from the major Commonwealth sporting powers: England, Australia, Canada, Kenya and of course the hosts Scotland. The sport embraces a great variety of activities and the basic skills of running, jumping and throwing can be, and are, practised enthusiastically worldwide. Medals at Olympic and Commonwealth Games are spread widely and there are always marvellous stories of achievements by athletes from less obvious areas, the Pacific islands, Caribbean islands, smaller African nations and so on.

Highlights

The men's distance running events have for many years provided highlights.

Traditionally, with the Africans, the British countries, Australia and New Zealand competing, we have seen a high proportion of the world's best runners take part at these Games.

Just look at the one mile or 1500 metres champions since that epic duel when Roger Bannister beat John Landy in 1954: Herb Elliott, Peter Snell, Kip Keino, Filbert Bayi, David Moorcroft and Steve Cram. In 1986 Cram will be aiming to emulate Keino, who won twice, in 1966 and 1970. On his 1985 form the Jarrow man, who is also the reigning World and European champion, must be the supreme favourite. Cram can take on and beat his rivals in all types of race, be it slowly run or fast. He has the long sustained drive to the finish, which could only be matched by the extra speed that Seb Coe has shown to be his forte. Coe showed his very special kick, off an already fast pace, in his great world record breaking years of 1979 and 1981, and again when he overcame severe illness and injury to retain his Olympic 1500m title in Los Angeles. He has never yet run at the Commonwealth Games, preferring to concentrate on the European Championships in 1978 and being sidelined by illness in 1982. Let us hope that both these men stay free of injury to give us another great race in Edinburgh together with that consummate racer Steve Ovett. Truly an event to savour, and one can add the amazing John Walker, who has run more than a hundred sub-four minute miles since he first burst on to the scene in 1974. Then at the Commonwealth Games he was second to Filbert Bayi, when the latter front-ran his way to a world record, and he won silver again in 1982. However, Walker may prefer to try the very much more open 5000 metres.

The Kenyan runners will be major medal threats, particularly at the

John Herbert (left) is the favourite to succeed Keith Connor as triple jump champion. (Below) Zola Budd set a world record at 5000m, and Commonwealth records at 1500m, 1 mile and 3000m in 1985.

men's events from 800 metres upwards, and I have selected Paul Kipkoech as a possible winner at both 5000m and 10000m, although at present there does not appear to be the really outstanding man at those distances as Henry Rono or Brendan Foster were. Remembering how the win of Lachie Stewart at 10000m, augmented by the 1-2 for Ian Stewart and Ian McCafferty, fired the Edinburgh crowds in 1970,

no doubt many will be looking to Nat Muir for home success this time. At 800 metres Sammy Koskei and Billy Konchellah head a group of highly talented Kenyans, but Cram has said that he wants to go for this event too, and as he showed last year when he beat the Olympic champion Joaquim Cruz, he need fear no one at this, his second-string distance.

Steve Jones will not be running the marathon, as he has chosen to contest this event at the European Championships. Instead he will run for Wales at 10000 metres. In his absence there could be renewed rivalry between the Brisbane medallists Rob de Castella and Juma Ikangaa with the Englishmen, perhaps Charlie Spedding and Hugh Jones, and the Kenyans well in contention.

The women's events from 400 to 3000 metres could be dominated by the British women. Kirsty McDermott of Wales is a clear favourite to retain her 800m title, having made a great breakthrough to world class in 1985, and may also go for the 1500m, where England's Chris Boxer bids to retain her title. Then there is Britain's woman athlete of the year in 1985, Zola Budd, who has said she will run this distance rather than 3000m. That may leave Wendy Sly, whom Budd has never beaten, as favourite for that longer event. Kathy Cook should win the 400m, to gain her first individual Commonwealth gold medal, although she has sprint relay golds from both 1978 and 1982. The longer distance titles however may go 'down under'. I have selected Lorraine Moller of New Zealand at 10000 metres, which is being held at the Games for the first time, and Lisa Martin of Australia at the marathon, although there are plenty of strong contenders for both, not least from the British, such as Angela Tooby of Wales at 10000m, and Sarah Rowell and Veronique Marot of England in the marathon. Another English woman, Paula Fudge, who won the 3000m at the 1978 Games, could beat them all at either 10000m or marathon, at which she made a successful debut last year.

Ben Johnson, the Canadian born in Jamaica, established himself in 1985 as the fastest man in the Commonwealth, and is clear favourite to repeat his World Cup win at 100 metres. However, we must not forget Allan Wells. He will be 34 years old, but he has shown a fine disregard for age and was the oldest ever Olympic 100m champion back in 1980. He has shown time and again the ability to peak for the big occasion. What a wondrous feat it would be if he could win his seventh Commonwealth medal in his hometown and on his home track, where his raking the long jump pit at the 1970 Games has attained legendary status. In the women's sprints we need surely look no further than to the graceful Jamaican Merlene Ottey-Page, unless the Canadian Angella Taylor, having given birth to a daughter in 1985, returns to top form.

Kirsty McDermott (681) on her way to 800m victory in 1982. No. 572 is Anne Clarkson (now Purvis) of Scotland, who was second, and who will be challenging again in Edinburgh.

History could be made in the women's high jump if Debbie Brill were to win her third title, for she won back in 1970 when aged 17. At the time she was a pioneer of the new flop style, which has become practically de rigueur for high jumpers. She slipped back a little in the 1970s, but came back to gain silver in 1978 and gold in 1982, and still in 1985 had a good margin over any other Commonwealth jumper. Her male team-mate Milt Ottey may also retain his high jump title. In 1982 there was a great triple jump battle between Keith Connor of England and Ken Lorraway of Australia. The former has retired and the latter has been seriously hampered by injuries, but Connor may well be succeeded by another Englishman, John Herbert, the European Cup winner last year. Even if Ken is not fully fit, gold may still go to the Lorraway household, for his wife Robyn could win the women's long jump battling against the enigmatic Bev Kinch.

Sadly, Commonwealth pole vault standards are not very good, but the event always provides great entertainment, and we could have

Medal selections - track and field athletics - men

100m:	Ben Johnson (CAN), Chidi Imo (NGR), Desai Williams (CAN)
200m:	Ade Mafe (ENG), Mike McFarlane (ENG) Desai Williams (CAN)
400m:	Innocent Egbunike (NGR), Darren Clark (AUS), Derek Redmond (ENG)
800m:	Steve Cram (ENG), Sammy Koskei (KEN), Billy Konchellah (KEN)
1500m:	Steve Cram, Seb Coe (ENG), Joseph Cheshire (KEN)
5000m:	Paul Kipkoech (KEN), Tim Hutchings (ENG), Nat Muir (SCO)
10000m:	Paul Kipkoech, Mike Musyoki (KEN), Steve Jones (WAL)
Marathon:	Rob de Castella (AUS), Charlie Spedding (ENG), Hugh Jones (ENG)
3000m steeplechase:	Julius Kariuki (KEN), Colin Reitz (ENG), Joshua Kipkemboi (KEN)
110m hurdles:	Mark McKoy (CAN), Jonathan Ridgeon (ENG), Don Wright (AUS)
400m hurdles:	Henry Amike (NGR), Mark Holtom (ENG), Max Robertson (ENG)
High jump:	Milt Ottey (CAN), Geoff Parsons (SCO), Alain Metellus (CAN)
Pole vault:	Andrew Ashurst (ENG), Jeff Gutteridge (ENG), Keith Stock (ENG)
Long jump:	Gary Honey (AUS), Yussuf Alli (NGR), Paul Emordi (NGR)
Triple jump:	John Herbert (ENG), Steve Hanna (BAH), Paul Emordi (NGR)
Shot:	Mike Spiritoso (CAN), Billy Cole (ENG), Mike Winch (ENG)
Discus:	Christian Okoye (NGR), Paul Nandapi (AUS), Paul Mardle (ENG)
Hammer:	David Smith (ENG), Martin Girvan (NIR), Matt Mileham (ENG)
Javelin:	David Ottley (ENG), Roald Bradstock (ENG), Mike O'Rourke (NZL)
Decathlon:	Daley Thompson (ENG), Dave Steen (CAN), Eugene Gilkes (ENG)
30km walk:	Guillaume Leblanc (CAN), Ian McCombie (ENG), Francois Lapointe (CAN)
4 x 100m relay:	Canada, Nigeria, England
4 x 400m relay:	England, Australia, Kenya

(Right) Merlene Ottey-Page won a complete set of medals: gold, silver and bronze in 1982, and also has three Olympic bronze medals.
(Far right) defending shot champion Judy Oakes.

an English 1-2-3. Similarly, Commonwealth throwing does not rate very highly in world terms, but a glowing exception to that is the javelin, particularly the women's, headed by Fatima Whitbread and Tessa Sanderson. The latter won in 1978, but missed the 1982 Games through injury, when the fast improving Whitbread won the bronze medal behind Australia's Sue Howland. Howland should challenge again, but only Sanderson can expect to get close to Fatima, who displayed marvellous 70-metre plus consistency last year. The English pair of David Ottley and Roald Bradstock have also made their presence felt in top-level men's javelin throwing, but one problem all have to face at this event is the new specification javelin to be used in 1986. This has a different centre of gravity to the old javelin, intended to reduce the distance thrown, now that the East German Uwe Hohn has ushered in the 100-metre era.

Other stars of the athletic arena may include the hurdlers Shirley Strong, Debbie Flintoff, Mark McKoy and Jonathon Ridgeon; the English 4 x 400 metres relay runners, Derek Redmond, Todd Bennett, Kriss Akabusi, Roger Black and Phil Brown; and the Nigerian sprinters. Once again, however, there will surely be maximum attention on the man fully entitled to be called the world's greatest athlete.

No decathlete in history has remotely approached the championships success of Daley Thompson. He won the Olympic titles of 1980 and 1984, the World title in 1983, European in 1982 and Commonwealth in both 1978 and

Medal selections - track and field athletics - women

100m:	Merlene Ottey-Page (JAM), Grace Jackson (JAM), Angella Taylor (CAN)
200m:	Merlene Ottey-Page (JAM), Kathy Cook (ENG), Grace Jackson (JAM)
400m:	Kathy Cook (ENG), Maree Chapman (AUS), Marita Payne (CAN)
800m:	Kirsty McDermott (WAL), Shireen Bailey (ENG), Bronwyn Fleming (AUS)
1500m:	Chris Boxer (ENG), Zola Budd (ENG), Lynn Williams (CAN)
3000m:	Wendy Sly (ENG), Lynn Williams (CAN), Donna Gould (AUS)
10000m:	Lorraine Moller (NZL), Angela Tooby (WAL), Lisa Martin (AUS)
Marathon:	Lisa Martin (AUS), Paula Fudge (ENG), Sarah Rowell (ENG)
100m hurdles:	Shirley Strong (ENG), Glynis Nunn (AUS), Judy Simpson (ENG)
400m hurdles:	Debbie Flintoff (AUS), P.T. Usha (IND), Sandra Farmer (JAM)
High jump:	Debbie Brill (CAN), Christine Stanton (AUS), Jeanne Cockcroft (CAN)
Long jump:	Robyn Lorraway (AUS), Shonel Ferguson (BAH), Joyce Oladapo (ENG)
Shot:	Gael Martin (AUS), Judy Oakes (ENG), Venissa Head (WAL)
Discus:	Gael Martin (AUS), Venissa Head (WAL), Sue Reinwald (AUS)
Javelin:	Fatima Whitbread (ENG), Tessa Sanderson (ENG), Sue Howland (AUS)
Pentathlon:	Glynis Nunn (AUS), Judy Simpson (ENG), Kim Hagger (ENG)
4 x 100m relay:	Canada, Jamaica, England
4 x 400m relay:	Canada, England, Australia

(Right) Daley Thompson OBE.
(Below left) Dave Ottley leads England's javelin challenge.
(Below right) Glynis Nunn uniquely qualified for three finals at both Brisbane and Los Angeles. She won the heptathlon on each occasion and was a finalist at 100m hurdles and long jump.

1982. Add to that four world records and you have the supreme all-rounder. Right from the first event, the 100 metres, where he invariably sprints to a resounding win, he dominates the event with his fierce competitiveness and wondrous ability to overcome each setback. He showed just such ability in the 1984 Olympics, when two mediocre throws in the discus threatened to cost him the lead to his West German rival Jürgen Hingsen, but his third and final effort winged out close to his best, and the adversity was behind him. He went on to seal his win in the pole vault, so that he could and did sail through the last two events, javelin and 1500 metres, on a confident cloud of knowing that once again he was the best at this supreme ten-event test.

I have been bold enough to list the medal candidates at each event. I find that Scots are few, but they will surely rise to the occasion and perhaps that is just one area where I will be wrong. Some of those in my table won't even make it to Edinburgh, but the mere preparation of this list whets my appetite for that day in July when again the Commonwealth Games athletics get underway and six days of magnificent competition unfold. I saw my first Commonwealth Games from the announcers' box in Edinburgh in 1970 and I have enjoyed the three Games that I have attended as much as any major meetings anywhere. I am sure that this year's fare will be at least as good.

Brother makes history with UK typewriters.

WHEN Brother Industries launched the first typewriter from its new Wrexham plant last August, it was an historic moment for British industry – the first time typewriters had been produced in this country for ten years.

This month the launch of its first Wrexham-produced range of commercial electronic typewriters is an even more significant milestone for Brother itself.

The three new models, the EM-501, 511 and 701, form the second of three ranges (domestic, compact and office) which will come on to the market this year and signal the start of the Japanese group's determined drive to dominate typewriter sales in the UK and Europe.

J. Cattini, General Manager, Brother Office Equipment Division.

The AX-10 was the first in its group and will be followed by the AX-20 and the AX-30 next month. Three compact typewriters and a further two EM models will be launched later in the year.

"We aim to substantially increase our share of the market within the next twelve months," says Jim Cattini, general manager of Brother's Office Equipment Division.

The company plans to be producing a phenomenal 20,000 machines a month at its plant in Wrexham, but Mr Cattini predicts that even this output is going to be overtaken by the demand throughout Europe.

"We sold more AX-10s in the UK and Europe in the first five months than even we predicted and we could have sold even more," he says. "And that was a basic electronic domestic model – the new EM Series has a much bigger market potential."

It is a series of sophisticated hi-tech electronic machines designed for heavy multiple use in big companies, financial institutions and local authorities. All EM machines are built and tested to withstand a minimum of 80 million cycles of operation, which is more than enough to cope with the demands of even the busiest office.

It was the EM Series that was chosen to be the official typewriter at the Los Angeles Olympic Games and 3,000 Brother machines took a pounding from 10,000 of the world's press.

The economics of UK production will enable Brother to become price competitive with other leading European models, but Brother is more concerned with creating the right reputation and building goodwill. Its traditional Japanese slogan is: "He who makes good products makes good friends."

Jim Cattini adds: "We have the capacity to produce even more machines than we are doing, but our production level is geared to guaranteeing quality. We aim to establish Brother as the leading brand and are emphasising design and reliability supported by a first-class dealer network for after sales service."

The western European electronic typewriter market is estimated to have been worth £1.5 billion last year and sales are currently growing at the rate of five per cent per annum. New product technology and fierce price wars have lowered the growth rate of revenue, but the potential of the market is still heady enough to attract more and more manufacturers.

The machines themselves have gone through a technological revolution in the last six years. Electric typewriters with 2,000 moving parts have been superseded by more efficient electronic models.

The boom in sales continues in spite of the growth of personal computers and word processors, largely because electronic typewriters are simpler to use, supply most office needs and the more sophisticated models can perform most of the functions of word processors.

Teenage Record Breakers.

TEENAGE Welsh girls at the new Brother Industries Wrexham factory are challenging the Japanese experts with their record levels of production.

Currently, local girls aged from 16 to 19 are achieving the production level of their counterparts at the Brother headquarters at Nagoya, Japan.

Not even the Brother factories at Taiwan and Korea have managed such an impressive rate. The Wrexham girls are now turning out a machine at the rate of one every 58 seconds. Brother is immensely proud of the Wrexham team and says it proves what a British workforce can do when highly motivated.

As their joint general manager Malcolm Newman puts it: "The kids are great. We hire girls because they have the manual dexterity and aptitude for fine assembly work. They are very keen and most of our recruitment now is by word of mouth."

Some of the secrets of success:

- Music is used instead of hooters or bells to mark tea and lunch breaks. It also marks the progress of work along the assembly line. It is speeded up only if the girls agree to lift production rates.
- Each group has its production target for the day displayed on a screen. Alongside, a counter ticks up each completed part so that they know from minute to minute how they are progressing.
- Competitions between groups stimulate quality assurance.
- From time to time the girls' roles are changed within the group to avoid boredom.

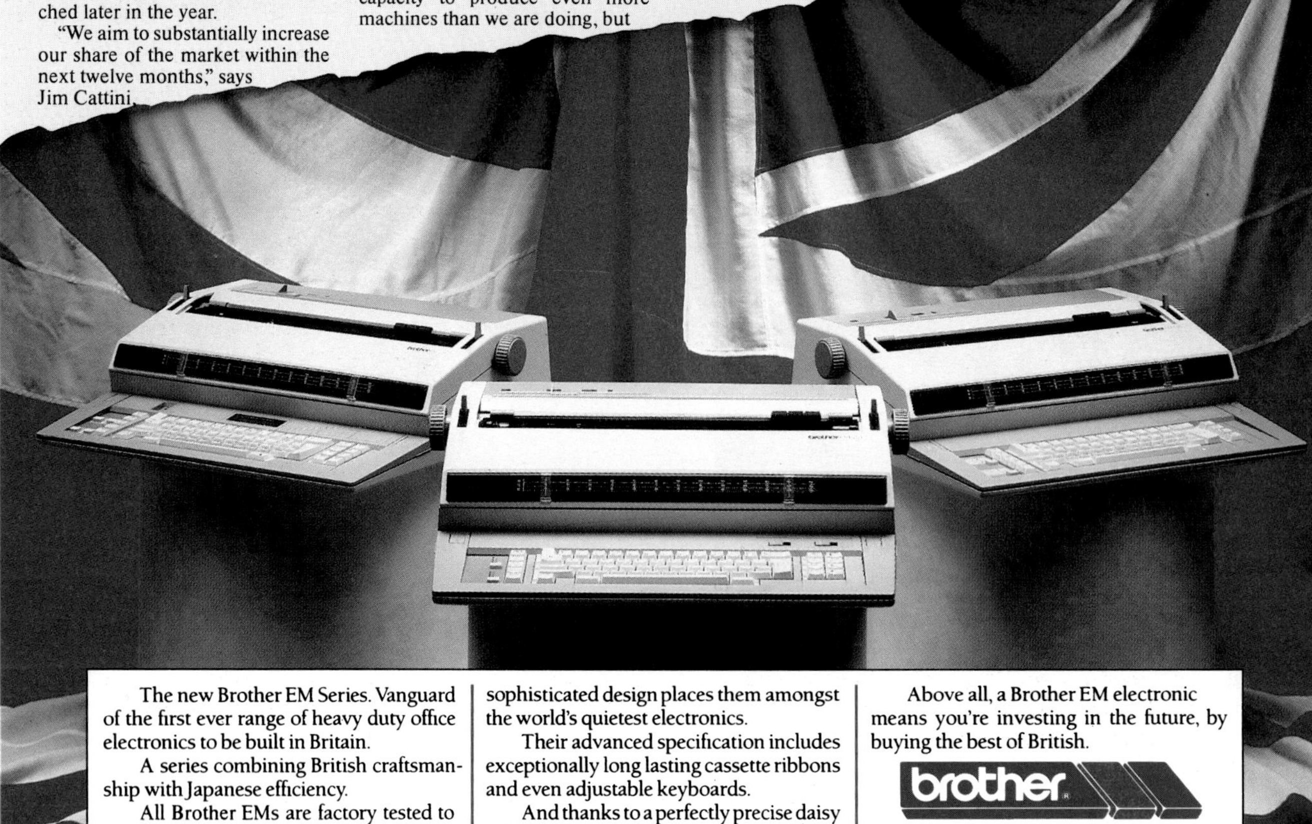

The new Brother EM Series. Vanguard of the first ever range of heavy duty office electronics to be built in Britain.

A series combining British craftsmanship with Japanese efficiency.

All Brother EMs are factory tested to an 80 million character capability. Whilst sophisticated design places them amongst the world's quietest electronics.

Their advanced specification includes exceptionally long lasting cassette ribbons and even adjustable keyboards.

And thanks to a perfectly precise daisy wheel, reproduction quality is superb.

Above all, a Brother EM electronic means you're investing in the future, by buying the best of British.

brother

The future at your fingertips.

DEPT. T, BROTHER OFFICE EQUIPMENT DIVISION, JONES + BROTHER, SHEPLEY STREET, AUDENSHAW, MANCHESTER M34 5JD. TEL: 061-330 6531
TELEX: 669092 TELECOM GOLD 84: JBT 003. BROTHER SHOWROOM: 83 EUSTON RD., LONDON NW1. BROTHER INDUSTRIES LIMITED, NAGOYA, JAPAN.

Sandy Sutherland

Feathers fly

The Scottish duo – Billy Gilliland and Dan Travers

There will be more feathers flying around than in a rookery at Meadowbank Sports Centre during the badminton events of the XIII Commonwealth Games.

An estimated 450 dozen (or well over 5,000) shuttles will be required for the team and individual events and, at current retail prices, a cost of over £5,000, all to be blasted to smithereens in a few minutes of smashing play. And, incidentally, in badminton, when players talk about getting the 'bird' they mean receiving the shuttle-cock, not being barracked.

The possibilities of top class action were greatly increased by a decision of the International Badminton Federation at the World Championships in Calgary last June, which reinstated many of the top players, previously ruled ineligible in their 'licensed player' status (which meant they could earn prize-money direct, as opposed to via their national federations). But, subsequently, moves to further professionalise the sport have once again put into question whether all the talented English team, for example, will choose to take part in an event where no prize-money is at stake.

It is hoped that Steve Baddeley, Nick Yates, Steve Butler and Helen Troke will spearhead the English challenge, but, in the meantime, Scotland are grateful for the IBF decision, which has made Billy Gilliland and Dan Travers available again. ' G & T ' will act as a great tonic to the home team and will be among the favourites for the men's doubles title, being the All-England runners-up in 1982. In addition, with the right partner, Gilliland is always a potential mixed doubles gold medallist.

The most exciting player in the Commonwealth at present, however, is a Chinese-born Australian from Sydney who won the Scottish Open men's singles title last November at Meadowbank and might well have been excused then for saying "Sze Yu in July".

Since then Sze Yu has gone on to further triumphs, including a victory over world champion Morten Frost in the Grand Prix finals. Baddeley, Yates and top Malaysian Misbun Sidek will be the men he has to fear most on his path to gold.

Helen Troke is a clear favourite for the women's title, provided she plays, and English team-mate Nora Perry is still capable of having a great influence on the final destination of the doubles medals. Since 1970, team competition has been added to the individual championships, making the overall tournament easily the largest ever staged in Scotland, with two halls required this time.

Between 13 and 19 countries will take part, although the medals will probably be confined to England, Australia, Canada, Malaysia, possibly Hong Kong and hopefully Scotland.

The team events go on for the first three days, starting on July 25, followed by a rest day, then four days of battle for the five individual titles: men's and women's singles, men's and women's doubles and mixed doubles.

Patrick Sullivan

Bowls ancient and modern

Peter Belliss (NZL)

Sporting Pictures (UK) Ltd.

Bowls is currently enjoying one of the most vigorous periods of expansion in its long history. The very image of this ancient sport has been transformed by that wonder of modern times - television; and the resulting wave of enthusiasm, especially among the young, has caused the welcome demise of the tag, 'old man's marbles'.

The advent of 'open bowls' in 1980 heralded the rise of sponsored tournaments with their ever-increasing cash prizes threatening to replace at least some of the traditional incentives for winning. At Edinburgh, however, you will see bowlers playing for the love of the game, the thrill of competition and the honour of representing their country, values which capture perfectly the very essence of sport in general and the Commonwealth Games in particular.

Bowls has been linked with the Games ever since the inaugural meeting at Hamilton, Ontario, in 1930 when, following a plea by Archibald McNaish, then treasurer of the English Bowling Association, and some determined lobbying by Canadian bowlers, the game was included as an 'optional sport'. With five countries entered in the bowling events - singles, pairs and fours - that first year saw England sweep the board by winning all three gold medals and the 1929 EBA singles champion, Robert George Colquhoun from Kent, becoming the first Commonwealth Games (then British Empire Games) singles champion.

Since that auspicious occasion English bowlers have compiled a more than useful record in the Games, none more so than the Clevedon Maestro, David J. Bryant, who won singles and fours gold medals in 1962 and repeated his singles success in 1970, 1974 and 1978. Robert Sprot, Scottish champion in 1929, took the singles gold in 1934 but our host country was forced to wait a long forty years before John Christie and Alex McIntosh were able to add to that meagre tally by winning the pairs in 1974. Once having acquired the habit, however, the Scots struck gold again in 1982 when Willie Wood survived one slip-up, a surprise 21-11 loss to Krishna Gauda of Fiji, before demolishing New Zealand's Peter Belliss 21-7 in the match which decided the outcome of the singles.

Further glory for Scotland came with the pairs success of John Watson and skip, David Gourlay, who took the gold medal on shot advantage over Wales. For Watson the victory was particularly sweet having earlier that year opted to forgo a £6,000 first prize earned for winning the World Indoor Singles Championship, thus retaining his eligibility for the Games in Brisbane. Overall pairs honours, however, belong to New Zealand who have won the event on no fewer than four occasions - 1938, 1950, 1958 and 1962, with England with just one success behind.

The fours find England top of the table with four wins - 1930, 1934, 1958 and 1962 - with New Zealand, Hong Kong and South Africa all tied with two each. Strangely enough, that giant among bowling nations, Australia, has but one gold medal to show for its efforts over the years, that coming in the 1982 fours event. Although, in bowling terms, little more than a minnow when compared with Australia, Hong Kong has earned an enviable record in the Games, winning the fours in 1970 and going one better in 1978 by taking both fours and pairs gold medals, and this with fewer players to choose from than some English counties! Triples were introduced on a trial basis at Brisbane in 1982, an innovation which also saw women bowlers make their debut performances in the Commonwealth Games and the winners of this important landmark were Florence Kennedy, Anna Bates and Margaret Mills of Zimbabwe. This year, although the triples are dropped,

SO RIGHT, IT NEVER VARIES.
DEWAR'S
12
AGED YEARS
ANCESTOR
SCOTCH WHISKY
Dewar's
FINE SCOTCH WHISKY
"White Label"
PERTH
SCOTCH
Dewar's
WHISKY
Distillers
Making friends throughout the world.
DEWAR'S NEVER VARIES.

Sporting Pictures (UK) Ltd.

women are eligible for selection in the three remaining events for the first time ever.

Since 1930, when bowlers from Canada, England, New Zealand, Scotland and South Africa took part in that historic sporting occasion, the number of participating bowling nations has risen steadily, apart from the first post-war meeting at Auckland in 1950 when only Australia, Canada, Fiji, New Zealand and South Africa were represented. Four years later the figure was up to ten, rising to a dozen in 1958 and thirteen in 1962.

The 1966 Games held at Kingston, Jamaica, found bowls excluded for the first time. With athletics and swimming the only compulsory sports, the host nation has the choice of seven out of nine other events and with bowls hardly played at all in Jamaica, the game was understandably omitted from the list. Since then, however, the numbers have continued to grow and for this year's event sixteen invitations have been despatched to all parts of the globe.

With the International Bowling Board's stringent guidelines on amateurism in mind, it is unlikely that many defending champions will be found at Edinburgh. The overall elevation of standards in the game, however, will ensure that bowling quality remains high and competition for medals as fierce as ever.

The exclusion of bowls from the 1966 Commonwealth Games led directly to the founding of the World Bowls Championships which first took place that year at the Kyeemagh Bowling Club, Sydney. England's David Bryant, who had won all 12 of his matches in the 1962 Commonwealth Games singles, won his first ten matches at Sydney, eventually winning the first World Championship singles with 14 victories and one loss.

Horace Harvey won the Commonwealth Games singles gold medal for South Africa in 1938, going one better than his father, Andrew, who took the runners-up medal in 1934. Willie Wood beat Peter Belliss of New Zealand 21-7 in the deciding singles match of the 1982 Commonwealth Games. Two years later, however, the big New Zealander took his revenge by defeating Wood 21-20 in the final of the World Championship singles at Aberdeen's Westburn Park.

Notes for Non-Bowlers

Unlike many of the televised indoor tournaments, the game on view at Edinburgh will be played to the traditional 21 shots for singles, 21 ends for pairs and fours rather than the seven-up sets game.

The jack must be delivered to a minimum of 25 yards (22.86m) from the front end of the mat and if this is not accomplished, the opposing player has the advantage of casting it to his own preferred length (providing that, too, is 25 yards or over) but does not play first.

Any bowl touching the jack in the course of its run is marked with chalk and remains 'live' during the course of the end, even if it runs, or is subsequently forced, into the ditch. Any bowl not touching the jack during the course of its run is 'dead' once it enters the ditch.

Singles and pairs matches are played with four bowls per player, fours with two.

NIGERIA IN BRIEF

Nigeria, with its population of over 90 million people of various customs and traditions, spans an area of 923,768 square kilometres in the West African sub-region. It is endowed with immense mineral resources and agricultural potentials. On attainment of independence on 1st October, 1960, it joined the Commonwealth and the United Nations, and has since remained faithful to the objectives of these organisations in promoting international peace, co-operation and mutual respect among all sovereign nations. Its commitment to decolonisation and the eradication of apartheid has been pursued with a single minded resolve.

Nigeria's great economic resources, such as petroleum, coal, uranium, iron ore, tin, columbite, limestone, et cetera, are being exploited to achieve rapid economic growth and social progress. Its agricultural resources amongst which are cocoa, rubber, timber, hides, skins, soya beans and palm products which suffered some neglect with the ascendancy of the oil economy, are now being actively revived to provide raw materials for local industries, consumption and export. For this purpose, the Federal Government has made it known that adequate arrangements have been made to create the right conditions and atmosphere that would attract foreign capital to supplement local resources. With her size, population and resources, Nigeria represents a new frontier for genuine investors.

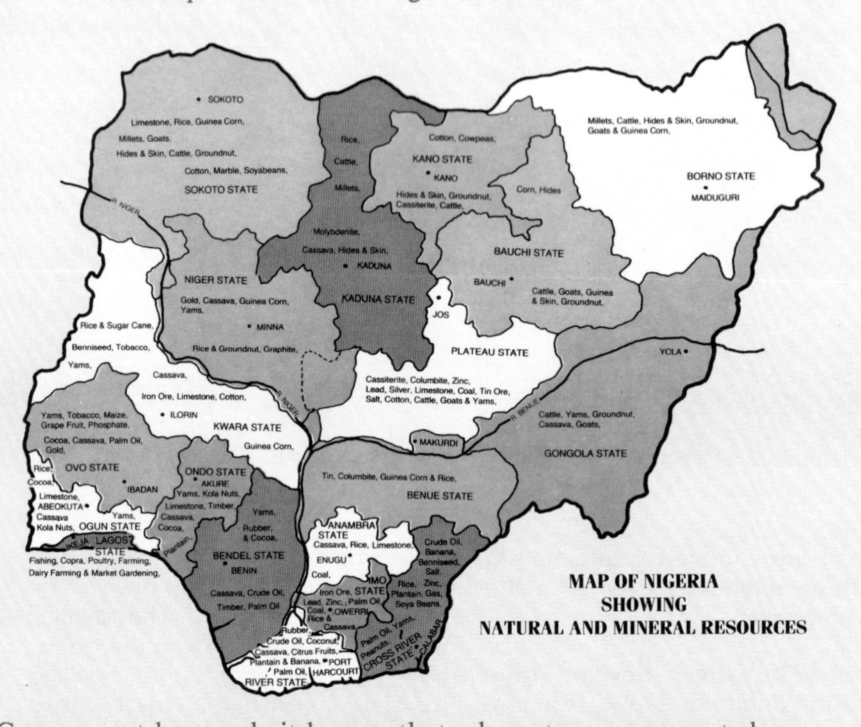

MAP OF NIGERIA SHOWING NATURAL AND MINERAL RESOURCES

As a sporting nation with a proud tradition and achievements in the international arena, Nigeria has continued to contribute to the development of sports amongst Commonwealth and other nations of the world. Nigeria considers, however, that the glory of sports is inconsistent with any form of discrimination on the basis of colour, sex or creed, and has therefore vigorously opposed apartheid in sports wherever it occurs. As the winner of the first ever FIFA/KODAK under-sixteen World Cup Championships held in China in 1985, coupled with its record of brilliant performances in other international sports competitions, the prospects for Nigeria in the field of sports are bright.

Harry Carpenter

with ringside reminiscences

I suppose it really *is* 28 years ago? I can see him as if it were yesterday . . . this curly-haired little Welshman, 19 years old, boxing like a born-again Jim Driscoll, sweeping up the bantamweight gold from under the nose of Australia's Ollie Taylor.

Howard Winstone, of course, in 1958, rousing the Cardiff crowd in Sophia Gardens to a frenzied rendition of 'Land of my Fathers'. Then, the extraordinary revelation by Winstone that a factory accident had chopped off the tops of three fingers on his right hand! Ten years later I watched him win the world professional featherweight crown with the same quicksilver skills.

Those Cardiff Games - still the Empire Games in those days - were my first. I have sat ringside at all of them since. Not one has ever disappointed me in the sheer quality of boxing. The political scene has changed. In 1958 South Africa was the leading boxing nation with four golds. Four years ago, in Brisbane, Kenya and Nigeria were most successful, three apiece. The standard needed to win has remained high throughout.

One more glance at '58 . . . to Dick McTaggart, the Scots magician, an elusive southpaw from Dundee who could handle - and beat - any man in the world at his weight over the amateur distance of three, three-minute rounds. Dick had that rare ability to judge precisely what he must do to win. He had the artist's deft touch, a mastery of the counterpunch, his eyes fixed on the opponent's gloves.

Pat Cowdell

McTaggart won competitions at every level, from junior titles to Olympic gold, the most successful British amateur of my time, with the intelligence not to take his subtle skills into the paid sport, where bludgeon can blunt rapier over the longer distance. It was a joy to see him in the Los Angeles Olympics, working with the British squad. I look forward to renewing friendship with him in Edinburgh.

The Games of '62, in Perth, Western Australia, saw the successful defence of the light-heavyweight title by Tony Madigan, a breezy Aussie who lived for a time in London. In 1954 he won the ABA championship at Wembley and sandwiched between his two Commonwealth golds was a remarkable bronze in the Rome Olympics... remarkable, because he came close to barring Cassius Clay's path to the gold. Madigan fought Clay in the semi-finals and gave him a tremendous battle before losing on points. To this day, Tony believes he won and I would not have argued in Rome had the verdict gone his way.

In 1966 we sat in the sun on the cricket field of Sabina Park in Kingston, Jamaica, to watch Mark Rowe (England) and Tom Imrie (Scotland) renew their light-middleweight rivalry. Three months earlier Imrie had KO'd Rowe in the ABA final. In Jamaica Rowe had revenge, and came close to knocking out Imrie! Tom, of course, was an Edinburgh man and four years later, in his own great city, had the satisfaction of winning the Commonwealth gold that Rowe had denied him in Kingston.

Another Jamaican memory: the amazing Philip Waruinge, of Kenya, featherweight champion, a man of outstanding ability, who won gold again in 1970, and later emigrated to Japan. He changed his name to Nakayama Waringe and at the age of 30 won a Japanese professional title and still later fought twice for the World Championship.

Now that we are back in Edinburgh after 16 years, I wonder if we shall

Elf
sponsor
energy
in
Edinburgh

Elf Aquitaine UK are a sponsor of the XIII Commonwealth Games

John Conteh - Commonwealth gold at Edinburgh in 1970.

see a winner of such abundant talent as John Conteh, middleweight victor here in 1970? It was no great surprise to see him win a world title four years later. The sadness came when his career was tossed away on a dubious point of principle, but the star quality was there for all to see at Murrayfield.

For comparison's sake, there were 136 entries for the 1970 boxing: Uganda was the leading nation with three golds. Light-flyweight was introduced for the first time, to make 11 weights. This year there will be 12, as super-heavy makes its debut. England enjoyed huge success in '74 in Christchurch, New Zealand. Billy Knight (light-heavy) and Neville Meade (heavy) were two of our winners. The other was Pat Cowdell (bantam), impressive then, and even more so in later career when he went to Houston, Texas, and gave the late Salvador Sanchez, of Mexico, a ferocious argument for 15 rounds in pursuit of a world crown. Neither must I forget to mention the brilliant Zambian, Lotte Mwale, winner of light-middle gold in '74, who went on to hold the Commonwealth professional light-heavyweight title for many years.

We come closer to the present day with the 1978 Games in Edmonton, Alberta, a boom town squatting on oil, and sure to go down in boxing history as the place where Barry McGuigan first made his impact internationally. Barry won the bantam gold and who should take the featherweight prize the same night, but Azumah Nelson, of Ghana, now McGuigan's arch rival for world supremacy!

So to Brisbane, four years ago, where England triumphantly placed seven men in the finals, only to wind up with just two golds, from Chris Pyatt (welter) and Jimmy Price (middle). These were the Games where Canada's mighty Shawn O'Sullivan and Willie de Wit showed their power. Neither was taken the distance in any contest. Both won silver in Los Angeles and today they are steadily accumulating wealth in U.S. rings.

Now another great festival is here, Games which call for technique and stamina. A boxer may be required to box four or even five times in less than a fortnight. He must make his weight before every contest. He must stay clear of injury. There is no seeding in the draw. A defending champion must take his place - and his chances - with the newcomers. The battle of a lifetime may well be needed simply to get through the opening series.

These are just a few of the problems awaiting the competitors from around the world. The Commonwealth Games are rightly called the Friendly Games and even in such a warlike sport as boxing, a punch on the nose can be given and taken and followed with a handshake at the end. The rewards, as we have seen, can be immense. Who knows? In these few days, another McGuigan, another Nelson, may emerge.

Hugh Porter

and skill on wheels

The last time the Games were held in Edinburgh a burly Aussie, Gordon Johnson, made a remarkable category change. After gaining the silver in the sprint, losing to fellow countryman John Nicholson, he immediately turned professional, travelled to Leicester where the World Championships were taking place, and defeated the great Italian Sante Gaiardoni, to win the World Crown. We will probably not see anyone repeat this performance, but what is certain is that the new 250 metre Afzelia hardwood timber velodrome, built ironically by another Aussie, Ron Webb, with its 12° straights and 44° angles on the banking will produce spectacular high speed racing.

The five track disciplines to be decided at this venue are the sprint, kilometre, individual pursuit, team pursuit and 10 mile scratch race. For those of you who are not au fait with the sport of cycling I will endeavour to explain a little about each of the events and where possible, although this could prove difficult not knowing who is to be selected, name a few likely favourites.

Riders will differ in physique according to their event. The sprinters tend to be heavily muscled while pursuiters are more honed down.

In the sprint, these powerfully built men with razor sharp reflexes, will watch each other for the slightest lack of concentration which will allow them to jump away, or they will try and manoeuvre their opponent to the front, sometimes by standing still, thus forcing him to lead out the sprint.

Times are taken over the final 200 metres and speeds in excess of 40mph (65km/h) are reached as they race for the line. In the early rounds it's sudden death with the losers trying to stay in the competition through the repêchage. From the quarter finals onwards it's the best of three with two-up rounds.

England's hope for the sprint gold lies with a Liverpudlian, Paul McHugh, the national champion, who was fourth in last year's World Juniors.

He will have to look out for Canada's Alex Ongaro who put him out of last year's Senior Worlds in the second round repêchage. Gary Neiwand (AUS), Curtis Harnett (CAN) and Eddie Alexander (SCO) are others expected to be through to the final stages.

Competitors in the kilometre time trial will cover four laps of the track alone with only the clock to beat. This is a pure test of speed from a standing start and they only get one chance. Using last year's World Championships as a guide Australia's Martin Vinnicombe who was placed third, speedy Trinidadian Gene Samuel fifth, one place lower than in L.A., and 1984 Olympic silver medallist, Curtis Harnett (CAN), who

Photo Library Internationa

Hugh Porter

Sporting Pictures (UK) Ltd.

Gary Trevsiol (CAN), 4000m pursuit

finished eighth, are likely to be among the medals.

British national champion for the kilometre, Eddie Alexander, riding in front of his own crowd could become Scotland's first ever cycling gold medallist.

The 4000 metre individual pursuiters require speed, strength and a dogged determination. Starting on opposite sides of the track, the optimum aim is to try to catch your opponent. This is not always possible, therefore the first man to complete his 16 laps is the winner.

After the qualifying round to find the top eight or sixteen according to strength of entry, the competition then progresses with the fastest against the slowest on a knockout basis. If one rider catches another he must complete the distance to record a time for seeding purposes in the next round, apart from the semis where obviously the winners will meet.

Favourite for this title must be Dean Woods (AUS), who struck gold in L.A. as part of his country's winning team pursuit squad. This former Junior World Champion was also fourth in last year's Senior World Individual Pursuit.

Australia are bidding for a hat trick of golds in the team pursuit which was introduced to the Games in 1974. New Zealand and England are the only other countries to have won medals in this event.

After the qualifying round to find the quickest eight teams, these are then matched fastest against slowest on a knock-out basis, as in the individual. The time is taken on the third team member to cross the line so each squad can shed one man.

Each rider takes a turn at the front, generally for a half or full lap, maintaining the speed whilst the others follow behind in line. He then swings up the banking towards the balustrade allowing the rest of the team to pass through, before dropping in at the back to wait his pacemaking turn again.

The ten mile race does not take place in the Olympics or World Championships. It is an exciting massed start event with one aim in mind, to be first over the line at the end of the final lap. It's a little like chess on wheels as individuals and groups make their bid for gold by attacking off the front of the bunch. The ever changing pattern of the race keeps the speed high, around 30mph (48km/h) with the final outcome always in doubt.

The 100 kilometre team time trial will use an undulating course based on the City of Edinburgh bypass. Racing against the clock, teams of four go off at two minute intervals, and the time is taken on the third man to finish. England are the defending champions and should be the last team to start.

Cycling's final event, the 105 mile Road Race, is the longest competition of the whole Games. Competitors face 15 laps of a seven mile loop primarily on the dual carriageway of the City of Edinburgh bypass which is at 500ft (150m), on the edge of the Pentland Hills.

Unlike the bikes used by the trackmen, which all have a single fixed gear, the roadmen's machines will be equipped with twelve or fourteen gears giving them a broad variety to cope with different terrain and conditions. To win this title, which will take around four hours, you need stamina and courage. Luck can also play a part. Mechanical trouble, a puncture at the wrong time or missing the vital winning break are all key factors.

England's John Tonks won the trial last year on this course and could be one of the favourites. Perhaps the most famous winner is Australia's Phil Anderson, who won back in 1978. Anderson is now one of the World's top professionals and has worn the Yellow Jersey as the race leader in the Tour de France.

FOUNDED 1556
TRADE MARK
TENNENT'S
80/-
Superior Ale
TENNENT'S
EXPORT
ALE
BRITAIN'S No.1 EXPORT ALE
TRADE MARK
TENNENT'S
FOUNDED 1556
SPECIAL
70/- ALE
Brewery Conditioned
TENNENT'S
LAGER
TENNENT'S
FOUNDED 1556
SPECIAL

John Goodbody

introduces judo

Men's judo, a regular part of the Olympic Games since 1972, will be a demonstration sport for the first time this year, preparing for its inclusion in the main programme in 1990. Yet the Commonwealth Games will still be more progressive than the Olympic movement in one feature - women's judo, blocked from full recognition at the Olympics until 1992, will be a demonstration sport this year and, alongside the men, will be on the full programme in 1990.

Of the eleven countries expected to take part in the seven weight categories, which will be fought out on Monday, July 28, England will field the strongest men's team. Three Olympic medallists, led by Neil Adams, the former world light-middleweight (under 78kgs) champion, are likely to be in the team. His precise throws and use of jujigatame (straight arm-lock) make him Europe's premier technician. But he is always attacked strongly by the talented Canadian Kevin Docherty. Scottish and Australian fighters should also be prominent. In the women's tournament, which will be held concurrently at Meadowbank, the most likely challengers to England's bantamweight (under 48kgs) world champion Karen Briggs and former world featherweight (under 52kgs) titleholder Loretta Doyle are, respectively, two Australians, Julie Reardon and Christina-Ann Boyd, who both took medals at the 1983 World Championships.

Neil Adams

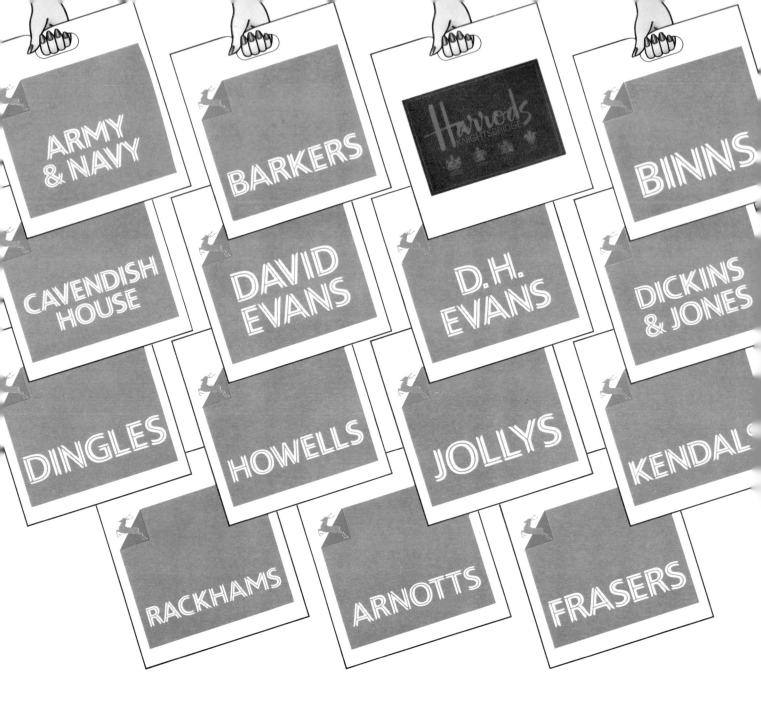

Richard Ayling

reviews rowing

Strathclyde Park will host the first Commonwealth Games Regatta since that at Perth, Australia in 1962.

During the 24 years that have elapsed, the sport of rowing has seen much change, and much growth. Rowing is now practised in most developed countries of the world. As a form of enjoyment and pursuit of good health it is now being promoted in developing nations. India is one emerging nation at rowing who will be hoping to contend final places at this year's events.

Since the first of the six Games Regattas held in Canada, in 1930 when there were only four events on offer, Australia has emerged as the strongest nation, recording eleven victories. England, always the strongest home nation, follows with nine, New Zealand with seven and Canada three in the six previous Commonwealth Games Regattas.

Of the other home nations, only Wales has won medals, with a bronze in 1958, followed by a silver behind England in the same event (coxless fours) in 1962. Scotland, on home water will be looking to open up their account in the enlarged programme of races.

In the men's heavyweight category there are the original six events that were last raced in 1962. The new categories include men's lightweight with two events,

Jon Clift (Rowing Magazine)

Canada's girls will be the crews to beat in the five new Women's Heavyweight events.

women's heavyweight with five events and women's lightweight with two events. All these categories are now raced annually as World Championships. Britain hosts the World Rowing Championships in August at Holme Pierrepont, Nottingham.

Prospects for racing are good

The likeliest medal winners in men's heavyweights will come from the 'Big Four', but there is no doubt that in the lightweight men's, and both women's events, some of the smaller nations will be waiting for their chance of success.

From the home nations England will spearhead the challenge with Martin Cross and Adam Clift. This coxless pair combination won a silver medal at the 1985 World Rowing Championships. Steven Redgrave, at 6ft 6in and 16 stone a veritable giant, is England's best chance of a gold medal in that most demanding event - the single sculls. Surprisingly, in the six Games Regattas contested to date, this event is the only one that England has not won. Both of these crews, are coached by Mike Spracklen,

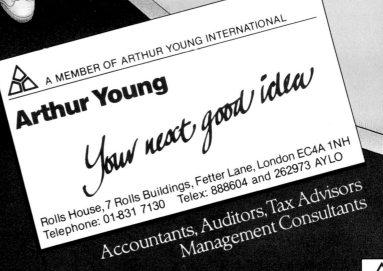

Jon Clift (Rowing Magazine)

Martin Cross and Adam Clift, England's spearhead for success.

who partnered by Geoff Baker won the double sculls event in Wales in 1958.

Another British Champion who will race under England's colours is Beryl Crockford, who may race in both women's heavyweight and lightweight classes of single sculls.

Heading Scotland's possible entry is the double Henley winning pair Ewan Pearson and David Riches, who will have tried for their Henley hat trick earlier in July. The possible confrontation between them and the English combination will be one of the major races.

In the men's and women's events the eights are the 'Blue Riband' races. The might of New Zealand, Australia and Canada battling against England for the three medals in the men's heavyweight event is likely to be one of the climaxes to the Regatta. The 'Kiwis' have never won the eights event, and their record at World and Olympic Regattas since 1971 of five gold medals makes them strong contenders. In the women's heavyweight eights Canada will start as strong favourites for the title.

Rowing has an active participation of over 25,000 in England alone, this at all levels and ages. In recent years rowing has also become a sport, when suitably adapted, for disabled people to participate.

Rowing dates back to the propulsion of galleys thousands of years ago. It has now well and truly become a 'Sport for all' in the United Kingdom and the Commonwealth.

We're covering the games from every angle.
As insurance brokers to the 1986 Commonwealth Games in Edinburgh, we have more reason than most to wish this important event in the athletics calendar every success.
Sedgwick
A commanding presence in worldwide insurance and reinsurance broking

David Parish

on the hotshots

Paul Bentley (GB), 1984 L.A. Olympics

Sporting Pictures (UK) Ltd.

Shooting is a sport of the will, trying to hold still and concentrate on releasing a perfectly aimed shot, whilst all the time nervousness tries to ruin a good result. Shooting is a vast competitive sport, with one major competition this year achieving an entry of some 100,000.

Events in the Commonwealth Games vary from small bore rifle three positions, lasting five hours, to the rapid fire pistol totalling in all 60 shots in 72 seconds. From the ultra precise prone rifle, through the efforts to hold the rifle or a pistol still whilst standing, to the sudden instant action of the shotgun shooter as the clay target leaves the trap at an astonishing speed.

Considerable physical and mental training have to be undertaken to perfect the co-ordination necessary for top performance just as in other sports, but size, sex and pure physical strength are not limiting factors.

The events are conducted under international shooting rules, except for the full bore rifle, as follows:

Small bore rifle 60 shots prone, fired at 50 metres with a .22 rifle on a target whose 10-ring or 'bull' is only only 12.4mm in diameter. A near perfect score is needed to win a medal, which can be far from easy even in the steady prone position, especially when there is a changeable wind to blow the bullet off course; the range to be used for these Commonwealth Games is likely to test the shooters' skill.

Small bore rifle 50 metres three positional event, 40 shots, prone, standing and kneeling. This match lasts 5 hours with 15 minutes for changeover between each position. This requires endurance and considerable powers of concentration, especially in the difficult standing position.

Air rifle 60 shots at 10 metres. It does not sound very far, but the 10-ring is only 1mm in diameter and this standing. The .177 rifles are very accurate, but owing to the low velocity of the pellet and the time taken for the mechanism to operate, it requires a very skilled approach, and a long 'follow through', holding the rifle on aim for what seems a long time after the trigger is pulled. It is a very demanding event and requires a very steady hold, and if the shooter has an off day it shows up here more than anywhere else.

The names to watch for in these three rifle events are: Alister Allan of Scotland, Olympic medallist, World Record holder in the 60 shot prone event with a perfect score of 600 and a previous Commonwealth Games gold medal winner; Malcolm Cooper of England, Olympic gold medallist; and Barry Dagger, also of England, Olympic medallist, and although of small size a giant in the world of shooting.

Air pistol 60 shots at 10 metres standing as with all pistol events. Very accurate .177 pistols and although naturally a bigger target is used than with the rifle, it has the same need of a steady prolonged hold to achieve top results.

Free pistol, 60 shots at 50 metres and the ultimate precision pistol match. The pistols used have long barrels, .22 calibre, form fitting grips and light triggers. Even so, they still have to be held very steadily indeed over this long course of fire.

Rapid fire pistol at 25 metres, shot with .22 pistols, on a series of five separate targets. When the targets turn to face the shooter the arm is raised from the ready position (45 degrees) and one shot fired on each target. The first two series in 8 seconds for five shots, the second two series in 6 seconds and the last two series in the meagre time of 4

THEY'LL NEED ALL THE HELP THEY CAN GET TO FIND YOU.

The Search and Rescue Dog Association and the Mountain Rescue Committee of Scotland are among the many Scottish groups we sponsor. Both would feel a little lost without our help.

YOU CAN BE SURE OF SHELL

Air Rifle. A left handed shooter, Adrian King. Because of the length of time the pellet is in the barrel it is important for accuracy that the weapon is recoilless.

Peter Hicks

seconds. This makes a total of 30 shots and the series are repeated again the next day for a total of 60 shots. Raising the pistol, aligning the sights, holding steady and carefully pulling the trigger without disturbing the aim, then moving to the next target and repeating the sequence until five shots are fired, is well worth seeing, especially in the 4 second series.

Centre fire pistol match may be shot with a pistol or revolver of from 7.62mm to 9.65mm calibre. There are 30 shots precision and 30 shots rapid. In the latter the pistol has to be raised, aimed and fired in the 3 seconds the target faces the shooter, and the shooter has to prepare for the next shot and return to the ready position in the 7 seconds that the target turns away. A name to watch is David Levene of England, who has been shooting very well and was placed highly in the European Championship in 1985.

Sporting Pictures (UK) Ltd.

Three Positional Rifle. Kneeling. Malcolm Cooper. The importance of the adjustments possible to the butt, allowing the rifle and its sights to be brought to its optimum position, are seen here.

Full bore rifle is the traditional Commonwealth event under National Rifle Association rules and is shot with 7.62mm rifles using 'as issued' ammunition (the competitors all use the same ammunition). Fired at distances of 300, 500 and 600 yards with the final being shot at 900 and 1000 yards. At the longest range one can imagine a bullet the size of a stub end of a pencil being sent to hit a bull the size of a large dinner plate at the best part of a mile. In a strong wind this can mean the barrel pointing well off the side of the 10 foot wide target, possibly pointing nearer an adjacent target, whilst the shooter hopes to have estimated the wind correctly so that it will blow the bullet into the centre of the bull. Even worse, of course, is a variable wind when the shooter may have to alter the reading on his rearsight for almost every shot. Such is the skill of the riflemen that there may be some truth to their claim to be the world's best meteorologists for the next 10 seconds. Two of the notables in this event are Arthur Clarke of Scotland, a previous Commonwealth Games winner, and Geoff Ayling of Tasmania, an excellent long range shot.

Trap is a shotgun event, fired at clay targets which are thrown from traps, hence the name, set in a line parallel to that from which the shooters fire. They speed away at various angles but always within 3.5 metres above the roof of the trap house, which is at ground level, when 10 metres away. So they come out very fast and fairly low and are a challenging target to hit. The shooter keeps the butt of his shotgun in his shoulder when calling for the next target, but even so the time between the first sighting of the target and when it is too far away to be broken is short indeed.

Skeet is a shotgun event fired at clay targets, but differs from Trap in that there is a 'high house' and a 'low house', as the structures are called, from which the clay target is thrown. These are placed on each side of the semi-circle from which the shooters fire so that a variety of singles and doubles, high and low are shot at in turn. The butt is kept at the hip so that the gun has to be raised, aimed and fired in a very short space of time.

At the time of writing, very few countries have selected their shooters for the various events or 'disciplines' as they are known, but a few of the outstanding performers have been mentioned.

Pat Besford

on swimming's hopefuls

Australia, Canada and England have always dominated the Commonwealth Games events in the pool. The forecasts for Edinburgh this summer do not suggest there will be any substantial change in this historic rule, although hosts Scotland, the fourth most successful over the years, have traditional south of the border rivals England as their target to beat.

The Scots, led by Director of Swimming Hamilton Smith, have taken elaborate steps to make their second Games at home an outstanding one. Their year-long 'Operation Edinburgh' included regular training week-ends, early selection of star competitors and many international-experience contests overseas.

Their memories of Edinburgh 1970 are not of the best. They won just one bronze medal thanks to a little-known 16 year old, David Wilkie, who went on to become Scotland's only Olympic swimming champion, for 200 metres breaststroke, in 1976. Smith summed things up: "We intend to take on England. We are nudging closer individually and on a group basis."

The top three countries between them have won 261 of the 289 titles and 741 of the 865 medals since 1930, leaving just 124 medals, 28 of them gold, to be shared amongst the six other teams to reach victory rostrums in 56 years.

Alex Baumann, Victor Davis and Anne Ottenbrite of Canada, all winners in Brisbane four years ago and who became Olympic champions in Los Angeles should all be in the hunt again. So should Jon Sieben of Australia, only a 200m butterfly bronze medallist in 1982 but who gained the shock Olympic victory of 1984 when he improved four seconds and beat West Germany's great Michael Gross in this event.

Anne Ottenbrite

Czechoslovakian-born Baumann, the Olympic champion and world record breaker for 200 and 400 metres medley, proudly bears the maple-leaf emblem of his adopted country as a coloured tattoo over his heart. He could be the swimming star of 1986.

Baumann's range of talent on all four strokes is immense. In addition to his two individual golds in Brisbane he won a bronze in the 4 x 100m freestyle relay, missed third place in the 200m freestyle by just three tenths of a second and swam in Canada's two other relay teams, both dramatically disqualified for flying take-overs after touching second in one and then first in the other. He was also entered in the 200m breaststroke, but did not swim . . . even a superman is not inexhaustible!

Scotland have two real hopes anxious to follow Baumann home in the shorter medley. Anglo-Scot Robin Brew, the international Super-Stars champion, took the silver in Brisbane and was fourth in the Olympics. He was edged out of third place in Los Angeles by Neil Cochran from Aberdeen, who at the end of last year broke Brew's British record in a world class time.

The temperamental Davis, the Olympic, World and Commonwealth champion and record holder for 200 metres breaststroke, suffered a salutary lesson four years ago when he was beaten over 100m by Adrian

The Olympic 200m Individual Medley was won by Alex Baumann (CAN) in a world record 2:01.42 from Pablo Morales (USA) and Neil Cochran of Scotland.

Moorhouse of England, whom the Canadians had not even considered as a remote rival.

Davis, whose ill-tempered display of bad manners in front of the Queen after his medley relay squad were disqualified in Brisbane will be long remembered, was only ninth and seventh in the 1985 World rankings for the 100 and 200m breaststroke. But he is a talented champion when he is motivated.

Moorhouse, from Leeds, reconfirmed his two-lap speed by winning the European title for the breaststroke sprint in Sofia last summer. The races between this pair, Australia's best, England's Murray Buswell and improving Scots like European junior champion Gary Watson are to be eagerly awaited.

Ottenbrite, like Davis, Olympic and Commonwealth champion for 200m breaststroke, returned home to Canada at the end of last year after some unsuccessful months training in California. Her task in Edinburgh may be the hardest of the pre-Games stars. In her absence a new Canadian champion, Cindy Ounpuu, emerged to take Anne's Commonwealth 100m record and come within eight hundredth of a second of her 200m figures.

Sieben, known as the 'Shrimp' at school because he was always the smallest in the class, stood only 5′ 9″ high as he lined up beside Gross, the mighty 6′ 7″ 'Albatross', in that memorable Los Angeles final. Not only did he have the temerity to beat Gross but he also took the West German's world record.

Last year Sieben also showed a nifty speed, despite his lack of inches, for 100m butterfly, finishing the year as No. 2 in the world, ahead of Gross, with a Commonwealth record.

England's Andy Jameson, close runner-up over 100m to Gross in the 1985 European championships, Tom Ponting and Vlastimil Cerny of Canada and New Zealand's Anthony Mosse, the top Commonwealth 200m man of last year are some to add glitter to the contests on this stroke.

Tracey Wickham of Australia, whose world records for 400 and 800m stood for more than seven years and England's June Croft, the 100 and 200m champion were the women freestyle stars in Brisbane. Both are now retired.

Stepping up in Miss Croft's place as England's best woman medal hope is Sarah Hardcastle. Four years ago, at 13, she was the baby of the team in Brisbane yet still managed to come fifth in the 800m.

Since that baptism of fire, the Essex girl, now six foot tall, has grown in swimming prowess as well as stature. In Los Angeles she became Britain's youngest ever summer Olympic medallist, with a silver over 400m and a bronze for 800m. Last August she came within a whisker of beating defending champion Astrid Strauss of East Germany in the European 800m.

Anna McVann of Australia is the most likely danger for Sarah while her countrywoman, all-rounder Michele Pearson, is a short distance freestyle hope and the outstanding candidate for the 200 and 400m medley for which she was the No. 1 in the Commonwealth in 1985.

Jon Sieben, who went into the Los

Chaucer's famous line could not have been more appropriately quoted than by a distinguished Irish missionary at the funeral of Eric Liddell.

Born in 1902, Liddell had become 'the most famous, the most popular and the best loved athlete Scotland ever produced' by the time he was 22.

Rugby international and Olympic gold medallist, he was universally admired for his athletic achievements, his high character, happy humour and for his Christianity–his unswerving commitment to which made him refuse to compete in the Sunday heats of the 100 metres at the Paris Olympics of 1924.

ERIC LIDDELL

"A VERRAY PARFIT GENTIL KNIGHT."

The commitment was lasting. In 1925 Liddell put fame aside and returned as a missionary to China, where he had been born. Apart from spells of leave, he remained there for the rest of his life.

That life was not to be a long one. Interned by the Japanese in 1942, Eric Liddell died of a brain tumour three years later in the camp at Weihsien.

Whom the gods love ...

The Royal Bank of Scotland

PART OF A SERIES 'SCOTS IN PORTRAIT'

The Royal Bank of Scotland plc.
Registered Office: 36 St. Andrew Square, Edinburgh EH2 2YB.
Registered in Scotland Number 90312.

Bankers to the Commonwealth Games 1986

Chris Snode

Angeles Olympics as the 16th best entry and emerged the champion is a good illustration of how favourites do not always come off on the night and a will to win can sometimes bring about miracles. This factor will add spice to what should be an enthralling six days of competition in the Edinburgh Commonwealth Pool.

The diving contests, two each for men and women, could produce a new crop of champions. England's Chris Snode, a double winner in 1978 and 1982, has retired while Canada's Olympic springboard gold medallist Sylvie Bernier, runner-up in Brisbane, is not a certain starter.

Bobby Morgan, the London-trained Welshman, could bring the Principality its first Commonwealth medals from the boards provided he can make up lost training and strength after months out of the water following breaking a wrist.

If there are doubts over the diving, the new Games discipline of synchronised swimming solo and duet titles seem certainties for Canada, the world's number two - and sometimes number one - nation, with England safe for the silvers.

Names to look for

MEN

Freestyle sprints	Mark Stockwell, Peter Dale & Neil Brooks (AUS), Blair Hicken & Sandy Goss (CAN), Mark Foster (ENG), Paul Easter (SCO), Per Siog-ang (SIN)
Freestyle distance	Justin Lemberg & Michael Mackenzie (AUS), Tony Day (WAL)
Backstroke	Mike West, Sean Murphy & Mark Tewkesbury (CAN), Gary Hurring & Paul Kingman (NZL), Andrew Phillips (JAM)
Breaststroke	Adrian Moorhouse & Murray Buswell (ENG), Victor Davis (CAN), Brett Stocks & Glenn Beringen (AUS), Gary Watson (SCO)
Butterfly	Jon Sieben, Barry Armstrong & Anthony MacDonald (AUS), Andrew Jameson & Steve Poulter (ENG), Tom Ponting & Vlastimil Cerny (CAN), Anthony Mosse (NZL)
Medley	Alex Baumann, Jon Kelly & Tom Ponting (CAN), Neil Cochran & Robin Brew (SCO), Rob Woodhouse (AUS), Steve Poulter (ENG)

WOMEN

Freestyle sprints	Jane Kerr (CAN), Michele Pearson (AUS), Caroline Cooper (ENG)
Freestyle distance	Sarah Hardcastle (ENG), Anna McVann (AUS), Debbie Wurzburger & Kim Milne (CAN)
Backstroke	Georgina Parkes & Audrey Moore (AUS), Kathy Read (ENG), Reema Abdo (CAN), Beverley Rose (SCO)
Breaststroke	Anne Ottenbrite, Cindy Ounpuu & Guylaine Cloutier (CAN), Dimity Douglas (AUS), Suki Brownsdon & Gaynor Stanley (ENG), Jean Hill (SCO)
Butterfly	Janet Tibbits, Donna McGinnis (AUS), Pam Rai & Jill Horstead (CAN), Caroline Cooper & Samantha Purvis (ENG)
Medley	Michele Pearson & Anna McVann (AUS), Jennifer McElroy & Donna McGinnis (CAN), Sarah Hardcastle, Kathy Read & Gaynor Stanley (ENG)

Sandy Sutherland

Called to the bar

David Morgan will carry the hopes of Wales in Edinburgh.

Edinburgh solicitor Charles Revolta was first 'called to the bar' for the 1970 Commonwealth Games. For Charles, who practises his legal profession at the Scottish Office, is a weight-lifter and a remarkably successful one at that. Yet he looks like one of those puny eight-stone weaklings into whose face you kick sand on the beach. Bespectacled and mild-mannered, Revolta is certainly not a stereotype, but he will be going for his fifth Commonwealth Games in July, when the event returns to his native city.

Revolta's most successful sortie was in Edmonton in 1978, when he took the silver medal, and perhaps the most remarkable aspect of this 36-year-old veteran's career is that he is still a flyweight despite the ravages of time and business lunches.

But, if his career is remarkable, it pales besides the longevity of the man who was the flyweight bronze medallist ahead of him in 1970 and a further bronze in 1974. John McNiven senior is now 50 and will be competing at a record sixth Games. The World Masters champion, he, too, has kept his waist-line well in trim over the years, although he has competed in three different classes, the fly (under 52 kg) bantam (under 56kg) and feather (under 60kg). Now he feels best at bantamweight.

The host nation's best chances probably lie with these gnarled veterans in the lighter divisions, where Scotland, just as in boxing, has a 'mighty midget' tradition.

But, overall, the battle for the medals will lie between England, Australia, Canada, India, Wales and Nigeria.

At the opposite end of the scales from the midgets is the massive Australian, Dean Lukin, the 1984 Olympic super-heavy champion whose massive 20-stone plus frame will fully test the stage at Edinburgh's Playhouse Theatre.

Nigeria have some fascinating characters including a lifter by the appropriate name of 'Ironbar', who holds the Commonwealth junior records for the super-heavy class.

England can boast Dean Willey, the featherweight champion of the last Games, in Brisbane in 1982, who has since moved up a class, and Wales include Dave Morgan, who broke the Commonwealth record in the under 75kg class on his last visit to Scotland in 1985, clean and jerking 195.5 kilos.

In all, ten weight divisions have to be settled with lifting taking place over five days and two sets of medals to be won on each day.

John Goodbody

on wrestling's giants

Canada, winners of five of the ten weight categories at last October's Commonwealth Championships in Glasgow, despite fielding a weakened team, are bound to dominate the freestyle events at the Games. As usual, the other Olympic wrestling style, Greco-Roman, where holds are barred below the waist, is not included in the Commonwealth events. Indeed, freestyle itself will be dropped from the 1990 Games - a sad omission of one of the most basic and ancient of all athletic activities - although it may return to future Commonwealth programmes. The sport has immense tradition. A pin or fall, scored when a wrestler forces an opponent's shoulders in contact with the mat, has been a method of securing an outright victory in some styles of the sport since antiquity.

When the Games were held in Edinburgh in 1970, India won five and Pakistan four of the titles. Since then Pakistan has left the Commonwealth and India's supremacy has been eroded by the Canadians, many of whom have been trained in the acutely competitive universities in the United States. Yet India still won two titles, the under 48kg and under 52kg, last October. In the lightest class Rajesh Kumar, whose silky movements are highlighted by a front head lock into take-downs, is favourite ahead of Canada's Ron Moncur. In the 52kg, Mahavir Singh took the title but should be challenged strongly by New Zealand's Shane Stannett and England's Nigel Donohue.

Mitch Ostberg is a likely winner of the 57kg and another Canadian, Gary Bohay, who is doing a pre-medical course at Arizona University, should be prominent in the under 62kg. But here he will meet England's Brian Aspen, whose use of fireman's carry and high crotch techniques brought him a European silver medal in 1984 and the Commonwealth title last year.

The under 68kg gold medal may be settled by the Canadian selection. Dave McKay won the Commonwealth title and his compatriot Pat Sullivan, a student from Concordia, Montreal, was third in last year's World Championships. But Australian Zsig Kelevitz is a determined fighter who was fifth in the Los Angeles Olympics. Another Australian, Craig Green, 22, has some stubborn opponents in the under 74kg class, including Martins Ubaha, a competitive Olympic weightlifter from Nigeria.

The under 82kg category should be dominated by Canadian Chris Rinke, the Olympic bronze medallist, with last year's winner of the Commonwealth title, Serge Marcil, moving up to 90kg where his compatriot Dick Cox will dispute selection. But England's Noel Loban, 1984 Olympic bronze medallist, is immensely experienced - he was US collegiate champion in 1980 and has long arms, which are useful for yanking opponents' legs.

Loban beat another Canadian, Clark Davis, in Los Angeles but Davis, a 1985 World Championships silver medallist, is now in the 100kg where Robert Algie, a raw-boned New Zealand sheepfarmer, should be among the medals. In the 100kg plus category, Albert Patrick, a CID Inspector in Brixton, still represents his native Scotland and could give the host country their best chance of a title despite the 20 stone Canadian Don Payne, second in the World Junior Championships and a keen American footballer at Penn State University.

Britain's No.1 bitter is now available on draught at No.17 Acacia Avenue.

Take-home bitter is nothing new. But a take-home draught bitter which stays fresh for days from the moment it's opened, was unheard of. Until now.

Some brewers said it couldn't be done.

But, mindful of the rewards to be gained, we at Allied-Lyons stuck to the task.

The beer posed no problem. It picked itself. Tetley is Britain's most popular bitter.

But bringing it home to you took eighteen months, £250,000 and the services of one of the country's leading packaging technologists.

The result. Tetley on Tap.

The best pint of bitter you'll ever drink at home. In an easy-to-carry pack.

Nearly 9 pints of Tetleys, that comes out clear and bright with a full frothy head just like down the pub.

Now we've the technology, we can apply it to other products, like Gaymer's Olde English Cyder.

Allied-Lyons now reach untapped markets.

Whether you live up North or down South you can now sup Britain's best-selling bitter at home.

Tetley on Tap is not the only innovation Allied-Lyons have in the pipeline.

In 1985 we launched over 100 new products worldwide. Which is something to write home about.

Allied-Lyons
GOING ON GROWING

EST. 1830
TEACHER'S.
A WELCOME
AWAITING.
TEACHER'S
HIGHLAND CREAM
PERFECTION OF OLD
SCOTCH WHISKY
HIGHLAND CREAM IS A UNIQUE
BLEND OF FINEST SCOTCH WHISKIES
Wm TEACHER & SONS LTD
GLASGOW SCOTLAND
40% vol 75cl
BOTTLED IN SCOTLAND

Allied-Lyons
GOING ON GROWING

The BBC

The Host Broadcaster

by Brendan J. Slamin

When Broadcasters from around the Commonwealth converge on Edinburgh they will share the common aim of reporting and reflecting the full drama and excitement of the Games to their home countries. Edinburgh will be presented to the world and some 800 million viewers and listeners around the world will be able to enjoy the Games through the medium of modern communications. Around the world, some 450 hours of television will be seen during the ten days of the Games and radio coverage will be more or less continuous to some 50 countries.

This vast amount of broadcasting can only be achieved by the provision of studio and outside broadcasting facilities and staff on a major scale. Each sport needs multi-camera coverage provided in such a way that the best performances from athletes of all the competing countries are seen. Commentary positions are needed for visiting broadcasters as well as for the BBC team, and all the requirements associated with modern sports coverage - such as slow motion replays and interview facilities - also need to be provided. All of these are required for the ten sports taking place at separate venues and up to eight occurring simultaneously.

Over 100 cameras are in use at the sports. As well as the normal complement of fixed cameras, helicopter shots will be used for the coverage of the opening ceremony, the men's and ladies' marathons, cycle road races and rowing. Shots from ground motorbike cameras, radio linked via a relay helicopter will be used to give live coverage. A specially developed low wash catamaran will house two cameras to allow viewers to keep abreast of the leading oarsman in each race at Strathclyde Park. From this plethora of television and radio coverage individual programmes are built and edited.

For example, when we in the UK may be watching athletics and badminton, the Canadian viewers may be watching rowing, and the Australians, boxing. So that each country's programmes can be tailored to their own requirements, the BBC as host broadcaster to the visitors, has equipped a specially provided Broadcast Centre in Edinburgh. This is the nerve centre of the whole broadcasting operation. As several sports are taking place simultaneously, some are recorded, edited and played back into the programmes at the earliest opportunity. Since each country is operating independently, this calls for the provision of more than 80 broadcast quality videotape recorders.

With some 450 hours of television and continuous coverage on radio to some 50 countries taking place, the Broadcast Centre will be operating on a 24 hour basis. When the last satellite transmission to Canada finishes at 3 am the editing for the next morning's early transmissions begins. With so much live broadcasting taking place, a complex communications network has been set up, in close association with British Telecom's national and international arms.

Within Edinburgh 90 microwave vision routes are being established and a network of audio and co-

Earth station in Edinburgh for feeding Canadian programmes by satellite to Toronto

ordination lines solely for the use of broadcasters. These serve to link the sporting venues into the Broadcast Centre and provide the air to ground circuits for the helicopter and motor cycle cameras.

To feed programmes to the home countries for their own transmissions, British Telecom has provided five southgoing vision circuits and a large number of audio lines for onward transmission by satellites hovering at 2,300 miles above the Atlantic, Pacific and Indian Oceans. There will be a satellite Earth station at Edinburgh, to feed a special satellite carrying the Canadian programmes to Toronto and Montreal.

The BBC is also, as part of its commitment to the Games, staging the first part of the opening ceremony. This is traditionally an opportunity for the host country to demonstrate fun and vitality, and the spirit of Scottish youth will come shining through in Stewart Morris's production.

In all, some 1,500 broadcasters, commentators, producers and technicians will be in Edinburgh using their skills to bring the Games to the world. The BBC in acting as their host is again demonstrating its commitment to the Games and the Commonwealth.

Total Commitment
Total Experience
Total Energy

David Wilkie

remembers how a Commonwealth medal set him on his way to Olympic Gold

Sporting Pictures (UK) Ltd.

The 1970 Edinburgh Commonwealth Games proved to be a significant event in my life, although I did not realise it at the time. A bronze medal in the 200 metres breaststroke was more than I could have dreamt of . . . in fact, at that time, I did not really dream of anything as far as swimming was concerned.

My coach at Warrender Baths Club in Edinburgh, Frank Thomas, kept telling me that I could do well but, at that stage, it was so far from anything I had already achieved, that I could not fully grasp the situation.

The 1970 Commonwealth Games made me realise what I could do without a great amount of training and dedication. I had only started training in 1968 and the team training and corporate spirit for the Games helped me to surge in Edinburgh. To be honest, the Games passed quickly for me and, like so many competitors, I failed to take the opportunities it afforded me because I did not really understand what was happening.

Nevertheless, the Games set me on the right path for future success. Training with the Scottish team gave me my first taste of disciplined conditioning and coupled with further training at Warrender in 1971, gave me a solid base for the 1972 Munich Olympics where I won a silver medal.

By the 1974 Commonwealth Games, I was much more experienced in world swimming terms. I was fortunate enough to win both the 200 metres individual medley and the 200 metres breaststroke. Scottish swimming continued to be prominent, and the size of our population was no obstacle to success. It was after 1974 that I had to make decisions about my future. I was used to training with a large squad of swimmers in Edinburgh but my school days were drawing to a close and the 1976 Olympics rapidly approaching. I decided to attend Miami University in Florida and in Montreal went on to win the Olympic gold medal.

Montreal was important but the 1970 Commonwealth Games helped me to develop my first sense of direction towards my ultimate goal. The memories I still retain of Edinburgh in 1970 are strong - the sense of real achievement in winning the bronze, the sight of a packed and colourful Royal Commonwealth Pool for the first time, the feeling of team spirit and national pride as part of the Scottish team - these memories come flooding back.

Bill Mahoney of Canada won the 200 metres breaststroke in 2:30:29. Swimming standards improved so rapidly that it hardly seems possible that some six years later, I was winning the Olympics in 2:15:11, some fifteen seconds faster. The event has now gone full circle. The outstanding performer who everyone will be wanting to beat is another Canadian, Victor Davis. The superb Davis lowered my world record three times, the last in winning the 1984 Olympic event.

Could it be that another unknown Scot might this time win a bronze and be set on a path of ultimate success, thus completing another ever upward moving aquatic circle? I hope so.

Mary Peters

talks of her pride

As an eighteen year old athlete just completing my first year as a student at the Belfast College of Domestic Science, I received a letter inviting me to represent Northern Ireland at the 1958 Empire Games. It was a thrill never to be forgotten. There were four women named on the athletic team. Thelma Hopkins (high and long jumper), Bridget Robinson (javelin thrower), Maeve Kyle (sprinter) and myself.

I was selected to compete in three events, high jump, shot, and 4 x 110 yards relay. I was eighth out of nine in the high jump, ninth out of ten in the shot and in the heat of the sprint relay we came in last of the four teams (by a long way). However, one of the other teams was disqualified and we made the final. How embarrassing! I had only just passed the baton to Maeve, who was on the final leg, when the winners were breaking the tape in a world record time. But what marvellous memories of friendship and competition. Enough to inspire me to train hard for the next Games to be held in Perth, Australia in 1962. It was reported to be over 110°F in the bowl of the stadium when I competed in the shot and finished fourth.

Although the pentathlon had been included in the 1964 Olympic programme, it still hadn't been introduced into the Commonwealth Games, and so my coach and I decided to really concentrate on winning a gold medal in the shot at the 1966 Games in Jamaica. With a heavy weight training programme and a weight gaining diet, I increased my weight from my usual ten and a half stones to thirteen stones. I hated every minute of the whole detestable operation - not only that, but on arrival in Kingston we were informed that the ladies would be submitted to the first ever 'Sex Tests' to prove that we were women. I assure you that I have a certificate on my wall to prove that I passed! I didn't, however, achieve my ambition. In a pre-Games meet I beat my nearest rival Val Young of New Zealand by three feet, but at the Games the shot, which I so desperately wanted to win, was delayed by an hour because the decathlon javelin event was still in progress near the shot circle. Somehow during the delay I lost my concentration and had to settle for the silver. It created a turning point in my career. I tried to put on a brave face and my coach suggested I had taken my defeat too lightly and that I may as well finish with athletics altogether. I knew that wasn't what I wanted and luck was on my side. The pentathlon was to be included in the 1970 Edinburgh Games, so I would make amends and go for two golds! In fact I had a very enjoyable Games. Walking along Princes Street, I saw a photograph of me displayed in a window - fame at last. However, I was in for a busy time.

At Meadowbank Stadium in the space of three days I took part in the five pentathlon events, the heats and finals of the hurdles and the qualifying round and final of the shot. I won the pentathlon with a new UK and Commonwealth record. Prince Charles presented me with my medal. I then went on to win a second gold in the shot event. Success was very sweet. The Scottish people were very generous to all the competitors and I have very special memories of my visit to Edinburgh. It had been worthwhile continuing my search for success and I was inspired to go for gold in Munich. My Olympic victory prompted the *Belfast Telegraph* newspaper to launch the Mary Peters Track Fund

to provide a synthetic track for the young people of Northern Ireland. Collecting money, making public appearances, party going, and doing promotional work took a great deal of time. This, along with the death of my coach, meant that training had to be neglected. I was getting on a bit - a veteran in athletic terms. At the age of thirty-four I decided I still wanted to have another go and create another record by contesting my fifth Commonwealth Games in Christchurch, New Zealand in 1974.

During the years of taking part in pentathlons all over the world, I had made so many friends, but two that I hold very dear, Ann Wilson (England) and Diane Jones (Canada) were to be rivals in my swan song. Ann was chirpy and bright and had been a tremendous support in Munich. Diane was one of the world's most talented multi-events exponents but had been plagued by a series of injuries. They, however, finished third and sixth respectively as an almost unknown Nigerian athlete called Modupe Oshikoya gave me a very close competition and it all depended on the final event. I ran as fast as my fitness would allow and just managed enough to retain my title and the last prize I would ever win as an athlete. But I still had one more competition in the high jump. As I failed at the third attempt at 5ft 8in the announcer solemnly told the spectators that my long career was over. I gathered up my tracksuit and ran to the exit tunnel with tears streaming down my face. It was a mixture of relief that all the hard training was over, and sadness that I would never feel again such rapport with athletic supporters, who had helped on so many occasions to raise my performances.

Sporting Pictures (UK) Ltd.

There was one final accolade. I was invited to carry the Northern Ireland flag at the closing ceremony. I decided that our flag should be noticed and asked the tallest man competing at the Games, Canadian shot putter Bruce Pirnie, to carry me on his shoulders with the flag held high. He even curtsied to the Queen as we passed the main stand.

I was very proud and honoured to represent my adopted country (I was born in Liverpool) over a period of sixteen years. I have so many wonderful memories and do not regret the sacrifices I made to succeed. Sport has given me so many rewards.

I look forward to seeing many old friends in Edinburgh in 1986.

A winning team.
GLENESK
YEARS 12 OLD
SINGLE MALT
VAT 69
RESERVE
12 YEARS OLD
THE ANTIQUARY
Finest old Scotch
WHISKY
Distilled, Blended and Bottled in Scotland
VAT 69
Distillers
Making friends throughout the world.
Wm. SANDERSON & SON LTD.
Braehead Mains, Edinburgh
and 63 Pall Mall, London.

Sport by Sport Review

The complete list of medallists for all sports

African champion Julius Kariuki of Kenya on his way to a World Cup steeplechase victory in 1985.

Serving the Commonwealth

The BCC Group has the privilege and distinction of serving 23 countries in the Commonwealth, giving it the second largest branch banking network in the Commonwealth.

The BCC Group's Capital Funds exceed US$1,200 million, Assets total US$17,000 million and it has offices in 72 countries. Its emphasis is on service – better service, in Edinburgh, in the Commonwealth and around the world.

And now, BCC VISA Travellers Cheques are also the Official Travellers Cheques of the XIII Commonwealth Games. BCC Travellers Cheques are also unique in one other respect. In addition to being welcome and refundable around the world, they offer a free Personal Accident Insurance cover up to US$275,000 – the only Travellers Cheques in the world to offer this facility.

BANK OF CREDIT AND COMMERCE INTERNATIONAL
SOCIETE ANONYME LICENSED DEPOSIT TAKER

45 BRANCHES IN UK. MAIN OFFICE: 100 LEADENHALL ST. LONDON EC3A 3AD. TEL: (01) 283 8566 TELEX: 892251 BCCLNA-G

ALSO INCLUDING A BRANCH AT 3 ST. ANDREWS SQUARE, EDINBURGH. TEL: (031) 557 2720 AND SPECIALLY DURING THE GAMES A BUREAU DE CHANGE AT MEADOWBANK STADIUM.

Argentina, Australia, Bahamas, Bahrain, Bangladesh, Barbados, Botswana, Brazil, Cameroon, Canada, China, Colombia, Cyprus, Djibouti, Egypt, France, Gabon, Germany (West), Gibraltar, Ghana, Grand Cayman, Hong Kong, India, Indonesia, Isle of Man, Italy, Ivory Coast, Jamaica, Japan, Jordan, Kenya, Korea (South), Lebanon, Liberia, Luxembourg, Macau, Malaysia, Maldives, Mauritius, Monaco, Morocco, Netherlands, Netherland Antilles, Niger, Nigeria, Oman, Pakistan, Panama, Paraguay, Philippines, Portugal, Senegal, Seychelles, Sierra Leone, Spain, Sri Lanka, Sudan, Swaziland, Switzerland, Thailand, Togo, Turkey, United Arab Emirates, United Kingdom, Uruguay, U.S.A., Venezuela, Yemen (North), Zambia, Zimbabwe.

The Official Travellers Cheques of the XIIIth Commonwealth Games

Archery

Archery has been selected as a Commonwealth Games sport just once to date, and is not on the programme for 1986. Men's and women's events were staged in 1982 at Brisbane on reclaimed swamp land at the Murarrie Recreation Reserve.

Each competition comprised double FITA rounds as prescribed by the International governing body for the sport; in each round a man shoots three dozen arrows at each of the following distances: 90m, 70m, 50m, 30m, and a woman shoots three dozen arrows at each of 70m, 60m, 50m, 30m.

The sport, which was first held in the Olympic Games in 1900, has not proved to be especially popular in Commonwealth countries, although eleven nations were represented in the 1982 tournament. The outstanding competitor was surely the remarkable women's winner, Neroli Fairhall of New Zealand, who shot from a wheelchair, as thirteen years earlier she had been disabled in a motorcycling accident. The 38-year-old competed on equal terms with non-handicapped archers, with the sole exception that her medication was accepted by the drug testing authorities. She tied on points with 17-year-old Janet Yates of Northern Ireland, but won the title on a higher number of 'inner golds', scoring the maximum ten points.

The men's title was won by Mark Blenkarne, with the same score that had earned him fourth place in the 1980 Olympic Games, and husband and wife Roger and Lucille LeMay won silver and bronze medals respectively.

Archery has advanced a long way from simple bows and arrows. The 1982 gold medallist Mark Blenkarne uses a highly sophisticated weapon.

ARCHERY MEDALLISTS

		MEN			WOMEN
1982	1.	Mark Blenkarne (ENG) 2446	1982	1.	Neroli Fairhall (NZ) 2373
	2.	Roger LeMay (CAN) 2426		2.	Janet Yates (NI) 2373
	3.	Michael Coen (AUS) 2411		3.	Lucille LeMay (CAN) 2349

ARCHERY - MEDAL TABLE BY NATIONS (1982 only)

Nation	Men			Women			Total
	G	S	B	G	S	B	
Canada	-	1	-	-	-	1	2
England	1	-	-	-	-	-	1
New Zealand	-	-	-	1	-	-	1
Northern Ireland	-	-	-	-	1	-	1
Australia	-	-	1	-	-	-	1
Total	1	1	1	1	1	1	6

ATHLETICS MEDALLISTS

Note that, where known, fully-automatic times are given as per the current regulations. Original official hand times may well have differed as, for instance, in the 1958 100 yards, when the winner Keith Gardner's time was given as 9.4 to 9.6 for Tom Robinson and Mike Agostini. The photo-finish showed Robinson a mere three-hundredths behind.

100 METRES

Run over 100 yards (91.44m) 1930-66

1930 1. Percy Williams (CAN) 9.9
2. Ernest Page (ENG) 10.2
3. John Fitzpatrick (CAN)
1934 1. Arthur Sweeney (ENG) 10.0
2. Martinus Theunissen (SAF) 10.0
3. Ian Young (SCO) 10.1
1938 1. Cyril Holmes (ENG) 9.7
2. John Mumford (AUS) 9.8
3. Edward Best (AUS) 9.8
1950 1. John Treloar (AUS) 9.7
2. Bill de Gruchy (AUS) 9.8
3. Donald Pettie (CAN) 9.9
1954 1. Mike Agostini (TRI) 9.6
2. Don McFarlane (CAN) 9.7
3. Hec Hogan (AUS) 9.7
1958 1. Keith Gardner (JAM) 9.66 (wind -1.67 m/s)
2. Tom Robinson (BAH) 9.69
3. Mike Agostini (CAN) 9.79
1962 1. Seraphino Antao (KEN) 9.50 (wind -1.8 m/s)
2. Tom Robinson (BAH) 9.63
3. Michael Cleary (AUS) 9.78
1966 1. Harry Jerome (CAN) 9.41
2. Tom Robinson (BAH) 9.44
3. Edwin Roberts (TRI) 9.52
1970 1. Don Quarrie (JAM) 10.24 (wind +3.6 m/s)
2. Lennox Miller (JAM) 10.32
3. Hasely Crawford (TRI) 10.33
1974 1. Don Quarrie (JAM) 10.38 (wind -0.5 m/s)
2. John Mwebi (KEN) 10.51
3. Ohene Karikari (GHA) 10.51
1978 1. Don Quarrie (JAM) 10.03 (wind +7.51 m/s)
2. Allan Wells (SCO) 10.07
3. Hasely Crawford (TRI) 10.09
1982 1. Allan Wells (SCO) 10.05 (wind +5.9 m/s)
2. Ben Johnson (CAN) 10.07
3. Cameron Sharp (SCO) 10.09

200 METRES

Run over 220 yards (201.17m) 1930-66

1930 1. Stanley Engelhart (ENG) 21.8
2. John Fitzpatrick (CAN)
3. William Walters (SAF)
1934 1. Arthur Sweeney (ENG) 21.9
2. Marthinus Theunissen (SAF) 22.0
3. Walter Rangeley (ENG) 22.1
1938 1. Cyril Holmes (ENG) 21.2
2. John Mumford (AUS) 21.3
3. Edward Best (AUS) 21.4
1950 1. John Treloar (AUS) 21.5
2. David Johnson (AUS) 21.8
3. Donald Jowett (NZL) 21.8
1954 1. Donald Jowett (NZL) 21.5
2. Brian Shenton (ENG) 21.5
3. Ken Jones (WAL) 21.9
1958 1. Tom Robinson (BAH) 21.08
2. Keith Gardner (JAM) 21.11
3. Gordon Day (SAF) 21.15
1962 1. Seraphino Antao (KEN) 21.28 (wind -2.5 m/s)
2. David Jones (ENG) 21.59
3. Johann du Preez (ZIM) 21.70
1966 1. Stanley Allotey (GHA) 20.65 (wind +1.0 m/s)
2. Edwin Roberts (TRI) 20.93
3. David Ejoke (NGR) 20.95
1970 1. Don Quarrie (JAM) 20.56 (wind +1.7 m/s)
2. Edwin Roberts (TRI) 20.69
3. Charles Asati (KEN) 20.74
1974 1. Don Quarrie (JAM) 20.73 (wind -0.6 m/s)
2. George Daniels (GHA) 20.97
3. Bevan Smith (NZL) 21.08
1978 1. Allan Wells (SCO) 20.12 (wind +4.31 m/s)
2. James Gilkes (GUY) 20.18
3. Colin Bradford (JAM) 20.43
1982 1= Alan Wells (SCO) 20.43 (wind +0.4 m/s)
1= Mike McFarlane (ENG) 20.43
3. Cameron Sharp (SCO) 20.55

400 METRES

Run over 440 yards (402.34m) 1930-66

1930 1. Alex Wilson (CAN) 48.8
2. William Walters (SAF) 48.9
3. George Golding (AUS)
1934 1. Godfrey Rampling (ENG) 48.0
2. Bill Roberts (ENG) 48.5
3. Crew Stoneley (ENG) 48.6
1938 1. Bill Roberts (ENG) 47.9
2. William Fritz (CAN) 47.9
3. Denis Shore (SAF) 48.1
1950 1. Edwin Carr (AUS) 47.9
2. Leslie Lewis (ENG) 48.0
3. David Batten (NZL) 48.8
1954 1. Kevan Gosper (AUS) 47.2
2. Donald Jowett (NZL) 47.4
3. Terry Tobacco (CAN) 47.8
1958 1. Milkha Singh (IND) 46.71
2. Malcolm Spence (SAF) 46.90
3. Terry Tobacco (CAN) 47.05
1962 1. George Kerr (JAM) 46.74
2. Robbie Brightwell (ENG) 46.86
3. Amos Omolo (UGA) 46.88
1966 1. Wendell Mottley (TRI) 45.08
2. Kent Bernard (TRI) 46.06
3. Don Domansky (CAN) 46.42
1970 1. Charles Asati (KEN) 45.01
2. Ross Wilson (AUS) 45.61
3. Saimoni Tamani (FIJ) 45.82
1974 1. Charles Asati (KEN) 46.04
2. Silver Ayoo (UGA) 46.07
3. Claver Kamanya (TAN) 46.16
1978 1. Rick Mitchell (AUS) 46.43
2. Joseph Coombes (TRI) 46.54
3. Glenn Bogue (CAN) 46.63
1982 1. Bert Cameron (JAM) 45.89
2. Rick Mitchell (AUS) 46.61
3. Gary Minihan (AUS) 46.68

800 METRES

Run over 880 yards (804.67m) 1930-66

1930 1. Thomas Hampson (ENG) 1:52.4
2. Reg Thomas (ENG) 1:56.4e
3. Alex Wilson (CAN) 1:56.5e
1934 1. Phil Edwards (GUY) 1:54.2
2. Johannes Botha (SAF) 1:55.0
3. James Stothard (SCO) 1:55.1
1938 1. Vernon Boot (NZL) 1:51.2
2. Frank Handley (ENG) 1:53.5
3. William Dale (CAN) 1:53.6
1950 1. John Parlett (ENG) 1:53.1
2. Jack Hutchins (CAN) 1:53.4
3. William Parnell (CAN) 1:53.4
1954 1. Derek Johnson (ENG) 1:50.7
2. Brian Hewson (ENG) 1:51.2
3. Ian Boyd (ENG) 1:51.9
1958 1. Herb Elliott (AUS) 1:49.32
2. Brian Hewson (ENG) 1:49.47
3. Michael Rawson (ENG) 1:50.94
1962 1. Peter Snell (NZL) 1:47.64
2. George Kerr (JAM) 1:47.90
3. Tony Blue (AUS) 1:48.99
1966 1. Noel Clough (AUS) 1:46.9
2. Wilson Kiprugut (KEN) 1:47.2
3. George Kerr (JAM) 1:47.2
1970 1. Robert Ouko (KEN) 1:46.89
2. Benedict Cayenne (TRI) 1:47.42
3. William Smart (CAN) 1:47.43
1974 1. John Kipkurgat (KEN) 1:43.85
2. Mike Boit (KEN) 1:44.4

One of the classic races of all time, as the front running Filbert Bayi (613) holds off John Walker and Ben Jipcho to win the 1974 1500m title and set a new world record.

Athletics

The track and field athletics events are undoubtedly the centrepiece of the Commonwealth Games, just as they are of the Olympic Games. Their events held in the main stadium, the runners, jumpers and throwers are, with no disrespect to the other sports, the focal point of much public and media interest.

The major athletics powers, England, Australia and Canada top the medal tables, but there have been many great athletes from all over the Commonwealth who have played their part in some of the greatest moments in the sport's history. The great Kenyan distance runners first made their mark on the international scene at the Commonwealth Games, with men like Kip Keino, Naftali Temu and Ben Jipcho leading the way. The first black African to win a gold medal was the Nigerian Emmanuel Ifeajuna at the high jump in 1954, and his country's tradition in the sport was brilliantly maintained in 1982 by the gaining of an upset victory by their men's sprint relay team. Caribbean sprinters, too, have had outstanding success and the first Pacific Island winner was shot putter Maitaika Tuicakau of Fiji in 1950. In all, medals have been won by athletes from 27 nations.

Wendy Sly (centre - 278) won the silver medal at 3000m in 1982. Others in view include Hilary Hollick (Wales - 677), Justina Chepchirchir (Kenya - 439), Lorraine Moller (New Zealand - 480), Yvonne Murray (Scotland) and Ruth Smeeth (England - 276).

Of all the great days in Games history, the final day of the 1954 Games, the 7th August, must be considered the most memorable. At 2.30 p.m. there was the long-awaited clash between Roger Bannister of England, who just three months earlier had run the first sub four-minute mile, and John Landy of Australia who seven weeks after that had improved Bannister's time of 3:59.4 to a new world record of 3:57.9. Bannister was considered the 'kicker' supreme, while Landy was one of the greatest front runners that the world had ever seen. The sports world was on tenterhooks for their duel in Vancouver and, although both men had problems, Bannister with a cold and Landy with a cut foot, the race lived up to all expectations. There were six other runners, but they were forgotten by the massed audience as Landy took the lead halfway into the first lap and set a remarkable pace, 58.2 for 440 yards and 1:58.2 for 880 yards. At this point he was some eight

PRICES EXCLUDE NUMBER PLATES, ROAD TAX AND DELIVERY AND ARE CORRECT AT THE TIME OF GOING TO PRESS. OFFICIAL D.O.E. FIGURES FOR PEUGEOT 309 SR: MPG (L/100KM) 55.4 (5.1) AT A CONSTANT 56 MPH. 42.2

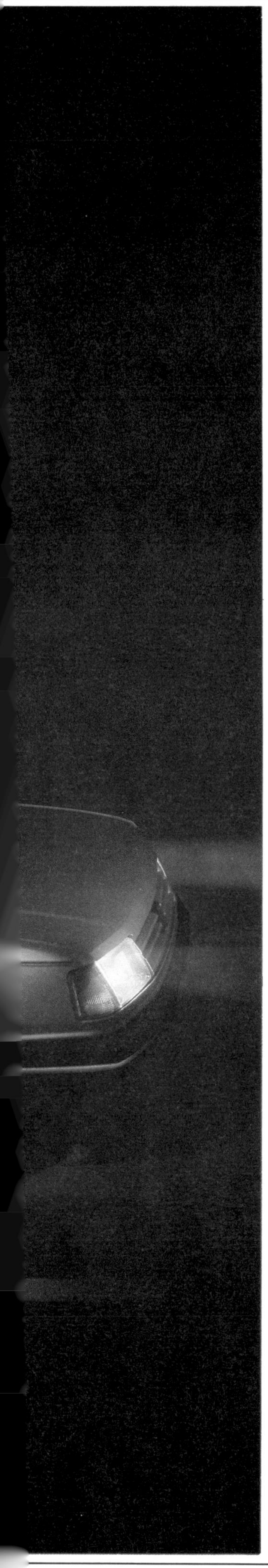

THE REALITY IS EVEN BETTER THAN THE DREAM.

When we set out to create the new Coventry-built Peugeot 309 we had one ambition. To take a fresh look at familiar design problems and find new, more intelligent answers.

Now, the 309 is no longer just a dream. So what's the reality?

The reality is a car so aerodynamically advanced that some models even have fairings under the bonnet.

A car so economical it can cover up to 640 miles on one tank of petrol. (So that, if you found yourself clocking up a typical yearly mileage at dead on 56 mph, you could expect to stop for petrol a mere sixteen times.)

MORE SPACE ALL ROUND.

Open up the hatch on the Peugeot 309 and you'll find plenty more to interest you. For not only is the 309's luggage space both wider and longer than anything its closest rivals can offer. It's also completely uncluttered.

Why? Because, just as in the famous Peugeot 205, we've set the rear shock absorbers horizontally under the floor.

So they don't waste space in the luggage area.

The Peugeot 309 has more space for people too. On the outside it's slimmer than any of its competitors. But inside, thanks to a body that's big on strength but small on bulk, it offers five grateful passengers more hip room than even its fiercest rival.

PERFORMANCE – AND PLEASURE.

With a choice of three alloy-headed engines – 1.1, 1.3 or 1.6 – the 309 has plenty of performance to offer.

Plenty of enjoyment too, with a five speed gear-box standard in every model except the GE 1.1.

And while you're being powered down the motorway, you'll be able to appreciate the 309's little extras. Like halogen headlamps, laminated windscreen and even rear seat belts on every model.

Plus, from the mid-range GR upwards, such luxuries as remote control door mirrors and tinted glass.

Not at all what you'd expect from an ordinary family hatchback – especially when its price ranges from just £5,145 to £7,495 for the 1.6 SR (shown here).

But then, the one thing we never dreamed the new Peugeot 309 could be, was ordinary.

THE NEW PEUGEOT 309

THE LION GOES FROM STRENGTH TO STRENGTH.

ANT 75 MPH. 33.2 (8.5) SIMULATED URBAN CYCLE.

FOR A COMPREHENSIVE INFORMATION PACK ON THE 309 RANGE, TELEPHONE 0272 217205.

800 metres continued

3. John Walker (NZL) 1:44.9
1978 1. Mike Boit (KEN) 1:46.39
2. Seymour Newman (JAM) 1:47.30
3. Peter Lemashon (KEN) 1:47.57
1982 1. Peter Bourke (AUS) 1:45.18
2. James Maina Boi (KEN) 1:45.45
3. Chris McGeorge (ENG) 1:45.60

1500 METRES
Run over 1 mile (1609.35m) 1930-66

1930 1. Reg Thomas (ENG) 4:14.0
2. William Whyte (AUS)
3. Jerry Cornes (ENG)
1934 1. Jack Lovelock (NZL) 4:12.8
2. Sydney Wooderson (ENG) 4:13.4
3. Jerry Cornes (ENG) 4:13.6
1938 1. Jim Alford (WAL) 4:11.6
2. Gerald Backhouse (AUS) 4:12.2
3. Vernon Boot (NZL) 4:12.6
1950 1. William Parnell (CAN) 4:11.0
2. Len Eyre (ENG) 4:11.8
3. Maurice Marshall (NZL) 4:13.2
1954 1. Roger Bannister (ENG) 3:58.8
2. John Landy (AUS) 3:59.6
3. Rich Ferguson (CAN) 4:04.6
1958 1. Herb Elliott (AUS) 3:59.03
2. Merv Lincoln (AUS) 4:01.80
3. Albert Thomas (AUS) 4:02.77
1962 1. Peter Snell (NZL) 4:04.58
2. John Davies (NZL) 4:05.12
3. Terrence Sullivan (ZIM) 4:06.61
1966 1. Kipchoge Keino (KEN) 3:55.34
2. Alan Simpson (ENG) 3:57.27
3. Ian Studd (NZL) 3:58.61
1970 1. Kipchoge Keino (KEN) 3.36.6
2. Dick Quax (NZL) 3:38.1
3. Brendan Foster (ENG) 3:40.6
1974 1. Filbert Bayi (TAN) 3:32.16
2. John Walker (NZL) 3:32.52
3. Ben Jipcho (KEN) 3:33.16
1978 1. David Moorcroft (ENG) 3:35.48
2. Filbert Bayi (TAN) 3:35.59
3. John Robson (SCO) 3:35.60
1982 1. Steve Cram (ENG) 3:42.37
2. John Walker (NZL) 3:43.11
3. Mike Boit (KEN) 3:43.33

5000 METRES
Run over 3 miles (4820.04m) 1930-66

1930 1. Stan Tomlin (ENG) 14:27.4
2. Alex Hillhouse (AUS) 14:27.6
3. Jack Winfield (ENG) 14:28.0e
1934 1. Walter Beavers (ENG) 14:32.6
2. Charles Allen (ENG) 14:37.8
3. Alex Burns (ENG) 14:45.4
1938 1. Cecil Matthews (NZL) 13:59.6
2. Peter Ward (ENG) 14:05.4
3. Robert Rankine (CAN)
1950 1. Len Eyre (ENG) 14:23.6
2. Harold Nelson (NZL) 14:27.8
3. Anthony Chivers (ENG) 14:28.1
1954 1. Chris Chataway (ENG) 13:35.2
2. Fred Green (ENG) 13:37.2
3. Frank Sando (ENG) 13:37.4
1958 1. Murray Halberg (NZL) 13:14.96
2. Albert Thomas (AUS) 13.24.37
3. Neville Scott (NZL) 13:26.06
1962 1. Murray Halberg (NZL) 13:34.15
2. Ron Clarke (AUS) 13:35.92
3. Bruce Kidd (CAN) 13:36.37
1966 1. Kipchoge Keino (KEN) 12:57.4
2. Ron Clarke (AUS) 12:59.2
3. Allan Rushmer (ENG) 13:08.6
1970 1. Ian Stewart (SCO) 13:22.8
2. Ian McCafferty (SCO) 13:23.4
3. Kipchoge Keino (KEN) 13:27.6
1974 1. Ben Jipcho (KEN) 13:14.4
2. Brendan Foster (ENG) 13:14.6
3. David Black (ENG) 13:23.6
1978 1. Henry Rono (KEN) 13:23.04
2. Mike Musyoki (KEN) 13:29.92
3. Brendan Foster (ENG) 13:31.35
1982 1. David Moorcroft (ENG) 13:33.00
2. Nick Rose (ENG) 13:35.97
3. Peter Koech (KEN) 13:36.95

10000 METRES
Run over 6 miles (9656.07m) 1930-66

1930 1. John Savidan (NZL) 30:49.6
2. Ernest Harper (ENG) 60y
3. Tom Evenson (ENG)
1934 1. Arthur Penny (ENG) 31:00.6
2. Robert Rankine (CAN) 31:01.6
3. Arthur Furze (ENG) 60y
1938 1. Cecil Matthews (NZL) 30:14.5
2. Robert Rankine (CAN) 180y
3. Wally Hayward (SAF) 250y
1950 1. Harold Nelson (NZL) 30:29.6
2. Andrew Forbes (SCO) 30:31.9
3. Noel Taylor (NZL) 30:31.9
1954 1. Peter Driver (ENG) 29.09.4
2. Frank Sando (ENG) 29:10.0
3. Jim Peters (ENG) 29:20.0
1958 1. David Power (AUS) 28:48.16
2. John Merriman (WAL) 28:48.84
3. Arere Anentia (KEN) 28:51.48
1962 1. Bruce Kidd (CAN) 28:26.13
2. David Power (AUS) 28:33.53
3. John Merriman (WAL) 28:40.26
1966 1. Naftali Temu (KEN) 27:14.21
2. Ron Clarke (AUS) 27:39.42
3. Jim Alder (SCO) 28:15.4
1970 1. Lachie Stewart (SCO) 28:11.71
2. Ron Clarke (AUS) 28:13.44
3. Dick Taylor (ENG) 28:15.34
1974 1. Richard Taylor (NZL) 27:46.4
2. David Black (ENG) 27:48.6
3. Richard Juma (KEN) 27:57.0
1978 1. Brendan Foster (ENG) 28:13.65
2. Mike Musyoki (KEN) 28:19.14
3. Mike McLeod (ENG) 28:34.30
1982 1. Gidamis Shahanga (TAN) 28:10.15
2. Zacharia Barie (TAN) 28:10.55
3. Julian Goater (ENG) 28:16.11

MARATHON
(26 miles 385 yards - 42,195 metres)

1930 1. Duncan McL.Wright (SCO) 2:43:43
2. Sam Ferris (ENG)
3. Johnny Miles (CAN)
1934 1. Harold Webster (CAN) 2:40:36
2. Donald McN. Robertson (SCO) 2:45:08
3. Duncan McL. Wright (SCO) 2:56:20
1938 1. Johannes Coleman (SAF) 2:30:49.8
2. Albert Norris (ENG) 2:37:57
3. Jack Gibson (SAF) 2:38:20
1950 1. Jack Holden (ENG) 2:32:57
2. Sydney Luyt (SAF) 2:37:02.2
3. James Clark (NZL) 2:39:26.4
1954 1. Joseph McGhee (SCO) 2:39:36
2. Jack Meckler (SAF) 2:40:57
3. Johannes Barnard (SAF) 2:51:49.8
1958 1. David Power (AUS) 2:22:45.6
2. Johannes Barnard (SAF) 2:22:57.4
3. Peter Wilkinson (ENG) 2:24:42
1962 1. Brian Kilby (ENG) 2:21:17
2. David Power (AUS) 2:22:15.4
3. Rod Bonella (AUS) 2:24:07
1966 1. Jim Alder (SCO) 2:22:07.8
2. Bill Adcocks (ENG) 2:22:13
3. Mike Ryan (NZL) 2:27:59
1970 1. Ron Hill (ENG) 2:09:28
2. Jim Alder (SCO) 2:12:04
3. Don Faircloth (ENG) 2:12:19
1974 1. Ian Thompson (ENG) 2:09:12
2. Jack Foster (NZL) 2:11:18.6
3. Richard Mabuza (SWZ) 2:12:54.4
1978 1. Gidamis Shahanga (TAN) 2:15:39.8
2. Jerome Drayton (CAN) 2:16:13.5

Ron Clarke tucks in behind Ian McCafferty in a heat of the 1970 5000 metres.

yards up, but Bannister closed the gap steadily to pass the bell three yards behind Landy's time of 2:58.7. On the final bend, as Landy turned his head inside to look over his left shoulder for the Englishman, Bannister drove past him and pushed on to the tape to win in a British record time of 3:58.8 with Landy second 0.8 sec. behind. It was the first time that two men had broken four minutes in a mile race.

Two hours before the mile had started the marathoners had left the stadium in 24°C (75°F) heat. Jim Peters from Essex in England was clearly the favourite, for he had set four world bests for the event, culminating in his 2 hours 17 minutes 39.4 seconds in the 1954 Poly Marathon, six weeks before the Games. He led from the start and entered the stadium for the last lap with an astonishing lead of some 20 minutes over any rival. In a spectacle never to be forgotten by all who saw it in the stadium, on film or on television, he then succumbed to dehydration, brought on by his efforts in the heat, so that he had little control over his arms and legs. He staggered and fell repeatedly, seemingly trying to climb non-existent stairs. Finally, a pitiable sight, he collapsed at what was the finishing line for the track events, although still with half a lap to go for the marathon finish, into the arms of colleagues and was rushed to hospital in a serious condition. There too was his team-mate Stan Cox, who, suffering from sun-stroke, had run into a telegraph pole with two miles to go. Long after Peters had left the scene, Scotland's Joe McGhee came in to win in 2:39.36. Peters remained in hospital for a week and never raced again.

The marathon has often been a high point of the Games. In 1950 Jack Holden became the oldest ever athletics gold medallist by winning this event at the age of 42 years 335 days. He did so despite having to run the last eight miles without shoes, which had split and caused blisters, and then, with two miles to run to the finish, he was attacked by a dog, a Great Dane.

In 1966 Jim Alder of Scotland led, but on arriving at the stadium was misdirected and reached the track to find that Bill Adcocks of England was somehow now ahead of him. Fortunately Alder was able to produce a finishing burst to overtake his rival and earn the gold medal, though by a mere 5.2 seconds.

Then too, there was an epic race in Brisbane in 1982, when Rob de Castella of Australia ran a beautifully

Marathon continued

3. Paul Bannon (CAN) 2:16:51.6

1982 1. Rob de Castella (AUS) 2:09:18
2. Juma Ikangaa (TAN) 2:09:30
3. Mike Grattan (ENG) 2:12:06

3000 METRES STEEPLECHASE

Held over 8 laps in 1930
and at 2 miles (3218.7m) in 1934

1930 1. George Bailey (ENG) 9:52.0
2. Alex Hillhouse (AUS)
3. Vernon Morgan (ENG)

1934 1. Stanley Scarsbrook (ENG) 10:23.4
2. Thomas Evenson (ENG)
3. George Bailey (ENG)

1962 1. Trevor Vincent (AUS) 8:43.4
2. Maurice Herriott (ENG) 8:45.0
3. Ron Blackney (AUS) 9:00.6

1966 1. Peter Welsh (NZL) 8:29.44
2. Kerry O'Brien (AUS) 8:32.58
3. Benjamin Kogo (KEN) 8:32.81

1970 1. Tony Manning (AUS) 8:26.2
2. Ben Jipcho (KEN) 8:29.6
3. Amos Biwott (KEN) 8:30.8

1974 1. Ben Jipcho (KEN) 8:20.8
2. John Davies (WAL) 8:24.8
3. Evans Mogaka (KEN) 8:28.6

1978 1. Henry Rono (KEN) 8:26.54
2. James Munyala (KEN) 8:32.21
3. George Kip Rono (KEN) 8:34.07

1982 1. Julius Korir (KEN) 8:23.94
2. Graeme Fell (ENG) 8:26.64
3. Greg Duhaime (CAN) 8:29.14

110 METRES HURDLES

Run over 120 yards (109.73m) 1930-66

1930 1. Lord Burghley (ENG) 14.6
2. Howard Davies (SAF) 14.7
3. Frederick Gaby (ENG)

1934 1. Don Finlay (ENG) 15.2
2. James Worrall (CAN) 15.5
3. Ashleigh Pilbrow (ENG) 15.7

1938 1. Tom Lavery (SAF) 14.0w
2. Larry O'Connor (CAN) 14.2
3. Sydney Stenner (AUS) 14.4

1950 1. Peter Gardner (AUS) 14.3
2. Ray Weinberg (AUS) 14.4
3. Tom Lavery (SAF) 14.6

1954 1. Keith Gardner (JAM) 14.2
2. Chris Higham (ENG) 14.9
3. Norman Williams (CAN) 14.9

1958 1. Keith Gardner (JAM) 14.20 (wind -3.5 m/s)
2. Jacobus Swart (SAF) 14.30
3. Ghulam Raziq (PAK) 14.32

1962 1. Ghulam Raziq (PAK) 14.34 (wind -2.1 m/s)
2. David Prince (AUS) 14.48
3. Laurie Taitt (ENG) 14.81

1966 1. David Hemery (ENG) 14.1
2. Michael Parker (ENG) 14.2
3. Ghulam Raziq (PAK) 14.3

1970 1. David Hemery (ENG) 13.66 (wind -2.9 m/s)
2. Mal Baird (AUS) 13.86
3. Godfrey Murray (JAM) 14.02

1974 1. Fatwel Kimaiyo (KEN) 13.69 (wind -0.1 m/s)
2. Berwyn Price (WAL) 13.84
3. Max Binnington (AUS) 13.88

1978 1. Berwyn Price (WAL) 13.70 (wind -6.15 m/s)
2. Max Binnington (AUS) 13.73
3. Warren Parr (AUS) 13.73

1982 1. Mark McKoy (CAN) 13.37 (wind -1.9 m/s)
2. Mark Holtom (ENG) 13.43
3. Don Wright (AUS) 13.58

400 METRES HURDLES

Run over 440 yards (402.34m) 1930-66

1930 1. Lord Burghley (ENG) 54.4
2. Roger Leigh-Wood (ENG) 55.9e
3. Douglas Neame (ENG)

1934 1. Alan Hunter (SCO) 55.2
2. Charles Reilly (AUS) 55.5
3. Ralph Brown (ENG) 55.6

1938 1. John Loaring (CAN) 52.9
2. John Park (AUS) 54.6
3. Alan McDougall (AUS) 55.2

1950 1. Duncan White (SRI) 52.5
2. John Holland (NZL) 52.7
3. Geoff Goodacre (AUS) 53.1

1954 1. David Lean (AUS) 52.4
2. Harry Kane (ENG) 53.3
3. Robert Shaw (WAL) 53.3

1958 1. Gerhardus Potgieter (SAF) 49.73
2. David Lean (AUS) 50.59
3. Bartonjo Rotich (KEN) 51.75

1962 1. Ken Roche (AUS) 51.5
2. Kimaru Songok (KEN) 51.9
3. Benson Ishiepai (UGA) 52.3

1966 1. Ken Roche (AUS) 50.95
2. Kingsley Agbabokha (NGR) 51.46
3. Peter Warden (ENG) 51.54

1970 1. John Sherwood (ENG) 50.03
2. William Koskei (UGA) 50.15
3. Charles K. Yego (KEN) 50.19

1974 1. Alan Pascoe (ENG) 48.83
2. Bruce Field (AUS) 49.32
3. William Koskei (KEN) 49.34

1978 1. Daniel Kimaiyo (KEN) 49.48
2. Garry Brown (AUS) 50.04
3. Alan Pascoe (ENG) 50.09

1982 1. Garry Brown (AUS) 49.37
2. Peter Rwamuhanda (UGA) 49.95
3. Greg Rolle (BAH) 50.50

4 x 100 METRES RELAY

Run over 4 x 110 yards (100.54m) 1930-66

1930 1. Canada 42.2
2. England 42.7
3. South Africa

1934 1. England 42.2
2. Canada 42.5
3. Scotland 43.0

1938 1. Canada 41.6
2. England 41.8
3. Australia 41.9

1950 1. Australia 42.2
2. England 42.5
3. New Zealand 42.6

1954 1. Canada 41.3
2. Nigeria 41.3
3. Australia 41.7

1958 1. England 40.72
2. Nigeria 41.05
3. Australia 41.64

1962 1. England 40.62
2. Ghana 40.74
3. Wales 40.80

1966 1. Ghana 39.8
2. Jamaica 40.0
3. Australia 40.0

1970 1. Jamaica 39.46
2. Ghana 39.82
3. England 40.05

1974 1. Australia 39.31
2. Ghana 39.61
3. Nigeria 39.70

1978 1. Scotland 39.24
2. Trinidad & Tobago 39.29
3. Jamaica 39.33

1982 1. Nigeria 39.15
2. Canada 39.30
3. Scotland 39.33

4 x 400 METRES RELAY

Run over 4 x 440 yards (402.34m) 1930-66

1930 1. England 3:19.4
2. Canada 3:19.8
3. South Africa

1934 1. England 3:16.8
2. Canada 3:17.4
3. Scotland

1938 1. Canada 3:16.9
2. England 3:19.2
3. New Zealand 3:22.0

1950 1. Australia 3:17.8
2. England 3:19.3
3. New Zealand 3:20.0

1954 1. England 3:11.2
2. Canada 3:11.6
3. Australia 3:16.0

1958 1. South Africa 3:08.21
2. England 3:09.61
3. Jamaica 3:10.08

1962 1. Jamaica 3:10.2
2. England 3:11.2
3. Ghana 3:12.3

1966 1. Trinidad & Tobago 3:02.8
2. Canada 3:04.9
3. England 3:06.5

1970 1. Kenya 3:03.63
2. Trinidad & Tobago 3:05.49
3. England 3:05.53

1974 1. Kenya 3:04.4
2. England 3:06.7
3. Uganda 3:07.5

1978 1. Kenya 3:03.54
2. Jamaica 3:04.00
3. Australia 3:04.23

1982 1. England 3:05.45
2. Australia 3:05.82
3. Kenya 3:06.33

HIGH JUMP

1930 1. Johannes Viljoen (SAF) 1.90
2. Colin Gordon (GUY) 1.88
3. William Stargratt (CAN) 1.85

Raelene Boyle takes over from Robyn Boak for the Australian relay team and flies on to complete the sprint treble at the 1970 Games.

judged race to catch the Tanzanians, Gidamis Shahanga, who had been a surprise winner in 1978, and Juma Ikangaa, who at one time built up a lead of a minute. Even when caught by de Castella, Ikangaa did not give up the struggle and actually repassed the Australian twice. 'Deke' however broke his rival to win by eleven seconds in what Ron Clarke described as "the best marathon ever run", for his time of 2:09.18 was magnificent on a hilly course.

The first world records set in Games athletics were by 18 year old Marjorie Jackson at Auckland in 1950 when she equalled the records at both 100 yards (10.8) and 220 yards (24.3). She repeated her individual sprint double in 1954 (by which time she had become Mrs Nelson) and, running on three Australian winning relay teams, won in all a record seven gold medals.

That tally was later matched by another Australian, Raelene Boyle, who started her Games career at the age of 19 in 1970 with a 100m/200m relay sprint treble. She repeated this success in 1974 and returned in 1982 to win a brilliant and ecstatically received, 400 metres victory on home ground at Brisbane in 1982. Boyle also won two silvers for a record total of nine medals, one ahead of her sprint relay team-mate Denise Boyd (née Robertson) in the years 1974-82. Denise Boyd, who won the 200m in 1978 as well as relay gold in 1974, is

The marathon medallists accept the applause of the Brisbane spectators in 1982. (left to right): Juma Ikangaa (2nd), Rob de Castella (1st) and Mike Gratton (3rd).

FUJI TAPE
G-SKSB
HIGH
QUALITY.

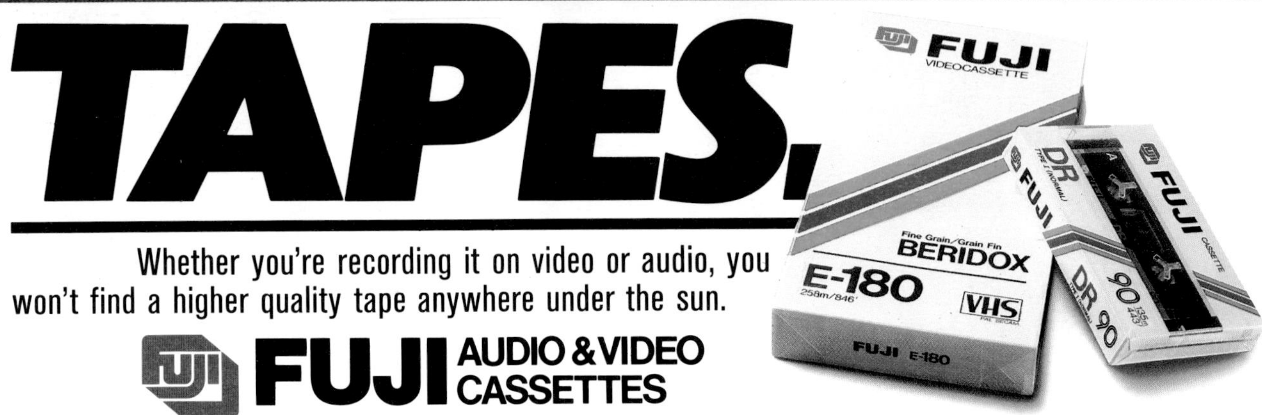
TAPES.
Whether you're recording it on video or audio, you won't find a higher quality tape anywhere under the sun.
FUJI AUDIO & VIDEO CASSETTES
FUJI
VIDEOCASSETTE
Fine Grain/Grain Fin
BERIDOX
E-180
VHS
FUJI E-180
DR
FUJI
FUJI CASSETTE
DR 90
90

High Jump continued

1934 1. Edwin Thacker (SAF) 1.90
2. Joseph Haley (CAN) 1.90
3. James Michie (SCO) 1.90
1938 1. Edwin Thacker (SAF) 1.96
2. Robert Heffernan (AUS) 1.88
3. Douglas Shetliffe (AUS) 1.88
1950 1. John Winter (AUS) 1.98
2= Joshua Majekodunmi (NGR) 1.95
2= Alan Paterson (SCO) 1.95
1954 1. Emmanuel Ifeajuna (NGR) 2.03
2. Patrick Etolu (UGA) 1.99
3. Nafiu Osagie (NGR) 1.99
1958 1. Ernest Haisley (JAM) 2.06
2. Charles Porter (AUS) 2.03
3. Robert Kotei (GHA) 2.00
1962 1. Percy Hobson (AUS) 2.11
2. Charles Porter (AUS) 2.08
3. Anton Norris (BAR) 2.03
1966 1. Lawrie Peckham (AUS) 2.08
2. Samuel Igun (NGR) 2.03
3. Anton Norris (BAR) 2.00
1970 1. Lawrie Peckham (AUS) 2.14
2. John Hawkins (CAN) 2.12
3. Sheikh Faye (GAM) 2.10
1974 1. Gordon Windeyer (AUS) 2.16
2. Lawrie Peckham (AUS) 2.14
3. Claude Ferragne (CAN) 2.12
1978 1. Claude Ferragne (CAN) 2.20
2. Greg Joy (CAN) 2.18
3= Dean Bauck (CAN) 2.15
3= Brian Burgess (SCO) 2.15
1982 1. Milt Ottey (CAN) 2.31
2. Stephen Wray (BAH) 2.31
3. Clarence Saunders (BER) 2.19

POLE VAULT

1930 1. Victor Pickard (CAN) 3.73
2. Howard Ford (ENG) 3.73
3. Robert Stoddard (CAN)
1934 1. Sylvanus Apps (CAN) 3.81 (3.88 in jump-off)
2. Alfred Gilbert (CAN) 3.81
3. Fred Woodhouse (AUS) 3.73
1938 1. Andries du Plessis (SAF) 4.11
2. Les Fletcher (AUS) 3.97
3. Stuart Frid (CAN) 3.88
1950 1. Tim Anderson (ENG) 3.97
2. Stan Egerton (CAN) 3.97
3. Peter Denton (AUS) 3.88
1954 1. Geoff Elliott (ENG) 4.26
2. Ron Miller (CAN) 4.20
3. Andries Burger (SAF) 4.13
1958 1. Geoff Elliott (ENG) 4.16
2. Robert Reid (CAN) 4.16
3. Mervyn Richards (NZL) 4.16
1962 1. Trevor Bickle (AUS) 4.49
2. Daniel Burger (ZIM) 4.42
3. Ross Filshie (AUS) 4.42
1966 1. Trevor Bickle (AUS) 4.80
2. Mike Bull (NIR) 4.72
3. Gerry Moro (CAN) 4.65
1970 1. Mike Bull (NIR) 5.10
2. Allan Kane (CAN) 4.90
3. Robert Raftis (CAN) 4.90
1974 1. Don Baird (AUS) 5.05
2. Mike Bull (NIR) 5.00
3. Brian Hooper (ENG) 5.00
1978 1. Bruce Simpson (CAN) 5.10
2. Don Baird (AUS) 5.10
3. Brian Hooper (ENG) 5.00
1982 1. Ray Boyd (AUS) 5.20
2. Jeff Gutteridge (ENG) 5.20
3. Graham Eggleton (SCO) 5.20

LONG JUMP

1930 1. Leonard Hutton (CAN) 7.20
2. Reginald Revans (ENG) 6.96
3. Johannes Viljoen (SAF) 6.86
1934 1. Sam Richardson (CAN) 7.17
2. Johann Luckhoff (SAF) 7.10
3. Jack Metcalfe (AUS) 6.93
1938 1. Harold Brown (CAN) 7.43
2. James Panton (CAN) 7.25
3. Basil Dickinson (AUS) 7.15
1950 1. Neville Price (SAF) 7.31
2. Bevan Hough (NZL) 7.20
3. David Dephoff (NZL) 7.08
1954 1. Ken Wilmshurst (ENG) 7.54
2. Karim Oluwu (NGR) 7.39
3. Sylvanus Williams (NGR) 7.22
1958 1. Paul Foreman (JAM) 7.47
2. Deryck Taylor (JAM) 7.47
3. Ramzan Ali (PAK) 7.33
1962 1. Michael Ahey (GHA) 8.05w
2. David Norris (NZL) 7.75
3. Wellesley Clayton (JAM) 7.73
1966 1. Lynn Davies (WAL) 7.99
2. John Morbey (BER) 7.89
3. Wellesley Clayton (JAM) 7.83
1970 1. Lynn Davies (WAL) 8.06w
2. Phil May (AUS) 7.94
3. Alan Lerwill (ENG) 7.94
1974 1. Alan Lerwill (ENG) 7.94
2. Chris Commons (AUS) 7.92
3. Joshua Owusu (GHA) 7.75
1978 1. Roy Mitchell (ENG) 8.06
2. Chris Commons (AUS) 8.04
3. Suresh Babu (IND) 7.94
1982 1. Gary Honey (AUS) 8.13
2. Steve Hanna (BAH) 7.79
3. Steve Walsh (NZL) 7.75

TRIPLE JUMP

1930 1. Gordon Smallacombe (CAN) 14.76
2. Reginald Revans (ENG) 14.29
3. Leonard Hutton (CAN) 13.90
1934 1. Jack Metcalfe (AUS) 15.63
2. Sam Richardson (CAN) 14.65
3. Harold Brainsby (NZL) 14.62
1938 1. Jack Metcalfe (AUS) 15.49
2. Lloyd Miller (AUS) 15.41
3. Basil Dickinson (AUS) 15.28
1950 1. Brian Oliver (AUS) 15.61
2. Leslie McKeand (AUS) 15.28
3. Ian Polmear (AUS) 14.67
1954 1. Ken Wilmshurst (ENG) 15.28
2. Peter Esiri (NGR) 15.25
3. Brian Oliver (AUS) 15.14
1958 1. Ian Tomlinson (AUS) 15.74
2. Jack Smyth (CAN) 15.69
3. David Norris (NZL) 15.45
1962 1. Ian Tomlinson (AUS) 16.20
2. John Baguley (AUS) 16.08
3. Fred Alsop (ENG) 16.03
1966 1. Samuel Igun (NGR) 16.40
2. George Ogan (NGR) 16.08
3. Fred Alsop (ENG) 15.96
1970 1. Phil May (AUS) 16.72
2. Michael McGrath (AUS) 16.41
3. Mohinder Singh Gill (IND) 15.90
1974 1. Joshua Owusu (GHA) 16.50
2. Mohinder Singh Gill (IND) 16.44
3. Moise Pomaney (GHA) 16.23
1978 1. Keith Connor (ENG) 17.21
2. Ian Campbell (AUS) 16.93
3. Aston Moore (ENG) 16.69
1982 1. Keith Connor (ENG) 17.81w
2. Ken Lorraway (AUS) 17.54
3. Aston Moore (ENG) 16.76

SHOT

1930 1. Hendrik Hart (SAF) 14.58
2. Robert Howland (ENG) 13.46
3. Charles Herman (CAN) 12.98
1934 1. Hendrik Hart (SAF) 14.67
2. Robert Howland (ENG) 13.53
3. Kenneth Pridie (ENG) 13.43
1938 1. Louis Fouche (SAF) 14.48
2. Eric Coy (CAN) 13.96
3. Francis Drew (AUS) 13.80
1950 1. Maitaika Tuicakau (FIJ) 14.64
2. Harold Moody (ENG) 13.92

Sheila Sherwood wins the long jump at Edinburgh in 1970. All her six jumps bettered those of runner-up Ann Wilson. Her best of 6.73m (22′0¾″) was a new Games and UK all-comers record.

one of several successful family combinations, for her husband Ray Boyd won the 1982 pole vault.

The Games of 1970 were particularly notable for such husband and wife feats as John and Sheila Sherwood of England won 400m hurdles and long jump respectively, and Howard and Rosemary Payne won at hammer and discus. Rosemary represented her native Scotland while Howard threw for England. This was his third title, and he went on to a silver medal in 1974. He had first competed in 1958 when he came fourth, representing Rhodesia. The 1966 and 1970 high jump gold medallist Lawrie Peckham of Australia also won a silver medal in 1974, at which Games Judy Canty won a relay silver. After their marriage Judy won the 1978 800 metres.

Perhaps the greatest Commonwealth family was from New Zealand. Les Mills won a gold, three silver and a bronze medal at shot and discus events between 1958 and 1970, but was omitted from the 1974 team, for which his wife Colleen (400 metres), daughter Donna (high jump) and son Philip (110 metres hurdles) were selected. Also from New Zealand, Yvette Williams won a unique treble at long jump, shot and discus as well as a silver for the javelin in 1950. Her younger brother Roy won the decathlon in 1966.

The winning of three individual gold medals was matched by Decima Norman of Australia with the 100 and 220 yards and long jump in 1938. To those she added two relay gold medals, for a record five gold medals at one Games. Another Australian, Shirley Strickland won five medals: three gold and two silver in 1950. The only man to win four medals at one Games has been Keith Gardner of Jamaica who, in 1958, not only retained his 120 yards hurdles title, but added a gold at 100 yards, silver at 220 yards and bronze in the relay.

The most successful male gold medallist in Games athletics history is the great Jamaican sprinter Don Quarrie. He won the 100/200m/relay treble at Edinburgh in 1970, retained both individual titles in 1974 and won the 100 metres for a third time in 1978. The only other athletes to win an event at three successive Games were Howard Payne, Valerie Young at shot and Pam Kilborn at hurdles, both in 1962-70. Young (née Sloper), from New Zealand, also won two shot titles and a silver and a bronze medal. Kilborn won three more gold medals, the long jump in 1962 and in Australia's sprint relay in 1966 and 1970.

The most successful competitor at the first Games in 1930 was Lord Burghley, who won both 120 and 440 yards hurdles and ran on England's winning 4 x 440 yards relay team. Hendrik Hart of South Africa won both shot and discus, a feat he repeated in 1934. He also won two javelin medals to equal Quarrie's men's record number of six medals. Tom Hampson of England won the 880 yards, and his subsequent Olympic 800m victory in 1932 made him the first man to follow a Commonwealth title with an Olympic one. Lord Burghley had achieved this double in the reverse order. Many

Shot continued

3. Leo Roininen (CAN) 13.68
1954 1. John Savidge (ENG) 16.77
2. John Pavelich (CAN) 14.95
3. Stephanus du Plessis (SAF) 14.93
1958 1. Arthur Rowe (ENG) 17.57
2. Martyn Lucking (ENG) 16.50
3. Barry Donath (AUS) 15.79
1962 1. Martyn Lucking (ENG) 18.08
2. Mike Lindsay (SCO) 18.05
3. David Steen (CAN) 17.90
1966 1. David Steen (CAN) 18.79
2. Les Mills (NZL) 18.37
3. George Puce (CAN) 17.14
1970 1. David Steen (CAN) 19.21
2. Jeff Teale (ENG) 18.43
3. Les Mills (NZL) 18.40
1974 1. Geoff Capes (ENG) 20.74
2. Mike Winch (ENG) 19.36
3. Bruce Pirnie (CAN) 18.68
1978 1. Geoff Capes (ENG) 19.77
2. Bruno Pauletto (CAN) 19.33
3. Bishop Dolegiewicz (CAN) 18.45
1982 1. Bruno Pauletto (CAN) 19.55
2. Mike Winch (ENG) 18.25
3. Luby Chambul (CAN) 17.46

DISCUS

1930 1. Hendrik Hart (SAF) 41.44
2. Charles Herman (CAN) 41.22
3. Abe Zvonkin (CAN) 41.18
1934 1. Hendrik Hart (SAF) 41.54
2. Douglas Bell (ENG) 40.44
3. Bernard Prendergast (JAM) 40.24
1938 1. Eric Coy (CAN) 44.76
2. David Young (SCO) 43.04
3. George Sutherland (CAN) 41.46
1950 1. Ian Reed (AUS) 47.72
2. Maitaika Tuicakau (FIJ) 43.96
3. Svein Sigfusson (CAN) 43.48
1954 1. Stephanus du Plessis (SAF) 51.70
2. Roy Pella (CAN) 49.54
3. Mark Pharaoh (ENG) 47.84
1958 1. Stephanus du Plessis (SAF) 55.94
2. Les Mills (NZL) 51.72
3. Gerald Carr (ENG) 51.62
1962 1. Warwick Selvey (AUS) 56.48
2. Mike Lindsay (SCO) 52.48
3. John Sheldrick (ENG) 50.68
1966 1. Les Mills (NZL) 56.18
2. George Puce (CAN) 55.94
3. Robin Tait (NZL) 55.02
1970 1. George Puce (CAN) 59.02
2. Les Mills (NZL) 57.84
3. Bill Tancred (ENG) 56.68
1974 1. Robin Tait (NZL) 63.08
2. Bill Tancred (ENG) 59.48
3. John Hillier (ENG) 57.22
1978 1. Borys Chambul (CAN) 59.70
2. Brad Cooper (BAH) 57.30
3. Rob Gray (CAN) 55.48
1982 1. Brad Cooper (BAH) 64.04
2. Rob Gray (CAN) 60.66
3. Bishop Dolegiewicz (CAN) 60.34

HAMMER

1930 1. Malcolm Nokes (ENG) 47.12
2. William Britton (IRE) 46.90
3. John Cameron (CAN) 44.46
1934 1. Malcolm Nokes (ENG) 48.24
2. George Sutherland (CAN) 46.24
3. William Mackenzie (SCO) 42.50
1938 1. George Sutherland (CAN) 48.70
2. Keith Pardon (AUS) 45.12
3. James Leckie (NZL) 44.34
1950 1. Duncan Clark (SCO) 49.94
2. Keith Pardon (AUS) 47.84
3. Herbert Barker (AUS) 45.62
1954 1. Muhammad Iqbal (PAK) 55.38
2. Johannes Dreyer (SAF) 54.74
3. Ewan Douglas (SCO) 52.80
1958 1. Mike Ellis (ENG) 62.90
2. Muhammad Iqbal (PAK) 61.70
3. Peter Allday (ENG) 57.58
1962 1. Howard Payne (ENG) 61.64
2. Dick Leffler (AUS) 59.82
3. Robert Brown (AUS) 57.64
1966 1. Howard Payne (ENG) 61.98
2. Praveen Kumar (IND) 60.12
3. Muhammad Iqbal (PAK) 59.56
1970 1. Howard Payne (ENG) 67.80
2. Bruce Fraser (ENG) 62.90
3. Barry Wiliams (ENG) 61.58
1974 1. Ian Chipchase (ENG) 69.56
2. Howard Payne (ENG) 68.02
3. Peter Farmer (AUS) 67.48
1978 1. Peter Farmer (AUS) 71.10
2. Scott Neílson (CAN) 69.92
3. Chris Black (SCO) 68.14
1982 1. Robert Weir (ENG) 75.08
2. Martin Girvan (NIR) 73.62
3. Chris Black (SCO) 69.84

JAVELIN

1930 1. Stanley Lay (NZL) 63.12
2. Doral Pilling (CAN) 55.94
3. Hendrik Hart (SAF) 53:22
1934 1. Robert Dixon (CAN) 60.02
2. Hendrik Hart (SAF) 58.28
3. Johann Luckhoff (SAF) 56.50
1938 1. James Courtwright (CAN) 62.80
2. Stanley Lay (NZL) 62.20
3. Jack Metcalfe (AUS) 55.52
1950 1. Leo Roininen (CAN) 57.10
2. Luke Tunabuna (FIJ) 56.02
3. Doug Robinson (CAN) 57.10
1954 1. James Achurch (AUS) 68.52
2. Muhammad Nawaz (PAK) 68.08
3. Jalal Khan (PAK) 67.50
1958 1. Colin Smith (ENG) 71.28
2. Jalal Khan (PAK) 70.82
3. Hans Moks (CAN) 70.42
1962 1. Alfred Mitchell (AUS) 8.10
2. Colin Smith (ENG) 77.94
3. Nicholas Birks (AUS) 75.06
1966 1. John FitzSimons (ENG) 79.78
2. Nicholas Birks (AUS) 76.16
3. Muhammad Nawaz (PAK) 69.94
1970 1. David Travis (ENG) 79.50
2. John McSorley (ENG) 76.74
3. John FitzSimons (ENG) 73.20
1974 1. Charles Clover (ENG) 84.92
2. David Travis (ENG) 79.92
3. Joseph Mayaka (KEN) 77.56
1978 1. Phil Olsen (CAN) 84.00
2. Michael O'Rourke (NZL) 83.18
3. Peter Yates (ENG) 78.58
1982 1. Michael O'Rourke (NZL) 89.48
2. Laslo Babits (CAN) 84.88
3. Zakayo Malekwa (TAN) 80.22

DECATHLON

All scored on the 1964 Scoring Tables

1966 1. Roy Williams (NZL) 7270 points
2. Clive Longe (WAL) 7123
3. Gerry Moro (CAN) 6983
1970 1. Geoff Smith (AUS) 7492
2. Peter Gabbett (ENG) 7469
3. Barry King (ENG) 7201
1974 1. Mike Bull (NIR) 7417
2. Barry King (ENG) 7277
3. Robert Lethbridge (AUS) 7270
1978 1. Daley Thompson (ENG) 8467
2. Peter Hadfield (AUS) 7623
3. Alan Drayton (ENG) 7484
1982 1. Daley Thompson (ENG) 8410
2. Dave Steen (CAN) 8004
3. Fidelis Obikwu (ENG) 7726

Above: Canadian Debbie Brill was high jump champion in 1970 and 1982.

Left: Geoff Capes dominated British and Commonwealth shot putting throughout the 1970s, and won gold medals at Christchurch and Edmonton.

Below: At his best Peter Snell was untouchable. The New Zealander won the Commonwealth 880 yards and 1 mile double in 1962.

others followed, with the first women being Marjorie Jackson, Shirley Strickland and Yvette Williams, who all followed 1950 Commonwealth success with Olympic golds in 1952. Lynn Davies, the great Welsh long jumper, went one better with Olympic, Commonwealth and European titles in 1964-70 and the ultimate has been achieved by Daley Thompson, who has not only won the decathlon at the World Championships as well as the aforementioned trio, but has added second Commonwealth and Olympic titles to his growing list.

In 1934 Sam Richardson of Canada won the long jump. At 16 years 263 days he remains the youngest champion. Three days earlier he gained the triple jump silver medal to become the youngest men's medallist. However, that age was bettered by the Kenyan girl Sabine Chebichi, who was reported to be under 15 when she was third in the 1974 800 metres. The youngest women's winner has been Canadian high jumper Debbie Brill who won in 1970 at 17 years 137 days, and who returned to win in 1982, thereby equalling Dorothy Tyler's record wait between wins of twelve years. The latter had first won the high jump in 1938 as Dorothy Odam.

In 1938 Cecil Matthews of New Zealand won both three and six miles. While nobody has replicated that feat, several of the greatest names in track history have won other distance event doubles: at 880 yards and 1 mile - Herb Elliott (AUS) 1958 and Peter Snell (NZL) 1962; at 1 and 3 miles - Kip Keino (KEN) 1966; at 6 miles and marathon - Dave Power (AUS) 1958;

GORE-TEX* FABRIC TECHNOLOGY.

THE WEATHER-BEATING RECORD HOLDERS.

Waterproof, windproof, breathable – the unrivalled weather-beating qualities of GORE-TEX Fabric make it a winner with amateurs and professionals the world over.

The reason? Gore's unique fabric technology.

It works like this. Sandwiched between the outer fabric (1) and the lining (3) is a unique, skin-like membrane (2) of PTFE (polytetrafluoroethylene) that keeps the weather out, but lets perspiration vapour escape freely.

Training hard, or just spectating, GORE-TEX Fabric will make a big difference to your comfort.

During these Games it is certain that there will be many outstanding performances, and many records broken.

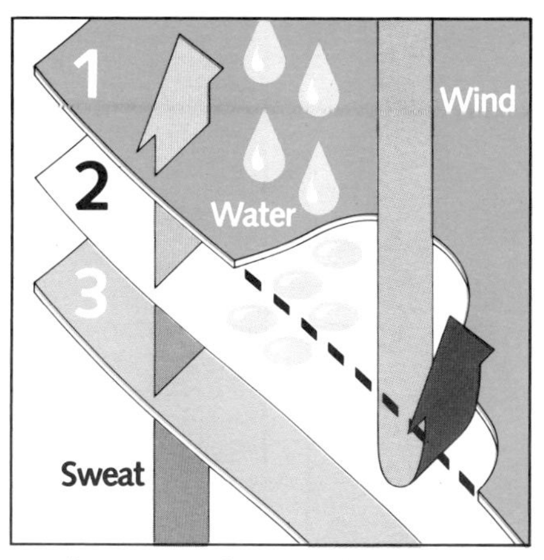

It's also certain that no other material stands to beat the record-breaking performance of GORE-TEX Fabric.

When it comes to beating the weather, there's just no competition.

W L Gore & Associates (UK) Ltd., Kirkton Campus, Livingston, West Lothian EH54 7BH Scotland. Telephone (0506) 412525 Telex 727236

Creative Technologies Worldwide

30 KILOMETRES ROAD WALK
Walked over 20 miles (32.187km) 1966-74

(Times in hours: minutes: seconds)

1966 1. Ron Wallwork (ENG) 2:44:42.8
2. Ray Middleton (ENG) 2:45:19.0
3. Norman Read (NZL) 2:46:28.2
1970 1. Noel Freeman (AUS) 2:33:33
2. Robert Gardiner (AUS) 2:35:55
3. Bill Sutherland (SCO) 2:37:24
1974 1. John Warhurst (ENG) 2:35:23.0
2. Roy Thorpe (ENG) 2:39:02.2
3. Peter Fullager (AUS) 2:42:08.2
1978 1. Ollie Flynn (ENG) 2:22:03.7
2. Willi Sawall (AUS) 2:22:58.6
3. Tim Erickson (AUS) 2:26:34.0
1982 1. Steve Barry (WAL) 2:10:16
2. Marcel Jobin (CAN) 2:12:24
3. Guillaume Leblanc (CAN) 2:14:56

WOMEN

100 METRES
Run over 100 yards (91.44m) 1934-66

1934 1. Eileen Hiscock (ENG) 11.3
2. Hilda Strike (CAN) 11.5
3. Lilian Chalmers (ENG) 11.6
1938 1. Decima Norman (AUS) 11.1
2. Joyce Walker (AUS) 11.3
3. Jeanette Dolson (CAN) 11.4
1950 1. Marjorie Jackson (AUS) 10.8
2. Shirley Strickland (AUS) 11.0
3. Verna Johnston (AUS) 11.1
1954 1. Marjorie Jackson (AUS) 10.7
2. Winsome Cripps (AUS) 10.8
3. Edna Maskell (ZAM) 10.8
1958 1. Marlene Willard (AUS) 10.70 (wind+0.22 m/s)
2. Heather Young (ENG) 10.73
3. Madeleine Weston (ENG) 10.81
1962 1. Dorothy Hyman (ENG) 11.2 (wind -5.8 m/s)
2. Doreen Porter (NZL) 11.3
3. Brenda Cox (AUS) 11.4
1966 1. Dianne Burge (AUS) 10.6
2. Irene Piotrowski (CAN) 10.8
3. Jill Hall (ENG) 10.8
1970 1. Raelene Boyle (AUS) 11.26 (wind+5.3 m/s)
2. Alice Annum (GHA) 11.32
3. Marion Hoffman (AUS) 11.36
1974 1. Raelene Boyle (AUS) 11.27 (wind+0.5 m/s)
2. Andrea Lynch (ENG) 11.31
3. Denise Robertson (AUS) 11.50
1978 1. Sonia Lannaman (ENG) 11.27 (wind+2.81 m/s)
2. Raelene Boyle (AUS) 11.35
3. Denise Boyd (née Robertson) (AUS) 11.37
1982 1. Angella Taylor (CAN) 11.00 (wind+1.4 m/s)
2. Merlene Ottey (JAM) 11.03
3. Colleen Pekin (néc Beazley) (AUS) 11.24

200 METRES
Run over 220 yards (201.17m) 1934-66

1934 1. Eileen Hiscock (ENG) 25.0
2. Aileen Meagher (CAN) 25.4
3. Nellie Halstead (ENG) 25.6e
1938 1. Decima Norman (AUS) 24.7
2. Jean Coleman (AUS) 25.1
3. Eileen Wearne (AUS) 25.3
1950 1. Marjorie Jackson (AUS) 24.3
2. Shirley Strickland (AUS) 24.5
3. Daphne Robb (SAF) 24.7
1954 1. Marjorie Jackson (AUS) 24.0
2. Winsome Cripps (AUS) 24.5
3. Shirley Hampton (ENG) 25.0
1958 1. Marlene Willard (AUS) 23.65
2. Betty Cuthbert (AUS) 23.77
3. Heather Young (ENG) 23.90
1962 1. Dorothy Hyman (ENG) 24.00 (wind -3.0 m/s)
2. Joyce Bennett (AUS) 24.21
3. Margaret Burvill (AUS) 24.42
1966 1. Dianne Burge (AUS) 23.73
2. Jennifer Lamy (AUS) 23.86
3. Irene Piotrowski (CAN) 23.92
1970 1. Raelene Boyle (AUS) 22.75 (wind+4.0 m/s)
2. Alice Annum (GHA) 22.86
3. Margaret Critchley (ENG) 23.16
1974 1. Raelene Boyle (AUS) 22.50 (wind+0.6 m/s)
2. Denise Robertson (AUS) 22.73
3. Alice Annum (GHA) 22.90
1978 1. Denise Boyd (née Robertson) (AUS) 22.82 (wind+5.01 m/s)
2. Sonia Lannaman (ENG) 22.89
3. Colleen Beazley (AUS) 22.93
1982 1. Merlene Ottey (JAM) 22.19 (wind+2.5 m/s)
2. Kathy Smallwood (ENG) 22.21 COOK
3. Angella Taylor (CAN) 22.48 ISSAJENKO

400 METRES
Run over 440 yards (402.34m) 1966

1966 1. Judy Pollock (AUS) 53.0
2. Deidre Watkinson (ENG) 54.1
3. Una Morris (JAM) 54.2
1970 1. Marilyn Neufville (JAM) 51.02
2. Sandra Brown (AUS) 53.66
3. Judith Ayaa (UGA) 53.77
1974 1. Yvonne Saunders (CAN) 51.67
2. Verona Bernard (ENG) 51.94
3. Charlene Rendina (AUS) 52.08
1978 1. Donna Hartley (ENG) 51.69
2. Verona Elder (née Bernard) (ENG) 52.94
3. Bethanie Nail (AUS) 53.06
1982 1. Raelene Boyle (AUS) 51.26
2. Michelle Scutt (WAL) 51.97
3. Joslyn Hoyte-Smith (ENG) 52.53

800 METRES
Run over 880 yards (804.67m) 1934-66

1934 1. Gladys Lunn (ENG) 2:19.4
2. Ida Jones (ENG) 2:21.0
3. Dorothy Butterfield (ENG) 2:21.4
1962 1. Dixie Willis (AUS) 2:03.85
2. Marise Chamberlain (NZL) 2:05.66
3. Joy Jordan (ENG) 2:05.96
1966 1. Abigail Hoffman (CAN) 2:04.3
2. Judy Pollock (AUS) 2:04.5
3. Anne Smith (ENG) 2:05.0
1970 1. Rosemary Stirling (SCO) 2:06.24
2. Pat Lowe (ENG) 2:06.27
3. Cheryl Peasley (AUS) 2:06.33
1974 1. Charlene Rendina (AUS) 2:01.1
2. Sue Haden (NZL) 2:02.0
3. Sabina Chebichi (KEN) 2:02.6
1978 1. Judy Peckham (AUS) 2:02.82
2. Tekla Chemabwai (KEN) 2:02.87
3. Jane Colebrook (ENG) 2:03.10
1982 1. Kirsty McDermott (WAL) 2:01.31
2. Anne Clarkson (SCO) 2:01.52 PURVIS
3. Heather Barralet (AUS) 2:01.70

1500 METRES

1970 1. Rita Ridley (ENG) 4:18.8
2. Joan Page (ENG) 4:19.0
3. Thelma Fynn (CAN) 4:19.1
1974 1. Glenda Reiser (CAN) 4:07.8
2. Joan Allison (née Page) (ENG) 4:10.7
3. Thelma Wright (née Fynn) (CAN) 4:12.3
1978 1. Mary Stewart (ENG) 4:06.34
2. Christine Benning (ENG) 4:07.53
3. Penny Werthner (CAN) 4:08.14
1982 1. Christina Boxer (ENG) 4:08.28 CAHILL
2. Gillian Dainty (ENG) 4:10.80
3. Lorraine Moller (NZL) 4:12.67

3000 METRES

1978 1. Paula Fudge (ENG) 9:13.0
2. Heather Thomson (NZL) 9:20.69
3. Ann Ford (ENG) 9:24.05
1982 1. Anne Audain (NZL) 8:45.53
2. Wendy Smith (ENG) 8:48.47
3. Lorraine Moller (NZL) 8:55.76

For years closely matched sprint rivals - in 1982 Kathy Smallwood (top) won a gold and a silver and Merlene Ottey (below) won gold, silver and bronze in the sprints. Now Mrs Cook and Page respectively, they should again be in contention for medals in Edinburgh.

and at 5000m and 3000m steeplechase - the Kenyans Ben Jipcho 1974 and Henry Rono 1978. Jipcho also had the time and stamina to gain a bronze medal at 1500 metres in a great race won by Filbert Bayi of Tanzania. Bayi was a sensational winner at Christchurch as he led from the gun with an awe-inspiring display of front running. His courage was rewarded with a world record time of 3:32.16 and another newcomer, New Zealander John Walker at 3:32.52 was also inside the previous record.

The athlete to have taken part at most Games is the New Zealand discus thrower Robin Tait, who was placed successively 4-3-6-1-4-8 from 1962 to 1982. Five Games were contested by Howard Payne, by New Zealand jumper Dave Norris (1958-74) and by one woman, Mary Peters, who represented Northern Ireland at five different events between 1958 and 1974. She won the shot in 1970 and the pentathlon in 1970 and 1974.

Two athletes have the slightly sad record of winning four silver medals but no gold. Ann Wilson of England was runner-up to Mary Peters in both those Pentathlon victories and gained further second places in 1970 at high and long jumps. Ron Clarke is surely the greatest non-gold medallist of all time. He had set world junior records for 1500 metres and 1 mile in 1956, in which year he had had the honour of running the Olympic Torch into the Olympic Stadium in Melbourne. Thereafter he concentrated on his accountancy studies, but came back

Mary Peters (centre) completed her Games career in 1974, with her third gold medal. Modupe Oshikoya (right) took the silver in the pentathlon. Sixth in that competition was Diane Jones of Canada (above), who as Diane Konihowski went on to win in 1978.

80 METRES HURDLES

1934 1. Marjorie Clark (SAF) 11.8
2. Betty Taylor (CAN) 11.9
3. Elsie Green (ENG) 12.2e
1938 1. Barbara Burke (SAF) 11.7
2. Isobel Grant (AUS) 11.7
3. Rona Tong (NZL) 11.8
1950 1. Shirley Strickland (AUS) 11.6
2. June Schoch (NZL) 11.6
3. Joan Shackleton (NZL) 11.7
1954 1. Edna Maskell (ZAM) 10.9
2. Gwendolyn Hobbins (CAN) 11.2
3. Jean Desforges (ENG) 11.2
1958 1. Norma Thrower (AUS) 10.72 (wind +4.89 m/s)
2. Carole Quinton (ENG) 10.77
3. Gloria Wigney (AUS) 10.94
1962 1. Pam Kilborn (AUS) 11.07 (wind -7.0 m/s)
2. Betty Moore (ENG) 11.40
3. Avis McIntosh (NZL) 11.47
1966 1. Pam Kilborn (AUS) 10.9
2. Carmen Smith (JAM) 11.0
3. Jenny Wingerson (CAN) 11.0

100 METRES HURDLES

1970 1. Pam Kilborn (AUS) 13.27 (wind -0.3 m/s)
2. Maureen Caird (AUS) 13.73
3. Christine Bell (ENG) 13.82
1974 1. Judy Vernon (ENG) 13.45 (wind +1.0 m/s)
2. Gaye Dell (AUS) 13.54
3. Modupe Oshikoya (NGR) 13.69
1978 1. Lorna Boothe (ENG) 12.98 (wind +3.56 m/s)
2. Shirley Strong (ENG) 13.08
3. Sharon Colyear (ENG) 13.17
1982 1. Shirley Strong (ENG) 12.78 (wind +4.5 m/s)
2. Lorna Boothe (ENG) 12.90
3. Susan Kameli (CAN) 13.10

400 METRES HURDLES

1982 1. Debbie Flintoff (AUS) 55.89
2. Ruth Kyalisiima (UGA) 57.10
3. Yvette Wray (ENG) 57.17

SPRINT RELAY - 2 x 110 yards, 1 x 220 yards

1934 1. England 49.4
2. Canada
3. Rhodesia
1938 1. Australia 49.1
2. Canada 49.9
3. England 51.3
1950 1. Australia 47.9
2. New Zealand 48.7
3. England 50.0

SPRINT RELAY - 2 x 220 yards, 2 x 110 yards

1934 1. Canada 1:14.4
2. England
3. Scotland
1938 1. Australia 1:15.2
2. England 1:16.9
3. Canada 1:18.7
1950 1. Australia 1:13.4
2. England 1:17.5
3. Canada

4 x 100 METRES RELAY

Run over 4 x 110 yards (100.54m) 1954-66

1954 1. Australia 46.8
2. England 46.9
3. Canada 47.8
1958 1. England 45.37
2. Australia 46.12
3. Canada 47.21
1962 1. Australia 46.71
2. England 46.81
3. New Zealand 46.93
1966 1. Australia 45.3
2. England 45.6
3. Jamaica 45.6
1970 1. Australia 44.14
2. England 44.28
3. Canada 44.68
1974 1. Australia 43.51
2. England 44.30
3. Ghana 44.35
1978 1. England 43.70
2. Canada 44.26
3. Australia 44.78
1982 1. England 43.15
2. Canada 43.66
3. Jamaica 43.69

4 x 400 METRES RELAY

1974 1. England 3:29.2
2. Australia 3:30.7
3. Canada 3:33.9
1978 1. England 3:27.19
2. Australia 3:28.65
3. Canada 3:35.83
1982 1. Canada 3:27.70
2. Australia 3:27.72
3. Scotland 3:32.92

HIGH JUMP

1934 1. Marjorie Clark (SAF) 1.60
2. Eva Dawes (CAN) 1.57
3. Margaret Bell (CAN) 1.52
1938 1. Dorothy Odam (ENG) 1.60
2. Dora Gardner (ENG) 1.57
3. Elizabeth Forbes (NZL) 1.57
1950 1. Dorothy Tyler (née Odam) (ENG) 1.60
2. Bertha Crowther (ENG) 1.60
3. Noeline Swinton (NZL) 1.55
1954 1. Thelma Hopkins (NIR) 1.67
2. Dorothy Tyler (ENG) 1.60
3. Alice Whitty (CAN) 1.60
1958 1. Michele Mason (AUS) 1.70
2. Mary Donaghy (NZL) 1.70
3. Helen Frith (AUS) 1.65
1962 1. Robyn Woodhouse (AUS) 1.78
2. Helen Frith (AUS) 1.73
3. Michele Mason (AUS) 1.73
1966 1. Michele Brown (née Mason) (AUS) 1.73
2. Dorothy Shirley (ENG) 1.70
3. Robyn Woodhouse (AUS) 1.70
1970 1. Debbie Brill (CAN) 1.78
2. Ann Wilson (ENG) 1.70
3. Moira Walls (SCO) 1.70
1974 1. Barbara Lawton (ENG) 1.84
2. Louise Hanna (CAN) 1.82
3. Brigitte Bittner (CAN) 1.80
1978 1. Katrina Gibbs (AUS) 1.93
2. Debbie Brill (CAN) 1.90
3. Julie White (CAN) 1.83
1982 1. Debbie Brill (CAN) 1.88
2. Christine Stanton (AUS) 1.88
3. Barbara Simmonds (ENG) 1.83

LONG JUMP

1934 1. Phyllis Bartholomew (ENG) 5.47
2. Evelyn Goshawk (CAN) 5.41
3. Violet Webb (ENG) 5.23
1938 1. Decima Norman (AUS) 5.80
2. Ethel Raby (ENG) 5.66
3. Thelma Peake (AUS) 5.55
1950 1. Yvette Williams (NZL) 5.90
2. Judith Canty (AUS) 5.78
3. Ruth Dowman (NZL) 5.74
1954 1. Yvette Williams (NZL) 6.08
2. Thelma Hopkins (NIR) 5.84
3. Jean Desforges (ENG) 5.84
1958 1. Sheila Hoskin (ENG) 6.02
2. Mary Bignal (ENG) 5.97
3. Beverley Watson (AUS) 5.97
1962 1. Pam Kilborn (AUS) 6.27
2. Helen Frith (AUS) 6.24
3. Janet Knee (AUS) 6.13
1966 1. Mary Rand (née Bignal) (ENG) 6.36
2. Sheila Parkin (ENG) 6.30
3. Violet Odogwu (NGR) 6.15
1970 1. Sheila Sherwood (née Parkin) (ENG) 6.73
2. Ann Wilson (ENG) 6.50
3. Joan Hendry (CAN) 6.28
1974 1. Modupe Oshikoya (NGR) 6.46
2. Brenda Eisler (CAN) 6.38
3. Ruth Martin-Jones (WAL) 6.38
1978 1. Sue Reeve (ENG) 6.59
2. Erica Hooker (AUS) 6.58
3. June Griffith (GUY) 6.52
1982 1. Shonel Ferguson (BAH) 6.91w
2. Robyn Strong (AUS) 6.88
3. Beverley Kinch (ENG) 6.78

Two multiple medallists: below: Howard Payne won his third hammer gold medal in 1970; right Don Quarrie at his last Games in 1982. He won six sprint gold medals at the Games from 1970 to 1978.

to win a surprise silver medal at 3 miles behind Murray Halberg (NZL) in 1962. Over the next few years he revolutionised distance running records, but at Commonwealth Games could do no better than second place, behind the Kenyans Kip Keino and Naftali Temu at 3 and 6 miles in 1966 and at 10,000 metres behind Lachie Stewart in 1970. The latter, in the blue vest of Scotland, ensured that the Edinburgh Games got off to a great start; a triumph that was added to later when the two Ians, Stewart and McCafferty staged a storming finish to win gold and silver at 5000 metres ahead of Keino, third, and Ron Clarke, in his last championships race, fifth.

The first dead heat in a Games final came in the 1982 Games in Brisbane, when the judges, even after the most careful scrutiny of the photo-finish picture were unable to separate Allan Wells of Scotland and Mike McFarlane of England in the 200 metres. Wells accumulated four gold, a silver and a bronze medal in the sprints in 1978 and 1982, record medal hauls for any British athlete. As a young Edinburgh Southern long jumper he had helped rake the pit at the 1970 Games and took up sprinting seriously at the age of 24, an age by which many of the great sprinters of the past had retired. His dedication and ability have been amply rewarded since then with Olympic 100m victory in 1980 as the pinnacle of a career in which he has long shown the knack of peaking for the major events. What a wonderful story it would be if at 34 he could win again in Edinburgh in 1986.

Above: A brilliant Scottish 1-2 at 5000 metres in 1970 thrilled the Meadowbank crowd. Ian Stewart raises his arm in triumph after a magnificent battle with Ian McCafferty down the home straight.

Left: Mike McFarlane (left) and Allan Wells (right) dead-heated at 200 metres in 1982, a unique achievement for an automatically timed sprint at a major Games.

SHOT

1954 1. Yvette Williams (NZL) 13.96
2. Jacqueline MacDonald (CAN) 12.98
3. Magdalena Swanepoel (SAF) 12.81
1958 1. Valerie Sloper (NZL) 15.54
2. Suzanne Allday (ENG) 14.44
3. Jacqueline Gelling (née MacDonald)(CAN) 14.03
1962 1. Valerie Young (née Sloper) (NZL) 15.23
2. Jean Roberts (AUS) 14.51
3. Suzanne Allday (ENG) 13.56
1966 1. Valerie Young (NZL) 16.50
2. Mary Peters (NIR) 16.29
3. Nancy McCredie (CAN) 15.34
1970 1. Mary Peters (NIR) 15.93
2. Barbara Poulsen (NZL) 15.87
3. Jean Roberts (AUS) 15.32
1974 1. Jane Haist (CAN) 16.12
2. Valerie Young (NZL) 15.29
3. Jean Roberts (AUS) 15.24
1978 1. Gael Mulhall (AUS) 17.31
2. Carmen Ionescu (CAN) 16.45
3. Judy Oakes (ENG) 16.14
1982 1. Judy Oakes (ENG) 17.92
2. Gael Mulhall (AUS) 17.68 MARTIN
3. Rosemarie Hauch (CAN) 16.71

DISCUS

1954 1. Yvette Williams (NZL) 45.02
2. Suzanne Allday (ENG) 40.02
3. Marie Dupree (CAN) 38.66
1958 1. Suzanne Allday (ENG) 45.91
2. Jennifer Thompson (NZL) 45.30
3. Valerie Sloper (NZL) 44.94
1962 1. Valerie Young (née Sloper) (NZL) 50.20
2. Rosslyn Williams (AUS) 46.66
3. Mary McDonald (AUS) 46.24
1966 1. Valerie Young (NZL) 49.78
2. Jean Roberts (AUS) 49.20
3. Carol Martin (CAN) 48.70
1970 1. Rosemary Payne (SCO) 54.46
2. Jean Roberts (AUS) 51.02
3. Carol Martin (CAN) 48.42
1974 1. Jane Haist (CAN) 55.52
2. Rosemary Payne (SCO) 53.94
3. Carol Martin (CAN) 53.16
1978 1. Carmen Ionescu (CAN) 62.16
2. Gael Mulhall (AUS) 57.60
3. Lucette Moreau (CAN) 56.44
1982 1. Margaret Ritchie (SCO) 62.98
2. Gael Mulhall (AUS) 58.64
3. Lynda Whiteley (ENG) 54.78

JAVELIN

1934 1. Gladys Lunn (ENG) 32.18
2. Edith Halstead (ENG) 30.94
3. Margaret Cox (ENG) 30.08
1938 1. Robina Higgins (CAN) 38.28
2. Antonia Robertson (SAF) 36.98
3. Gladys Lunn (ENG) 36.40
1950 1. Charlotte MacGibbon-Weeks (AUS) 38.84
2. Yvette Williams (NZL) 37.96
3. Cleo Rivett-Carnac (NZL) 34.42
1954 1. Magdalena Swanepoel (SAF) 43.82
2. Pearl Thornhill-Fisher (ZAM) 41.96
3. Shirley Couzens (CAN) 38.98
1958 1. Anna Pazera (AUS) 57.40
2. Magdalena Swanepoel (SAF) 48.72
3. Averil Williams (ENG) 50.24
1962 1. Susan Platt (ENG) 50.24
2. Rosemary Morgan (ENG) 49.62
3. Anna Pazera (AUS) 48.68
1966 1. Margaret Parker (AUS) 51.38
2. Anna Bocson (formerly Pazera) (AUS) 47.80
3. Jay Dahlgren (CAN) 47.68
1970 1. Petra Rivers (AUS) 52.00
2. Anne Farquhar (ENG) 50.82
3. Jay Dahlgren (CAN) 49.54
1974 1. Petra Rivers (AUS) 55.48
2. Jenny Symon (AUS) 52.14
3. Sharon Corbett (ENG) 50.26
1978 1. Tessa Sanderson (ENG) 61.34
2. Alison Hayward (CAN) 54.32
3. Laurie Kern (CAN) 53.60
1982 1. Suzanne Howland (AUS) 64.46
2. Petra Rivers (AUS) 62.28
3. Fatima Whitbread (ENG) 58.86

PENTATHLON (all scored on 1971 tables)

1970 1. Mary Peters (NIR) 4515 (5148 on tables used)
2. Ann Wilson (ENG) 4416 (5037)
3. Jenny Meldrum (née Wingerson) (CAN) 4120 (4736)
1974 1. Mary Peters (NIR) 4455
2. Modupe Oshikoya (NGR) 4423
3. Ann Wilson (ENG) 4236
1978 1. Diane Konihowski (CAN) 4768
2. Susan Mapstone (ENG) 4222
3. Yvette Wray (ENG) 4211

HEPTATHLON

1982 1. Glynis Nunn (AUS) 6282
2. Judy Livermore (ENG) 6214 SIMPSON
3. Jill Ross (CAN) 5981

Daley Thompson leads his fellow decathletes on a lap of honour after his second Commonwealth gold in 1982.

Injury caused Tessa Sanderson to miss the 1982 Games, but she will be hoping to regain her title in 1986 against arch-rival Fatima Whitbread.
Right: Shonel Ferguson, the first woman from the Bahamas to win a medal, gold at long jump in 1982.

ATHLETICS - MEDAL TABLE BY NATIONS

Nation		Men			Women		Total
	G	S	B	G	S	B	
England	74	62	56	33	43	34	302
Australia	45	52	41	49	36	25	248
Canada	32	40	43	13	17	34	179
New Zealand	18	15	23	10	11	11	88
South Africa	16	13	14	4	2	2	51
Kenya	21	9	17	-	1	1	49
Scotland	11	9	18	3	2	3	46
Jamaica	14	7	8	2	2	3	36
Nigeria	3	8	4	1	1	2	19
Ghana	4	4	5	-	2	2	17
Wales	5	4	4	1	1	1	16
Trinidad & Tobago	3	7	3	-	-	-	13
Northern Ireland	2	4	-	4	2	1	12
Pakistan	2	3	6	-	-	-	11
Bahamas	2	6	1	1	-	-	10
Uganda	-	4	3	-	1	1	9
Tanzania	3	3	2	-	-	-	8
India	1	2	2	-	-	-	5
Fiji	1	2	1	-	-	-	4
Guyana	1	2	-	-	-	1	4
Zimbabwe	-	1	2	-	-	1	4
Zambia	-	-	-	1	1	1	3
Bermuda	-	1	1	-	-	-	2
Barbados	-	-	2	-	-	-	2
Sri Lanka	1	-	-	-	-	-	1
The Gambia	-	-	1	-	-	-	1
Swaziland	-	-	1	-	-	-	1

C&A wish all competitors every success.
RODEO
The name for active sportswear at C&A
C&A

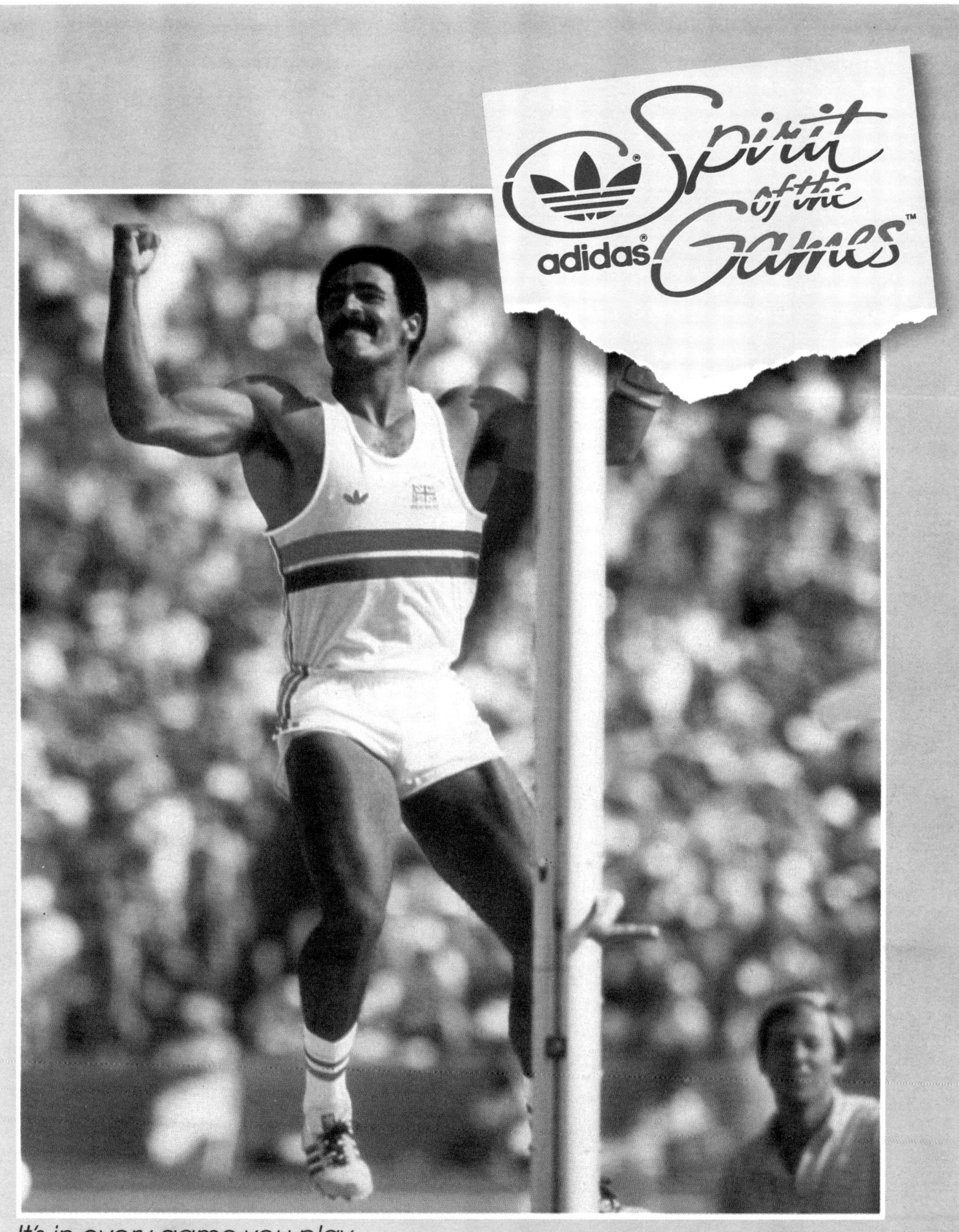

It's in every game you play.

BADMINTON MEDALLISTS

MEN'S SINGLES

1966 1. Tan Aik Huang (MAL)
2. Yew Cheng Hoe (MAL)
3. Dinesk Khanna (IND)
1970 1. Jamie Paulson (CAN)
2. Paul Whetnall (ENG)
3. Raymond Sharp (ENG)
1974 1. Punch Gunalan (MAL)
2. Jamie Paulson (CAN)
3. Derek Talbot (ENG)
1978 1. Padukone Prakash (IND)
2. Derek Talbot (ENG)
3. Ray Stevens (ENG)
1982 1. Syed Modi (IND)
2. Nick Yates (ENG)
3. Razif Sidek (MAL)

MEN'S DOUBLES

1966 1. Tan Aik Huang & Yew Cheng Hoe (MAL)
2. Ng Boon Bee & Tan Yee Khan (MAL)
3. Roger Mills & David Horton (ENG)
1970 1. Ng Boon Bee & Punch Gunalan (MAL)
2. Tan Soon Hooi & Ng Tat Wai (MAL)
3. Jamie Paulson & Yves Paré (CAN)
1974 1. Derek Talbot & Elliot Stuart (ENG)
2. Ray Stevens & Michael Tredgett (ENG)
3. Punch Gunalan & Dominic Soong Chok Soong (MAL)
1978 1. Ray Stevens & Michael Tredgett (ENG)
2. Foot Lian Moo & Beng Teong Ong (MAL)
3. Richard Purser & Bryan Purser (NZL)
1982 1. Razif Sidek & Beng Teong Ong (MAL)
2. Martin Dew & Nick Yates (ENG)
3. Patrick Tryon & Paul Johnson (CAN)

WOMEN'S SINGLES

1966 1. Angela Bairstow (ENG)
2. Sharon Whittaker (CAN)
3. Ursula Smith (ENG)
1970 1. Margaret Beck (ENG)
2. Gillian Perrin (ENG)
3. Margaret Boxall (ENG)
1974 1. Gillian Gilks (née Perrin) (ENG)
2. Margaret Beck (ENG)
3. Sylvia Ng (MAL)
1978 1. Sylvia Ng (MAL)
2. Katherine Swee Phek Teh (MAL)
3. Wendy Clarkson (CAN)
1982 1. Helen Troke (ENG)
2. Sally Podger (ENG)
3. Gillian Clark (ENG)

WOMEN'S DOUBLES

1966 1. Helen Horton & Ursula Smith (ENG)
2. Angela Bairstow & Iris Rogers (ENG)
3. Rosalind Ang & Teoh Siew Yong (MAL)
1970 1. Margaret Boxall & Susan Whetnall (ENG)
2. Gillian Perrin & Julie Rickard (ENG)
3. Rosalind Ang & Teoh Siew Yong (MAL)
1974 1. Margaret Beck & Gillian Gilks (née Perrin) (ENG)
2. Susan Whetnall & Margaret Boxall (ENG)
3. Sylvia Ng & Rosalind Ang (MAL)
1978 1. Nora Perry & Anne Statt (ENG)
2. Jane Youngberg & Claire Backhouse (CAN)
3. Ami Ghia & Kanwal Singh (IND)
1982 1. Claire Backhouse & Johanne Falardeau (CAN)
2. Gillian Clark & Karen Beckman (ENG)
3. Karen Chapman & Sally Podger (ENG)

MIXED DOUBLES

1966 1. Roger Mills & Angela Bairstow (ENG)
2. Anthony Jordan & Helen Horton (ENG)
3. Robert McCoig & Muriel Ferguson (SCO)
1970 1. Derek Talbot & Margaret Boxall (ENG)
2. Roger Mills & Gillian Perrin (ENG)
3. David Eddy & Susan Whetnall (ENG)
1974 1. Derek Talbot & Gillian Gilks (née Perrin) (ENG)
2. Paul Whetnall & Nora Gardner (ENG)
3. Elliott Stuart & Susan Whetnall (ENG)
1978 1. Michael Tredgett & Nora Perry (née Gardner) (ENG)
2. Billy Gilliland & Joanna Flockhart (SCO)
3. Derek Talbot & Barbara Sutton (ENG)
1982 1. Martin Dew & Karen Chapman (ENG)
2. Duncan Bridge & Karen Beckman (ENG)
3. Steve Wilson & Robin Denton (NZL)

TEAM

1978 1. England
2. Canada
3. Malaysia
1982 1. England
2. Canada
3. Australia

Commonwealth medallists both, but here on the same side: Billy Gilliland of Scotland and Karen Chapman of England.

BADMINTON - MEDAL TABLE BY NATIONS

Nation	G	S	B	Total
England	17	16	11	44
Malaysia	6	5	7	18
Canada	2	5	3	10
India	2	-	2	4
Scotland	-	1	1	2
New Zealand	-	-	2	2
Australia	-	-	1	1

Badminton

Gillian Gilks, triple gold medallist in 1974.

Both England and India have strong claims to have been the originators of the game, so it is fitting that badminton has become established as a Commonwealth Games sport since 1966. The events are men's and women's singles and doubles, mixed doubles; and, since 1978, a team competition. Badminton has been added to the Olympic Games programme for 1992.

The first star of the Games was Tan Aik Huang of Malaysia who won gold medals in singles and doubles in 1966 without losing a single game en route. However, the most successful competitors have been England's Gillian Gilks (née Perrin) who, after three silver medals in 1970, won a unique three gold medals four years later, and Derek Talbot, who amassed four golds, a silver and two bronze medals from 1970 to 1978. Two more England players, Nora Perry and Michael Tredgett, won three gold medals in 1978, including the team event, which was not included when Gilks won her triple. Despite their domination of the event, winning over half the medals, England have not provided a men's singles champion. In contrast, the only occasion on which an English woman has not won the singles was in 1978, when the event was staged in 30°C heat. The 1982 champion Helen Troke, was at 17 years 335 days, the youngest champion.

Badminton is an unusual sport in that it has been estimated that shuttle speed on leaving the racquet head can reach 300km/h (186mph), but this is dissipated so fast that the shuttle will fall to the ground within 12-13 metres (39-42 feet). During a single game a player may cover over a mile in distance. The shuttle, usually made of 14-16 feathers fixed in a cork base, weighing between 4.7 and 5.5 grams, takes a tremendous battering. In the 1982 Games events some 9,600 shuttles were supplied.

The badminton court is rectangular, measuring 13.4m by 6.1m for doubles or 5.2m for singles. The net is 1.5m high. Doubles games and men's singles consist of 15 points, but with an option to play a further 5 points if the score reaches 13-all and a further option to play an additional 3 points if the score reaches 14-all. Women's singles are to 11 points with an option of a further 3 points at 9-all and an additional 2 points at 10-all. A match is the best of three games.

BOWLS MEDALLISTS

SINGLES - MEN

1930 1. Robert Colquhoun (ENG)
2. J. Thomas (SAF)
3. William Fielding (NZL)
1934 1. Robert Sprot (SCO)
2. W.S. MacDonald (CAN)
3. Andrew Harvey (SAF)
1938 1. Horace Harvey (SAF)
2. Frank Livingstone (NZL)
3. Jack Low (AUS)
1950 1. James Pirret (NZL)
2. Albert Newton (AUS)
3. Lionel Garnett (FIJ)
1954 1. Ralph Hodges (ZIM)
2. James Pirret (NZL)
3. Arthur Saunders (SAF)
1958 1. Phineas Danilowitz (SAF)
2. Percy Baker (ENG)
3. William Jackson (ZIM)
1962 1. David Bryant (ENG)
2. Joseph Black (SCO)
3. Alan Bradley (ZIM)
1970 1. David Bryant (ENG)
2. Neal Bryce (ZAM)
3. Roy Fulton (NIR)
1974 1. David Bryant (ENG)
2. Clive White (AUS)
3. William Wood (SCO)
1978 1. David Bryant (ENG)
2. John Snell (AUS)
3. John Evans (WAL)
1982 1. William Wood (SCO)
2. Robert Parrella (AUS)
3. Peter Belliss (NZL)

PAIRS - MEN

1930 1. Tommy Hills & George Wright (ENG)
2. Peter McWhannell & William Fielding (NZL)
3. Arthur Reid & W. Moore (CAN)
1934 1. Tommy Hills & George Wright (ENG)
2. W.G. Hutchinson & A.A. Langford (CAN)
3. Thomas Davies & Stan Weaver (WAL)
1938 1. Lance Macey & William Denison (NZL)
2. Percy Hutton & Howard Mildren (AUS)
3. D. Anderson & J.R. Appleford (SAF)
1950 1. Robert Henry & Phil Exelby (NZL)
2. W. Gibb & H. van Zyl (SAF)
3. James Poulton & Leslie Brown (FIJ)
1954 1. William Rosbotham & Percy Watson (NIR)
2. Samuel Gardiner & Richard Williams (CAN)
3. George Budge & John Carswell (SCO)
1958 1. John Morris & Richard Pilkington (NZL)
2. John Myrdal & Wilf Randall (SAF)
3. B. Wells & Hector Philp (ZIM)
1962 1. Robert McDonald & Hugh Robson (NZL)
2. Michael Purdon & Thomas Hamill (SCO)
3. Charles Bradley & William Jackson (ZIM)
1970 1. Norman King & Peter Line (ENG)
2. Robert McDonald & Hugh Robson (NZL)
3. James Donnelly & Sid Thompson (NIR)
1974 1. John Christie & Alex McIntosh (SCO)
2. John Evans & Peter Line (ENG)
3. Phil Skoglund & Robert McDonald (NZL)
1978 1. Eric Liddell & Clementi Delgado (HGK)
2. Alex McIntosh & William Wood (SCO)
3. James Morgan & Ray Williams (WAL)
1982 1. John Watson & David Gourlay (SCO)
2. Lyn Perkins & Spencer Wilshire (WAL)
3. Denis Dalton & Peter Rheuben (AUS)

FOURS - MEN

1930 1. England
2. Canada
3. Scotland
1934 1. England
2. Northern Ireland
3. Scotland
1938 1. New Zealand
2. South Africa
3. Australia
1950 1. South Africa
2. Australia
3. New Zealand
1954 1. South Africa
2. Hong Kong
3. Southern Rhodesia
1958 1. England
2. South Africa
3. Rhodesia
1962 1. England
2. Scotland
3. Rhodesia
1970 1. Hong Kong
2. Scotland
3. Northern Ireland
1974 1. New Zealand
2. Australia
3. Scotland
1978 1. Hong Kong
2. New Zealand
3. Wales
1982 1. Australia
2. New Zealand
3. Northern Ireland

TRIPLES - WOMEN

1982 1. Zimbabwe
2. New Zealand
3. England

The Hong Kong bowls team, fours gold medallists in 1978.

BOWLS - MEDAL TABLE BY NATIONS

Nation	G	S	B	Total
New Zealand	7	7	4	18
England	12	2	1	15
Scotland	4	5	5	14
South Africa	4	5	3	12
Australia	1	7	3	11
Zimbabwe (Rhodesia)	2	-	7	9
Northern Ireland	1	1	4	6
Canada	-	4	1	5
Wales	-	1	4	5
Hong Kong	3	1	-	4
Fiji	-	-	2	2
Zambia	-	1	-	1

Lawn Bowls

Colorsport

Willie Wood (SCO)

Bowls, although not an Olympic sport, has been held at every Commonwealth Games except 1966. The first women's bowls event was a triples competition in 1982, but from 1986 the women's events are the same as for the men - singles, pairs and fours. The bowling fraternity in Canada fought vigorously to have the sport included in the inaugural Games of 1930, and their efforts were rewarded by entries from four other countries: England, New Zealand, Scotland and South Africa. The tragic death of one of the Scots left their fours team one short, so the Canadian hosts provided an extra player, Tom Chambers, who assisted his new team-mates to a bronze medal - a gesture indicative of the friendly atmosphere of the competition.

In 1934 no Australian team entered originally, but E.W. 'Ted' Walker was visiting Britain at the time and summoned some Australian players who were also on private visits so that a team did compete. Since then Australia have always been represented, although they did not win a gold medal until 1982.

After the Sydney Games of 1938, when for financial reasons there were no UK teams, there was a move to remove bowls from the programme and have it replaced by another sport. Such a move was, however, defeated, as it was again after the 1950 Games. The sport was not held in 1966 as there were no bowling greens in Jamaica, but it has since been well supported, with a record 17 countries in 1978.

Until a separate competition was introduced in 1966 the Commonwealth Games bowls events were considered as unofficial world championships, as to that time nearly all the sport's major players were from Commonwealth countries.

It is possible to stay at the top for many years in bowls, so it is perhaps not surprising that overall Games age records have been set at this sport. David Bryant of England won four consecutive singles titles from 1962 to 1978. His 16-year winning span has not been exceeded and at 46 years 288 days when he won his last title he is the oldest singles winner. He won a record fifth gold medal with the fours in 1962.

Scotland's Willie Wood compiled a complete set of medals, moving up in the singles from bronze in 1974 to a silver in 1978 to gold in 1982. Percy Watson of Northern Ireland won medals at Games 20 years apart, a silver in 1934 and a gold in 1954. He went on to compete twice more to achieve a unique 28-year Games competitive span. Other remarkable veterans include the Englishmen Percy Baker, who won a silver medal in the 1958 singles aged 63, and Edwin Bateman who competed in the 1954 pairs in his 75th year.

The most notable bowls family accomplishment is that of the Harveys of South Africa. Andrew took the singles bronze in 1934, while his son Horace won the 1938 gold medal. Incidentally, Horace's son Tom, the third generation, won medals at the 1972 World Championships.

The sport provides a good example of the success that can come to one of the smaller members of the Commonwealth family of nations, in this case Hong Kong. The Hong Kong Bowls Association was formed in 1910 and was originally affiliated to the English Bowling Association. Sixty years later there were still only some 600 bowlers in the Crown Colony, but they created a major surprise by winning the fours in Edinburgh. Three of their players were of Portugese descent and the fourth, Abdul Kitchell, was Malaysian and, at 54, one of the oldest gold medallists. In 1934 Hong Kong had entered a team of people on leave in England and in 1954 they had taken the fours silver medal. This success has continued as in 1978 Hong Kong repeated its fours win and added the pairs title. The latter team comprised Clementi Delgado, who had been in the winning 1970 foursome, and Eric Liddell, aged 54, who was competing in his sixth Games, to equal the record for any sport.

Nation strives with nation to win the world's greatest sporting honours at the Olympic Games.

City strives with city to win the greatest honour of all – the right to host the Olympic Games.

Amsterdam, Barcelona, Belgrade, Brisbane and Paris are the international competition Birmingham faces in its spirited bid to host the XXVth Olympiad in 1992.

Worthy opponents for a city that has been centre stage for the whole world many times over.

20,000 International Rotarians, for instance, chose Birmingham's National Exhibition Centre for their World Conference in 1984. In preference to anywhere else in the world.

·BIRMINGHAM·ONE OF

’s Olympic Finalist.

Last year the NEC celebrated its tenth successful year. An event the est of the country, who did not share the vision and vitality of Birmingham’s ity fathers, can now only stand back and applaud.

Birmingham’s foresight and imagination has put its name high on ny list of the world’s great cities.

And the world’s greatest sporting event is a prize this great multi-racial Commonwealth city is determined to win.

City of Birmingham, Council House, Victoria Square, Birmingham. 021-235 2903.

The Big Heart of England

BOXING MEDALLISTS

48kg - LIGHT-FLYWEIGHT

1970 1. James Odwori (UGA)
2. Anthony Davies (WAL)
3. Peter Butterfield (AUS)
Michael Abrams (ENG)
1974 1. Stephen Muchoki (KEN)
2. James Odwori (UGA)
3. Syed Kedir (SIN)
John Bambrick (SCO)
1978 1. Stephen Muchoki (KEN)
2. Francis Musankabala (ZAM)
3. Kid Sumalia (GHA)
Birender Thapa (IND)
1982 1. Abraham Wachire (KEN)
2. John Lyon (ENG)
3. Lucky Siame (ZAM)
Leonard Makhanya (SWA)

51kg - FLYWEIGHT

1930 1. Jacob Smith (SAF)
2. Thomas Pardoe (ENG)
3. Ross Galloway (CAN)
1934 1. Patrick Palmer (ENG)
2. Maxie Berger (CAN)
3. Jackie Pottinger (WAL)
1938 1. Johannes Joubert (SAF)
2. Joseph Gagnon (CAN)
3. Hugh Cameron (SCO)
1950 1. Hugh Riley (SCO)
2. K. Edwin (SRI)
3. Marcus Temple (SAF)
1954 1. Richard Currie (SCO)
2. Abel Becker (ZAM)
3. Warren Batchelor (AUS)
1958 1. Jackie Brown (SCO)
2. Tommy Bache (ENG)
3. Donald Braithwaite (WAL)
Peter Lavery (NIR)
1962 1. Robert Mallon (SCO)
2. Cassis Aryee (GHA)
3. Michael Pye (ENG)
Philip Waruinge (KEN)
1966 1. Sulley Shittu (GHA)
2. Kenneth Campbell (JAM)
3. Frank Scott (CAN)
John Rakowski (AUS)
1970 1. David Needham (ENG)
2. Leo Rwabogo (UGA)
3. David Larmour (NIR)
Alex McHugh (SCO)
1974 1. David Larmour (NIR)
2. Chandra Narayanan (IND)
3. John Byaruhanga (UGA)
Saliu Ishola (NGR)
1978 1. Michael Irungu (KEN)
2. Ian Clyde (CAN)
3. Peter Wighton (AUS)
Hugh Russell (NIR)
1982 1. Michael Mutua (KEN)
2. Joseph Kelly (SCO)
3. Albert Musankabala (ZAM)
Grant Richards (AUS)

54kg - BANTAMWEIGHT

1930 1. Hyman Mizler (CAN)
2. Tommy Holt (SCO)
3. John Kellar (CAN)
1934 1. Freddy Ryan (ENG)
2. Albert Barnes (WAL)
3. Thomas Wells (SCO)
1938 1. William Butler (ENG)
2. Hendrik Knoeson (SAF)
3. Jack Dillon (AUS)
1950 1. Johannes van Rensburg (SAF)
2. Albert Perera (SRI)
3. Leonard Walters (CAN)
1954 1. John Smillie (SCO)
2. Gordon Smith (ZIM)
3. Abubakar Idi Garuba (NGR)
1958 1. Howard Winstone (WAL)
2. Oliver Taylor (AUS)
3. Richard Hanna (NIR)
Alfred Owen (SCO)
1962 1. Jeffery Dynevor (AUS)
2. Samwell Abbey (GHA)
3. Peter Bennyworth (ENG)
John Sentongo (UGA)
1966 1. Edward Ndukwu (NGR)
2. Darryl Norwood (AUS)
3. Nderu Mwaura (KEN)
Brian Kendall (NZL)
1970 1. Sulley Shittu (GHA)
2. Samuel Mbogwa (KEN)
3. Courtney Atherly (GUY)
Stewart Ogilvie (SCO)
1974 1. Pat Cowdell (ENG)
2. Ali Rojo (UGA)
3. Newton Chisanga (ZAM)
Isaac Maina (KEN)
1978 1. Barry McGuigan (NIR)
2. Tumat Sogolik (NGU)
3. Douglas Maina (KEN)
William Rannelli (CAN)
1982 1. Joe Orewa (NGR)
2. Roy Webb (NIR)
3. Raymond Gilbody (ENG)
Richard Reilly (AUS)

57kg - FEATHERWEIGHT

1930 1. F.R. Meacham (ENG)
2. Lawrence Stevens (SAF)
3. Alex Lyons (SCO)
1934 1. Charles Catterall (SAF)
2. J.D. Jones (WAL)
3. William Fulton (ZIM)
1938 1. Anadale Henricus (SRI)
2. James Watson (SCO)
3. Kenneth Moran (NZL)
1950 1. Henry Gilliland (SCO)
2. Andrew Vercueil (ZIM)
3. Peter Brander (ENG)
1954 1. Leonard Leisching (SAF)
2. Malcolm Collins (WAL)
3. Dave Charnley (ENG)
1958 1. Wally Taylor (AUS)
2. Malcolm Collins (WAL)
3. Gert Coetzee (SAF)
John McClory (NIR)
1962 1. John McDermott (SCO)
2. Ali Juma (KEN)
3. Turori George (NZL)
Edward Stone (AUS)
1966 1. Philip Waruinge (KEN)
2. Patrick Maguire (NIR)
3. Amos Ajao (GHA)
Harold West (JAM)
1970 1. Philip Waruinge (KEN)
2. Deogratias Musoke (UGA)
3. Alan Richardson (ENG)
1974 1. Edward Ndukwa (NGR)
2. Shadrack Odhiambo (UGA)
3. Dale Anderson (CAN)
Samuel Mbugua (KEN)
1978 1. Azumah Nelson (GHA)
2. John Sichula (ZAM)
3. Guy Boutin (CAN)
Maurice O'Brien (ENG)
1982 1. Peter Konyegwachie (NGR)
2. Peter Hanlon (ENG)
3. Rodney Harberger (AUS)
Winfred Kabunda (ZAM)

60kg - LIGHTWEIGHT

1930 1. James Rolland (SCO)
2. Cosmo Canzano (CAN)
3. Albert Love (ENG)
1934 1. Leslie Cook (AUS)
2. Frank Taylor (WAL)
3. H.J. Moy (ENG)
1938 1. Harry Groves (ENG)
2. Harry Hurst (CAN)
3. William Fulton (ZIM)
1950 1. Ronald Latham (ENG)
2. William Barber (AUS)
3. Edward Haddad (CAN)
1954 1. Piet van Staden (ZIM)
2. Frank McQuillan (SCO)
3. Brian Cahill (AUS)
1958 1. Dick McTaggart (SCO)
2. James Jordan (NIR)
3. John Cooke (ENG)
Thomas Donovan (NZL)
1962 1. Eddie Blay (GHA)
2. Kesi Odongo (UGA)
3. Thomas Donovan (NZL)
Brian Whelan (ENG)
1966 1. Anthony Andeh (NGR)
2. Ronald Thurston (ENG)
3. Stephen Baraza (KEN)
Samuel Lockhart (NIR)
1970 1. Abayomi Adeyemi (NGR)
2. John Gillan (SCO)
3. Tatu Ghionga (MAW)
Mosesk Mbogwa (KEN)
1974 1. Ayub Kalule (UGA)
2. Kayin Amah (NGR)
3. Robert Colley (NZL)
Muniswami Venu (IND)
1978 1. Gerard Hamil (NIR)
2. Patrick Waweru (KEN)
3. John McAllister (SCO)
Teddy Makofi (ZAM)
1982 1. Hussein Khalili (KEN)
2. James McDonnell (ENG)
3. Stephen Larrimore (BAH)
Brian Tink (AUS)

63.5kg LIGHT-WELTERWEIGHT

1954 1. Mickey Bergin (CAN)
2. Aubrey Harris (ZIM)
3. Desmond Duguid (AUS)
1958 1. Henry Loubscher (SAF)
2. Robert Kane (SCO)
3. Raymond Galante (CAN)
Joseph Jacobs (ENG)
1962 1. Clement Quartey (GHA)
2. Dick McTaggart (SCO)
3. Brian Brazier (ENG)
Harvey Reti (CAN)
1966 1. James McCourt (NIR)
2. Aaron Popoola (GHA)
3. Raymond Maguire (AUS)
Alex Odhiambo (UGA)
1970 1. Muhamad Muruli (UGA)
2. Dai Davies (WAL)
3. Paul Kayula (ZAM)
Odartey Lawson (GHA)
1974 1. Obisia Nwakpa (NGR)
2. Anthony Martey (GHA)
3. James Douglas (SCO)
Philip Mathenge (KEN)
1978 1. Winfield Braithwaite (GUY)
2. James Douglas (SCO)
3. Michial Mawangi (KEN)
John Raftery (CAN)
1982 1. Christopher Ossai (KEN)
2. Charles Owiso (KEN)
3. David Chibuye (ZAM)
Clyde McIntosh (ENG)

67 kg - WELTERWEIGHT

1930 1. Leonard Hall (SAF)
2. Howard Williams (CAN)
3. F. Brooman (ENG)
1934 1. David McCleave (ENG)
2. Richard Barton (SAF)
3. William Duncan (NIR)
1938 1. Bill Smith (AUS)
2. Darcy Heeney (NZL)
3. Andrew Tsirindanis (ZIM)

Boxing

Boxing has been included at all Games and medal winning has been shared in a more widespread fashion than for any other sport, with 28 nations being represented. New weight categories have been introduced and in 1986 an additional one, at super-heavyweight, has been added. The heavyweight now has a top weight limit of 91kg. Note that two bronze medals per event have been awarded since 1958.

Australia's Tony Madigan has been the most successful boxer, winning light-heavyweight gold medals in 1958 and 1962 as well as the silver in 1954. He lost to Muhammad Ali (then Cassius Clay) in the semi-finals of the 1960 Olympic Games. Close behind Madigan is Philip Waruinge of Kenya with two golds, at featherweight in 1966 and 1970, and a bronze at flyweight in 1962; he also won Olympic silver and bronze medals. In fact, a dozen Commonwealth champions have also gained Olympic medals, although only one, Scotland's Dick McTaggart, has won titles at both Games: Olympics in 1956 and Commonwealth in 1958.

The youngest winner was Johannes Van Rensburg (SAF) at 17 years 277 days with the 1950 bantamweight title. He later became Empire professional champion, but failed in his attempts at the world title. Four boxers have won Commonwealth titles and then gone on to world professional crowns. First the 1958 bantamweight gold medallist Howard Winstone, who

Barry McGuigan won the Commonwealth bantamweight title in 1978. Seven years later the pride of Northern Ireland took the world professional title.

67kg Welterweight continued

1950 1. Terence Ratcliffe (ENG)
2. William Seewitz (NZL)
3. Alex Obeyesekere (SRI)
1954 1. Nicholas Gargano (ENG)
2. Rodney Litzow (AUS)
3. Hendrik van der Linde (SAF)
1958 1. Joseph Greyling (SAF)
2. Thomas Kawere (UGA)
3. Brian Nancurvis (ENG)
Robert Scott (SCO)
1962 1. Wallace Coe (NZL)
2. John Pritchett (ENG)
3. Albert Turmel (JER) - only one bronze
1966 1. Eddie Blay (GHA)
2. Robert Arthur (ENG)
3. Andrew Peace (SCO)
Frank Young (NIR)
1970 1. Emma Ankudey (GHA)
2. John Olulu (KEN)
3. Shivaji Bhonsle (IND)
Thomas Joyce (SCO)
1974 1. Muhamad Muruli (UGA)
2. Errol McKenzie (WAL)
3. Steven Cooney (SCO)
John Rodgers (NIR)
1978 1. Michael McCallum (JAM)
2. Ken Beattie (NIR)
3. Anthony Freal (WAL)
Derrick Hoyt (CAN)
1982 1. Christopher Pyatt (ENG)
2. Laston Mukobe (ZAM)
3. Chenanda Machaiah (IND)
Charles Nwokolo (NGR)

71kg - LIGHT-MIDDLEWEIGHT

1954 1. Wilfred Greaves (CAN)
2. Frederick Wright (ZAM)
3. Bruce Wells (ENG)
1958 1. Grant Webster (SAF)
2. Stuart Pearson (ENG)
3. Bill Brown (WAL)
James Walters (CAN)
1962 1. Harold Mann (CAN)
2. Brian Benson (ZIM)
3. Kenneth Hopkins (NGU)
Francis Nyangweso (UGA)
1966 1. Mark Rowe (ENG)
2. Tom Imrie (SCO)
3. Nojim Maiyegun (NGR)
R. Okine (GHA)
1970 1. Tom Imrie (SCO)
2. Julius Luipa (ZAM)
3. David Attan (KEN)
Patrick Doherty (NIR)
1974 1. Lotti Mwale (ZAM)
2. Alex Harrison (SCO)
3. Robert Davies (ENG)
Lance Revill (NZL)
1978 1. Kelly Perlette (CAN)
2. Abdulahman Athuman (KEN)
3. Enock Chama (ZAM)
Ropati Samu (WSA)
1982 1. Shawn O'Sullivan (CAN)
2. Nicholas Croombes (ENG)
3. Tommy Corr (NIR)
Roland Omoruyi (NGR)

75kg - MIDDLEWEIGHT

1930 1. Frederick Mallin (ENG)
2. Dudley Gallagher (AUS)
3. Teddy Phillips (CAN)
1934 1. Alf Shawyer (ENG)
2. Leonard Wadsworth (CAN)
3. Jimmy Magill (NIR)
1938 1. Denis Reardon (WAL)
2. Maurice Dennis (ENG)
3. Rex Carey (CAN)
1950 1. Theunis van Schalkwyk (SAF)
2. James Beal (NZL)
3. William Pinkus (CAN)
1954 1. Johannes van der Kolff (SAF)
2. Arthur Crawford (ZAM)
3. Marcel Piau (CAN)
1958 1. Terry Milligan (NIR)
2. Phillipus du Plessis (SAF)
3. John Caiger (ENG)
Robert Piau (CAN)
1962 1. Cephas Colquhoun (JAM)
2. Thomas Arimi (GHA)
3. Moses Evans (FIJ) - only one bronze
1966 1. Joe Darkey (GHA)
2. Arthur Trout (JAM)
3. Mathias Ouma (UGA)
John Turpin (ENG)
1970 1. John Conteh (ENG)
2. Titus Simba (TAN)
3. Samuel Kasongo (ZAM)
Robert Murphy (AUS)
1974 1. Frankie Lucas (SVI)
2. Julius Luipa (ZAM)
3. Les Rackley (NZL)
Carl Speare (ENG)
1978 1. Philip McElwaine (AUS)
2. Delroy Parkes (ENG)
3. Richard Betham (WSA)
Roddy MacDonald (CAN)
1982 1. Jimmy Price (ENG)
2. Douglas Sam (AUS)
3. Kevin McDermott (CAN)
Jeremiah Okorodudu (NGR)

81kg - LIGHT-HEAVYWEIGHT

1930 1. Joe Goyder (ENG)
2. Al Pitcher (CAN)
3. Joey Basson (SAF)
1934 1. George Brennan (ENG)
2. George Holton (SCO)
3. Sydney Leibrandt (SAF)
1938 1. Nicholaas Wolmarans (SAF)
2. Cecil Overell (AUS)
3. Joseph Wilby (ENG)
1950 1. Donald Scott (ENG)
2. Chris Rollinson (NZL)
3. Jack Taylor (AUS)
1954 1. Piet Van Vuuren (SAF)
2. Tony Madigan (AUS)
3. Norman Misselbrook (CAN)
1958 1. Tony Madigan (AUS)
2. Robert Higgins (WAL)
3. William Bannan (SCO)
Gerhardus de Bruyn (SAF)
1962 1. Tony Madigan (AUS)
2. Jojo Miles (GHA)
3. Hans Christie (NIR)
Thomas Menzies (SCO)
1966 1. Roger Tighe (ENG)
2. Fatai Ayinla (NGR)
3. Dennis Booth (AUS)
Sylvester Hines (JAM)
1970 1. Fatai Ayinla (NGR)
2. Oliver Wright (JAM)
3. Victor Attivor (GHA)
John Rafferty (SCO)
1974 1. Billy Knight (ENG)
2. William Byrne (NZL)
3. Gordon Ferris (NIR)
Isaac Ikhuoria (NGR)
1978 1. Roger Fortin (CAN)
2. Ronald Smith (ENG)
3. Faitala Su'A (WSA)
Edward Thande (KEN)
1982 1. Fine Sani (FIJ)
2. Jonathan Kirisa (UGA)
3. Kevin Barry (NZL)
Joseph Poto (ZAM)

Over 81kg - HEAVYWEIGHT

1930 1. Victor Stuart (ENG)
2. William Skimming (CAN)
Only two boxers
1934 1. Pat Floyd (ENG)
2. Jan van Rensburg (SAF)
3. Lord David Douglas-Hamilton (SCO)
1938 1. Thomas Osborne (CAN)
2. Claude Sterley (SAF)
3. Les Harley (AUS)
1950 1. Frank Creagh (NZL)
2. Sidney Cousins (AUS)
Only two boxers
1954 1. Brian Harper (ENG)
2. Gerald Buchanan (CAN)
3. George Jenkins (SAF)
1958 1. Daniel Bekker (SAF)
2. David Thomas (ENG)
3. Robert Pleace (WAL)
Gbadegesin Salawu (NGR)
1962 1. Geroge Oywello (UGA)
2. William Kini (NZL)
3. Holgar Johansen (FIJ)
Graham Robinson (AUS)
1966 1. William Kini (NZL)
2. Adonis Ray (GHA)
3. Daniel McAlinden (NIR)
Benon Ocan (UGA)
1970 1. Benson Masanda (UGA)
2. John McKinty (NIR)
3. Jack Meda (CAN)
Leslie Stevens (ENG)
1974 1. Neville Meade (ENG)
2. Fatai Ayinla (NGR)
3. Benson Masanda (UGA)
Vai Samu (WSA)
1978 1. Julius Awome (ENG)
2. Adamah Mensah (GHA)
3. George Stankovich (NZL)
1982 1. Willie DeWit (CAN)
2. Harold Hylton (ENG)
3. Willy Isangura (TAN)
Mohamed Abdallah Kent (KEN)

Associated Sports Photography

Pat Cowdell, another Games Champion to move on to professional success.

took the world title ten years later, then John Conteh won at middleweight for England in 1970 and went on to the world professional title at light-heavyweight four years later. Most recently Barry McGuigan and Azumah Nelson won world featherweight titles in 1985.

In the 1911 Festival of Empire, which preceded the Games proper, heavyweight boxing was included and most remarkably the winner, Harold Hardwick of Australia, had previously won the 100 yards freestyle swimming.

Boxing at the Commonwealth Games has at various times been plagued by indifferent judging and disputed decisions. Surely one of the most unfortunate competitors was John Coker, the Sierra Leone heavyweight who, in 1966, was unable to find a pair of gloves large enough for his enormous hands anywhere in Kingston and was disqualified prior to the competition for failing to be properly equipped. Not all decisions have unhappy endings. After the 1962 light-welterweight final Clement Quartey of Ghana was given the decision over Dick McTaggart, whereupon he fainted and had to be revived by officials.

A member of the British House of Lords won a boxing medal in 1934, Lord David Douglas-Hamilton at heavyweight for Scotland. It is unlikely that his achievement will be matched in Edinburgh.

Billy Knight of England (right), the 1974 light-heavyweight gold medallist, beat Gordon Ferris of Northern Ireland in the semi-final.

BOXING - MEDAL TABLE BY NATIONS

Nation	G	S	B	Total
England	27	15	24	66
Canada	9	10	22	41
Scotland	10	11	17	38
Australia	7	9	18	34
South Africa	14	6	7	26
Kenya	8	6	12	26
Northern Ireland	5	5	15	25
Ghana	8	8	5	21
Uganda	6	8	7	21
Nigeria	9	3	8	20
New Zealand	3	6	10	19
Zambia	1	8	10	19
Wales	2	9	5	16
Zimbabwe	1	4	3	8
Jamaica	2	3	2	7
India	-	1	4	5
Sri Lanka	1	2	1	4
Western Samoa	-	-	4	4
Fiji	1	-	2	3
Guyana	1	-	1	2
Papua-New Guinea	-	1	1	2
Tanzania	-	1	1	2
St. Vincent	1	-	-	1
Bahamas	-	-	1	1
Jersey	-	-	1	1
Malawi	-	-	1	1
Singapore	-	-	1	1
Swaziland	-	-	1	1

RUN WITH THE TRACK SPECIALISTS

Events like the Commonwealth Games present a real challenge. To organisers, competitors — and companies like ScotRail.

Visitors to Edinburgh want to get there quickly and with the minimum of fuss. Just the areas where our track record stands comparison with anyone.

High Speed Trains speed our customers into Edinburgh throughout the day — just 4½ hours, for example, from London or around 2½ hours from Aberdeen.

Luxury modern coaches provide on-train catering, air conditioning, comfortable seats and spacious luggage facilities.

InterCity sleepers have steward service available throughout the night. And in the morning, a refreshing cup of tea or coffee delivered to your compartment.

And on the West coast, you can enjoy the same facilities on Electric Scot daytime services and overnight sleepers, with a half hourly service linking Glasgow and Edinburgh when you arrive.

Whatever your choice of track, it's one run you're sure to enjoy . . . with ScotRail.

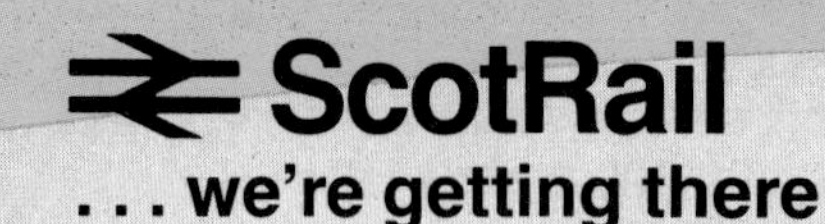
ScotRail
. . . we're getting there

CYCLING MEDALLISTS

SPRINT

(times given are for final 200m in the final)

1934 1. Ernest Higgins (ENG)
2. Horace Pethybridge (AUS)
3. Edward Clayton (SAF)
1938 1. Edgar Gray (AUS)
2. Robert Porter (AUS)
3. George Giles (NZL)
1950 1. Russell Mockridge (AUS) 12.3
2. Sidney Patterson (AUS)
3. George Avery (NZL)
1954 1. Cyril Peacock (ENG) 11.8
2. not awarded - Lionel Cox (AUS) disqualified in final
3. Tom Shardelow (SAF)
1958 1. Dick Ploog (AUS) 11.9
2. Karl Barton (ENG)
3. Lloyd Binch (ENG)
1962 1. Thomas Harrison (AUS) 12.0
2. Karl Barton (ENG)
3. Ian Browne (AUS)
1966 1. Roger Gibbon (TRI) 11.8 and 11.3
2. James Booker (ENG)
3. Daryl Perkins (AUS)
1970 1. John Nicholson (AUS) 12.21
2. Gordon Johnson (AUS)
3. Leslie King (TRI)
1974 1. John Nicholson (AUS) 12.71
2. Xavier Mirander (JAM)
3. Ian Atherley (TRI)
1978 1. Kenrick Tucker (AUS) 11.24
2. Trevor Gadd (ENG)
3. David Weller (JAM)
1982 1. Kenrick Tucker (AUS)
2. Michael McRedmond (NZL)
3. Murray Steele (NZL)

1000 METRES TIME TRIAL

1934 1. Edgar Gray (AUS) 1:16.4
2. Robert McLeod (CAN) 1:18.0
3. Edward Clayton (SAF) 1:8.6
1938 1. Robert Porter (AUS) 1:15.2
2. Tasman Johnson (AUS) 1:15.7
3. Ernest Mills (ENG) 1:15.9
1950 1. Russell Mockridge (AUS) 1:13.4
2. Sidney Patterson (AUS) 1:13.5
3. Thomas Godwin (ENG) 1:13.6
1954 1= Dick Ploog (AUS) 1:12.5
1= Alfred Swift (SAF) 1:12.5
3. Keith Harrison (ENG) 1:12.7
1958 1. Neville Tong (ENG) 1:12.1
2. Warren Scarfe (AUS) 1:12.4
3. Warwick Dalton (NZL) 1:12.6
1962 1. Peter Bartels (AUS) 1:12.9
2. Ian Chapman (AUS) 1:13.2
3. Roger Whitfield (ENG) 1:13.5
1966 1. Roger Gibbon (TRI) 1:09.6
2. Philip Bristow-Stagg (AUS) 1:10.9
3. Richard Hine (AUS) 1:11.0
1970 1. Harry Kent (NZL) 1:08.69
2. Leslie King (TRI) 1:10.40
3. Jocelyn Lovell (CAN) 1:10.53
1974 1. Dick Paris (AUS) 1:11.85
2. John Nicholson (AUS) 1:11.92
3. Ian Hallam (ENG) 1:12.15
1978 1. Jocelyn Lovell (CAN) 1.06.00
2. Kenrick Tucker (AUS) 1:06.96
3. Gordon Singleton (CAN) 1:07.56
1982 1. Craig Adair (NZL) 1:06.954
2. Chris Wilson (AUS) 1:07.926
3. Terence Tinsley (ENG) 1:07.932

4000 METRES INDIVIDUAL PURSUIT

1950 1. Cyril Cartwright (ENG) 5:16.3
2. Russell Mockridge (AUS) 5:27.0
3. Leslie Lock (NZL)
1954 1. Norman Sheil (ENG) 5:03.5
2. Peter Brotherton (ENG) 5:09.1
3. Robert Fowler (SAF)
1958 1. Norman Sheil (ENG) 5:10.2
2. Tom Simpson (ENG) 5:10.5
3. Warwick Dalton (NZL) 5:14.7
1962 1. Maxwell Langshaw (AUS) 5:08.2
2. Richard Hine (AUS) 5:13.2
3. Harry Jackson (ENG) 5:14.2
1966 1. Hugh Porter (ENG) 4:56.6
2. John Bylsma (AUS) 4:59.0
3. Richard Hine (AUS) 5:03.7
1970 1. Ian Hallam (ENG) 5:01.41
2. Danny Clark (AUS) 5:04.93
3. Blair Stockwell (NZL)
1974 1. Ian Hallam (ENG) 5:05.46
2. William Moore (ENG) 5:11.81
3. Gary Sutton (AUS)
1978 1. Michael Richards (NZL) 4:49.74
2. Gary Campbell (AUS) 4:55.68
3. Anthony Doyle (ENG) 4:55.87
1982 1. Michael Turtur (AUS) 4:50.990
2. Shaun Wallace (ENG) 4:51.347
3. Alex Stieda (CAN) 4:54.254

4000 METRES TEAM PURSUIT

1974 1. England 4:40.50
2. Australia 4:49.22
3. New Zealand
1978 1. Australia 4:29.43
2. New Zealand 4:37.73
3. England 4:51.18
1982 1. Australia 4:26.090
2. New Zealand 4:29.733
3. England 4:34.783

100 KILOMETRES ROAD TEAM TIME TRIAL

1982 1. England 2:09:27.00
2. Australia 2:09:33.62
3. New Zealand 2:10:55.96

TANDEM SPRINT

1970 1. Gordon Johnson & Ron Jonker (AUS) 11.43
2. Jocelyn Lovell & Barry Harvey (CAN)
3. John Hatfield & John Beswick (WAL)
1974 1. Geoffrey Cooke & Ernest Crutchlow (ENG) 10.74
2. John Rush & Danny O'Neil (AUS) 10.93
3. Paul Medhurst & Phil Harland (NZL) 11.10
1978 1. Jocelyn Lovell & Gordon Singleton (CAN) 15.52
2. Trevor Gadd & David Le Grys (ENG)
3. Ron Boyle & Stephen Goodall (AUS)

10 MILES TRACK

1934 1. Robert McLeod (CAN) 24:26.2
2. Edward Clayton (SAF)
3. William Harvell (ENG)
1938 1. William Maxfield (ENG) 24:44.0
2. Ray Hicks (ENG)
3. Sydney Rose (SAF)
1950 1. William Heseltine (AUS) 23:23.4
2. Leslie Lock (NZL) 23:23.4
3. Kenneth Caves (AUS)
1954 1. Lindsay Cocks (AUS) 21:59.5
2. Keith Harrison (ENG)
3. Donald Skene (WAL)
1958 1. Ian Browne (AUS) 21:40.2
2. Warren Johnston (NZL)
3. Donald Skene (WAL)
1962 1. Douglas Adams (AUS) 22:10.8
2. Warren Johnston (NZL)
3. John Clarey (ENG)
1966 1. Ian Alsop (ENG) 21:46.0
2. Hilton Clarke (AUS) 21:46.4
3. Trevor Bull (ENG) 21:46.8
1970 1. Jocelyn Lovell (CAN) 20:46.72
2. Brian Temple (SCO) 20:47.56
3. Vernon Stauble (TRI) 20:47.72
1974 1. Stephen Heffernan (AUS) 20:51.25
2. Stepehn Heffernan (AUS) 20:51.61
3. Ian Hallam (ENG) 20:51.66
1978 1. Jocelyn Lovell (CAN) 20:05.81

Cycling

Associated Sports Photography

Intense concentration for competitors in the Games' longest event, the cycling road race in 1974.

Cycling events have been included at all Games except the first, but so far only for men. Women's events, at sprint, 3000m individual pursuit and 60km road race, are to be staged for the first time in Auckland in 1990.

In 1934 when cycling was first included, all three events, 1000m time trial, 1000m sprint and the 10 miles, were held on the same day. It was thus outstanding for Ed Clayton of Canada to win medals at all three disciplines. One of the winners, Edgar 'Dunc' Gray of Australia, became the first man to win Olympic and Commonwealth titles in the sport. Five more of his countrymen were to emulate this achievement over the years: Russell Mockridge, Ian Browne, Michael Turtur, Kevin Nichols and Michael Grenda, but only Mockridge matched Gray's feat of individual gold medals at both Games.

The most successful cyclist at the Games has been Jocelyn Lovell of Canada, who uniquely won three gold medals in one year, when in 1978 he won the 1000m time trial, the 10 miles, and teamed up with Gordon Singleton to win the tandem. He had previously won gold, silver and bronze medals in 1970. He later married the speed skater Sylvia Burka, but was tragically struck down by a lorry while out training in 1983 and is now a quadraplegic. The Australian cyclist Russell Mockridge was killed in a similar accident in 1958 when he collided with a bus during a professional road race. He had won two gold medals at Auckland in 1950, but then retired from the sport to study for the Ministry. However, he came to feel that he could not aspire to the high ideals required for such a calling and returned to further cycling successes.

The most medals won at one Games are four, two gold and two bronze, by Ian Hallam of England in 1974, while New Zealand's Blair Stockwell uniquely won medals over a span of twelve years, 1970 to 1982. Probably

10 Mile Track continued

	2.	Shane Sutton (AUS) 20:06.00
	3.	Gary Sutton (AUS) 20:06.10
1982	1.	Kevin Nichols (AUS) 19:56.559
	2.	Gary Hammond (AUS) 19:56.639
	3.	Michael Turtur (AUS) 19:56.660

ROAD RACE

Raced over 100km 1938-54, 120 miles (193km) 1958-66, 164.6km 1970, 183km 1974, 117 miles (188km) 1978 184km 1982

1938	1.	Hendrik Binneman (SAF) 2:53:29.6
	2.	John Brown (NZL) 2:53:29.8
	3.	Raymond Jones (ENG) 2:53:29.9
1950	1.	Hector Sutherland (AUS) 3:13:06.4
	2.	Richard Carter (NZL) 3:13:06.5
	3.	John Fowler (AUS) 3:13:06.6
1954	1.	Eric Thompson (ENG) 2:44:08.1
	2.	John Baird (NZL)
	3.	Bernard Pusey (ENG)
1958	1.	Ray Booty (ENG) 5:16:33.7
	2.	Frank Brazier (AUS) 5:19:21.7
	3.	Stuart Slack (IOM) 5:19:21.7
1962	1.	Wesley Mason (ENG) 5:20:26.2
	2.	Anthony Walsh (NZL) 5:20:27.0
	3.	Laurence Byers (NZL) 5:20:27.2
1966	1.	Peter Buckley (IOM) 5:07:52.5
	2.	Desmond Thompson (NZL) 5:12:11.2
	3.	Laurence Byers (NZL) 5:12:19.8
1970	1.	Bruce Biddle (NZL) 4:38:05.8
	2.	Raymond Bilney (AUS) 4:39:05.9
	3.	John Trevorrow (AUS) 4:40:03.0
1974	1.	Clyde Sefton (AUS) 5:07:16.87
	2.	Phil Griffiths (ENG) 5:07:45.95
	3.	Remo Sansonetti (AUS) 5:17:26.80
1978	1.	Philip Anderson (AUS) 4:22:34.41
	2.	Pierre Harvey (CAN) 4:22:34.55
	3.	Garry Bell (NZL) 4:22:35.06
1982	1.	Malcolm Elliott (ENG) 4:34:40.06
	2.	Stephen Bauer (CAN) 4:34:41.00
	3.	Roger Sumich (NZL) 4:34:41.35

CYCLING - MEDAL TABLE BY NATIONS

Nation	G	S	B	Total
Australia	27	26	12	65
England	19	12	17	48
New Zealand	4	11	14	29
Canada	5	4	3	12
South Africa	2	1	5	8
Trinidad & Tobago	2	1	3	6
Wales	-	-	3	3
Isle of Man	1	-	1	2
Jamaica	-	1	1	2
Scotland	-	1	-	1

the youngest gold medallist was 17-year-old Dick Ploog of Australia, who tied for the 1000m time trial title in 1954. That was the only tie in Games history until the celebrated 200m athletics final in 1982. Ploog won a further gold medal, this time all to himself, in the sprint in 1958. Only Russell Mockridge won both sprint and time trial at the same Games.

The tallest gold medallist was the 2.01m (6ft 7in) Mike Richards of New Zealand, the winner of the 4000m individual pursuit in 1978, and the first brothers to win gold medals were Gary and Shane Sutton (AUS) in the team pursuit at the same Games.

Perhaps the most curious decision to affect medals came in the 1978 tandem sprint. The English pair, Trevor Gadd and David Le Grys, were disqualified in the semi-finals for forcing the New Zealand pair, Eric MacKenzie and Charles Fabish, off the track. Because one of the New Zealanders was so shaken by the resulting fall that he could take no further part in the proceedings, the English team was reinstated and allowed to compete in the final. In the first race of the final series they suffered a burst tyre and crashed. Both Gadd and Le Grys were carried off on stretchers and the gold medal went to Canada. Despite their semi-final disqualification they were awarded the silver medals, and the luckless New Zealanders missed out completely.

There have been many close races which have caused the judges considerable difficulties in determining placings. In the 10 miles track race in 1950 just a fifth of a second separated the first three finishers, and in that year in the road race there was only half a second between first and fifth. In the 1958 road race Ray Booty (ENG) won by nearly three minutes, but the next five riders all shared the same time. In contrast the biggest margin of victory has been 4 minutes 18.7 seconds for Peter Buckley in the 1966 road race over 120 miles. This was the only gold medal won by an Isle of Man competitor in Games history.

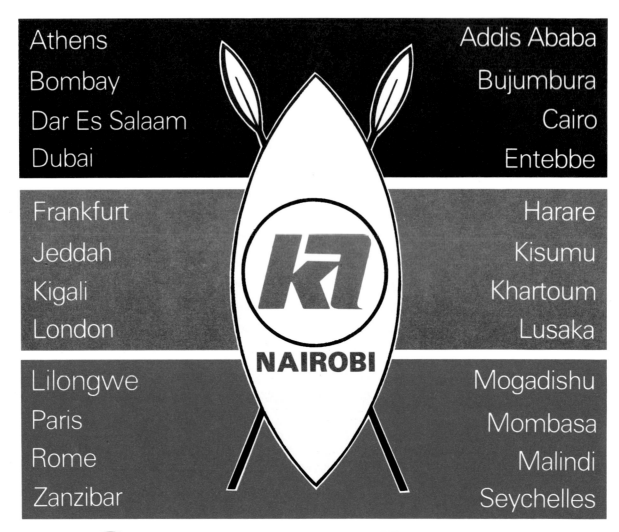

A great track record.
WM. McEWAN
BREWER
80/-
CASK CONDITIONED
FOUNTAIN BREWERY EDINBURGH
WM. McEWAN
BREWER
80/-
FOUNTAIN BREWERY EDINBURGH

FENCING MEDALLISTS

MEN'S FOIL - INDIVIDUAL

1950 1. René Paul (ENG)
2. John Fethers (AUS)
3. George Pouliot (CAN)
1954 1. René Paul (ENG)
2. John Fethers (AUS)
3. Allan Jay (ENG)
1958 1. Raymond Paul (ENG)
2. Ivan Lund (AUS)
3. René Paul (ENG)
1962 1. Alexander Leckie (SCO)
2. Allan Jay (ENG)
3. Ralph Cooperman (ENG)
1966 1. Allan Jay (ENG)
2. William Hoskyns (ENG)
3. Graham Paul (ENG)
1970 1. Mike Breckin (ENG)
2. Barry Paul (ENG)
3. Graham Paul (ENG)

MEN'S FOIL - TEAM

1950 1. England
2. New Zealand
3. Canada
1954 1. England
2. Australia
3. Canada
1958 1. England
2. Australia
3. Wales
1962 1. England
2. Australia
3. Canada
1966 1. England
2. Australia
3. Scotland
1970 1. England
2. Australia
3. Canada

MEN'S EPEE - INDIVIDUAL

1950 1. Charles-Louis de Beaumont (ENG)
2. Robert Anderson (ENG)
3. Ivan Lund (AUS)
1954 1. Ivan Lund (AUS)
2. René Paul (ENG)
3. Carl Schwende (CAN)
1958 1. William Hoskyns (ENG)
2. Michael Howard (ENG)
3. Allan Jay (ENG)
1962 1. Ivan Lund (AUS)
2. John Pelling (ENG)
3. Peter Jacobs (ENG)
1966 1. William Hoskyns (ENG)
2. John Pelling (ENG)
3. Robert Reynolds (WAL)
1970 1. William Hoskyns (ENG)
2. Lester Wyong (CAN)
3. Peter Jacobs (ENG)

MEN'S EPEE - TEAM

1950 1. Australia
2. England
3. Canada
1954 1. England
2. Canada
3. Australia
1958 1. England
2. Canada
3. Australia
1962 1. England
2. Australia
3. Canada
1966 1. England
2. Canada
3. Australia
1970 1. England
2. Scotland
3. Canada

MEN'S SABRE - INDIVIDUAL

1950 1. Arthur Pilbrow (ENG)
2. Robert Anderson (ENG)
3. George Pouliot (CAN)
1954 1. Michael Amberg (ENG)
2. Ralph Cooperman (ENG)
3. John Fethers (AUS)
1958 1. William Hoskyns (ENG)
2. Ralph Cooperman (ENG)
3. Mike Amberg (ENG)
1962 1. Ralph Cooperman (ENG)
2. Benedek Simo (CAN)
3. John Andru (CAN)
1966 1. Ralph Cooperman (ENG)
2. Alexander Leckie (SCO)
3. Gabor Arato (AUS)
1970 1. Alexander Leckie (SCO)
2. Rodney Craig (ENG)
3. Richard Cohen (ENG)

MEN'S SABRE - TEAM

1950 1. England
2. Canada
3. Australia
1954 1. Canada
2. England
3. Australia
1958 1. England
2. Australia
3. Wales
1962 1. England
2. Canada
3. New Zealand
1966 1. England
2. Australia
3. Canada
1970 1. England
2. Scotland
3. Australia

WOMEN'S FOIL INDIVIDUAL

1950 1. Mary Glen-Haig (ENG)
2. Patricia Woodroffe (NZL)
3. Catherine Pym (AUS)
1954 1. Mary Glen-Haig (ENG)
2. Gillian Sheen (ENG)
3. Aileen Harding (WAL)
1958 1. Gillian Sheen (ENG)
2. Barbara McCreath (AUS)
3. Mary Glen-Haig (ENG)
1962 1. Melody Coleman (NZL)
2. Johanna Winter (AUS)
3. Janet Hopner (AUS)
1966 1. Janet Wardell-Yerburgh (ENG)
2. Shirley Parker (ENG)
3. Gaye McDermitt (NZL)
1970 1. Janet Wardell-Yerburgh (ENG)
2. Marion Exelby (AUS)
3. Susan Youngs (SCO)

WOMEN'S FOIL - TEAM

1966 1. England
2. Australia
3. New Zealand
1970 1. England
2. Scotland
3. Canada

FENCING - MEDAL TABLE BY NATIONS

Nation	Men			Women			Total
	G	S	B	G	S	B	
England	30	14	10	7	2	1	64
Australia	3	11	9	-	4	2	29
Canada	1	7	12	-	-	1	21
Scotland	2	3	1	-	1	1	8
New Zealand	-	1	1	1	1	2	6
Wales	-	-	3	-	-	1	4

Fencing

Although fencing was only included in the Games from 1950 to 1970, some competitors accumulated remarkable collections of medals. The most was 13 collected by the Australian Ivan Lund, equalled at any sport only by the swimmer Mike Wenden. Lund's three gold, six silver and four bronze were won between 1950 and 1962 at all three disciplines of foil, épée and sabre. Bill Hoskyns of England achieved a record number of gold medals at any sport with nine, again with all three weapons, as well as a silver. Other multiple medallists were the Englishmen René Paul, eight gold, one silver, one bronze; Ralph Cooperman, seven, three and one; and Allan Jay, eight, one and two respectively. Jay won his first gold in 1950 as a member of the Australian épée team, but won the rest of his medals for England. His medal winning over five Games is a record for any sport.

The most successful fencers at one Games were René Paul and Bill Hoskyns who each won three gold medals and a silver in 1954 and 1966 respectively. The women's record was set by Janet Wardell-Yerburgh, who won a record four medals in 1966 and 1970 at individual and team foil events, but the team event had not been included prior to 1966, so that double gold medallist Mary Glen-Haig of England did not have the opportunity of matching her. Glen-Haig, later Britain's first woman International Olympic Committee representative, also won a bronze medal in 1958, ten days after her fortieth birthday.

The oldest fencing gold medallist was Charles-Louis de Beaumont of England who won the individual épée title when just short of his 48th birthday, and was then a member of the winning épée team in 1954 at the age of 52. England's Arthur Pilbrow won the sabre title and two team golds in 1950 when just two weeks younger than de Beaumont. One of the youngest medallists was Graham Paul who was just 19 when he fenced on two winning teams in 1966. His family, with his father René, uncle Raymond and brother Barry, won 13 gold, 2 silver and 2 bronze at the Commonwealth Games.

HAND WOVEN
Harris Tweed
THE HARRIS TWEED ASSOCIATION LIMITED
REGISTERED TRADE MARK No.319214
HARRIS TWEED
HANDWOVEN IN THE OUTER HEBRIDES
FROM SCOTTISH GROWN WOOL
100% WOOL
225037

GYMNASTICS MEDALLISTS

MEN'S INDIVIDUAL

1978 1. Philip Delesalle (CAN) 56.40 points
2. Lindsay Nylund (AUS) 54.95
3. Jean Choquette (CAN) 54.25

MEN'S TEAM

1978 1. Canada 165.55
2. England 161.95
3. Australia 158.50

WOMEN'S INDIVIDUAL

1978 1. Elfi Schlegel (CAN) 38.25
2= Sherry Hawco (CAN) 37.25
2= Monica Goermann (CAN) 37.25

WOMEN'S TEAM

1978 1. Canada 113.25
2. England 107.40
3. New Zealand 106.35

Gymnastics

Although a popular international sport, gymnastics has been held at just one Commonwealth Games - at Edmonton in 1978. The host country, Canada, won all four golds, with Elfi Schlegel, in the women's events, and Philip Delesalle, in the men's, winning two golds each.

Unfortunately the standard of gymnastics in Commonwealth countries is not particularly high, and only Great Britain, Australia and Canada were represented at the sport at the 1984 Olympic Games.

GYMNASTICS - MEDAL TABLE BY NATIONS

Nation	G	S	B	Total
Canada	4	2	1	7
England	-	2	-	2
Australia	-	1	1	2
New Zealand	-	-	1	1

Elfi Schlegel on the beam, 1978.

ROWING MEDALLISTS

SINGLE SCULLS

1930 1. Bobby Pearce (AUS) 8:03.6
2. Jack Beresford (ENG)
3. Fred Bradley (ENG)

1938 1. Herbert Turner (AUS) 8:24.0
2. Peter Jackson (ENG) 5 lengths
3. Robert Smith (NZL) 4 lengths

1950 1. Mervyn Wood (AUS) 7:46.8
2. Anthony Rowe (ENG) 7:54.0
3. Ian Stephen (SAF) 8:03.0

1954 1. Donald Rowlands (NZL) 8:28.2
2. Sidney Rand (ENG) 8:43.4
3. Robert Williams (CAN) 8:51.3

1958 1. Stuart Mackenzie (AUS) 7:20.1
2. James Hill (NZL) 7:23.9
3. Russell Carver (ENG) 7:26.8

1962 1. James Hill (NZL) 7:39.7
2. William Barry (ENG) 7:44.9
3. Ian Tutty (NZL) 7:48.9

DOUBLE SCULLS

1930 1. Elswood Bole & Bob Richards (CAN) 7:48.0
US crews finished 2nd and 3rd as guest competitors

1938 1. William Bradley & Cecil Pearce (AUS) 7:29.4
2. Robert Offer & Jack Offer (ENG) 9 lengths
3. Angus Jackson & Robert Smith (NZL) 10 lengths
No medals awarded as the event was described as an invitation event.

1950 1. Mervyn Wood & Murray Riley (AUS) 7:22.0
2. Joe Schneider & Des Simonsen (NZL) 7:32.0
3. Kenneth Tinegate & Jack Brown (ENG) 7:39.0

1954 1. Mervyn Wood & Murray Riley (AUS) 7:54.5
2. Robert Parker & Reginald Douglas (ENG) 8:05.2 NZL
3. Donald Guest & Lawrence Stephan (CAN) 8:28.5

1958 1. Michael Spracklen & Geoffrey Baker (ENG) 6:54.4
2. Mervyn Wood & Stuart Mackenzie (AUS) 7:01.4
3. Norman Suckling & James Hill (NZL)

1962 1. George Justice & Nicholas Birkmyre (ENG) 6:52.4
2. Peter Watkinson & Murray Watkinson (NZL) 6:54.3
3. Barclay Wade & Graeme Squires (AUS) 7:01.4

COXLESS PAIRS

1950 1. Walter Lambert & Jack Webster (AUS) 7:58.0
2. David Gould & Humphrey Gould (NZL) 8:10.0
Only two crews

1954 1. Robert Parker & Reginald Douglas (NZL) 8:23.9
2. Thomas Christie & Nicholas Clack (ENG) 8:24.1
3. David Anderson & Geoffrey Williamson (AUS) 8:29.7

1958 1. Robert Parker & Reginald Douglas (NZL) 7:11.1
2. Michael Hall & Stewart Douglas-Mann (ENG) 7:13.7
3. Steven Roll & Kevin Webb (AUS)

1962 1. Stewart Farquharson & James Lee-Nicholson (ENG) 7:03.7
2. Graham Lawrence & Murray Lawrence (NZL) 7:08.5
3. Rodger Ninham & William Hatfield (AUS)

COXLESS FOURS

1930 1. England 7:04.6
2. Canada
3. New Zealand

1958 1. England 6:34.4
2. Canada 6:38.9
3. Wales 6:47.9

1962 1. England 6:31.1
2. Wales 6:32.5
3. Canada 6:34.9

COXED FOURS

1930 1. New Zealand 8:02.0
2. Canada 4 lengths
3. British Guiana 2 lengths

1938 1. Australia 7:16.8
2. New Zealand 1¼ lengths
3. Canada ¾ length

1950 1. New Zealand 7:17.2
2. Australia 7:24.0
Only two crews

1954 1. Australia 7:58.3
2. New Zealand 8:04.4
3. England 8:04.5

1958 1. England 6:46.5
2. Canada 6:53.2
3. Australia

1962 1. New Zealand 6:48.2
2. Australia 6:48.8
3. England 7:04.9

EIGHTS

1930 1. England 6:37.0
2. New Zealand ¾ length
3. Canada 5 lengths

1938 1. England 6:29.0
2. Australia ¾ length
3. New Zealand 2 lengths

1950 1. Australia 6:27.0
2. New Zealand 6:27.5
3. England 6:40.0

1954 1. Canada 6:59.0
2. England 7:10.5
Only two crews

1958 1. Canada 5:51.1
2. Australia 5:56.1
3. England 6:10.2

1962 1. Australia 5:53.4
2. New Zealand 5:53.6
3. England 6:09.4

ROWING - MEDAL TABLE BY NATIONS (1930, 1938-62)

Nation	G	S	B	Total
England	9	9	8	26
New Zealand	7	10	5	22
Australia	11	5	5	21
Canada	3	4	5	12
Wales	-	1	1	2
Guyana	-	-	1	1
South Africa	-	-	1	1

Joy for the British eights crew at the Olympic Games in 1980, when they won the silver medal.

Associated Sports Photography

Rowing

Having last been held in 1962, rowing is being re-introduced to the Games in 1986, when for the first time women's events will be included.

Rowing was one of the original sports staged at the 1930 Games when, somewhat curiously, American oarsmen were invited to compete in certain events. In the double sculls an English pair were the only opposition against the host country, Canada, and when they withdrew two American crews were allowed to row. Canada won the race and the gold medals, but the Americans did not count in the medal tables.

Single sculler Steven Redgrave of England - a name to look for in 1986.

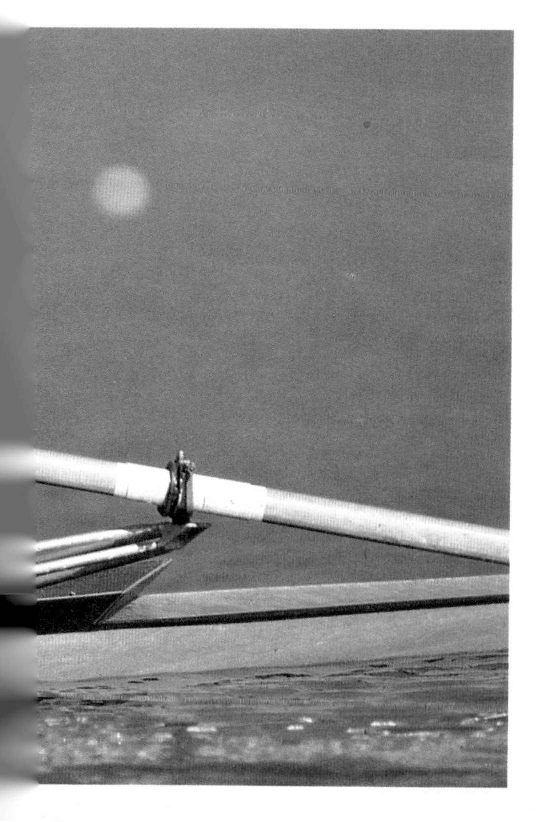

Although a number of oarsmen have won medals at both Commonwealth and Olympic Games, reflecting the high standard of rowing in the Commonwealth, only two have won individual gold medals at both Games, the Australians Bobby Pearce and Mervyn Wood. Pearce was the reigning Olympic champion at the time of the 1930 Games and was a big attraction in Hamilton, with thousands turning out to watch him train. Although matched against a former Olympic champion, England's Jack Beresford, Pearce won easily. He so liked Canada that he stayed there, even after retaining his Olympic title in 1932. His father, Harry, who coached him, had been a world professional champion. Bobby, too, turned professional, won the world title and retired undefeated at the beginning of the War. Mervyn Wood competed at three Commonwealth Games, 1950-8, winning three golds and a silver medal. He was the oldest champion when he took first place in the double sculls and coxed fours on the same afternoon in 1954 when aged 37 years 96 days. In 1958 he won a silver medal aged 41 years 83 days, another record. All this despite being slightly handicapped by a partially withered hand. He was a fingerprint expert with the New South Wales police force, and ended his career as their Police Commissioner.

The nearest that anyone has come to winning two single sculls titles was when James Hill (NZL) won gold in 1962 after silver in 1958. The title has never been won by any sculler from outside Australasia. Just one man has won medals in single sculls and eights contests, Peter Jackson of England, a gold in the eights and a silver in the sculls in 1938.

The most successful partnership was that of Robert Parker and Reg Douglas of New Zealand. They started their Games career with a silver medal at double sculls in 1954 and later the same day won the coxless pairs. They retained the latter in 1958.

Perhaps the smallest man ever to win a gold medal at the Games was the cox of the New Zealand fours in 1930. He was Arthur Eastwood, who was a top-class jockey and who had ridden the winner of the New Zealand Cup in 1929. A member of that foursome, Jack Macdonald, also a rugby player, became the first Maori to win a Commonwealth gold medal.

The South African sculler Ian Stephen caused some merriment at the post-Games dinner in 1950. He won the bronze medal but as his country's sole representative was also the team manager and coach, so in the latter roles he praised his team, as a member of the team he praised his team manager and the coach, and as coach he praised the team and team manager!

SHOOTING MEDALLISTS

SMALL BORE RIFLE
(.22 rifle)

1966 1. Gilmour Boa (CAN) 587
2. Brian Lacey (NZ) 585
John Murphy (AUS) 584

1974 1. Yvonne Gowland (AUS) 594
2. Bill Watkins (WAL) 591
3. Alister Allan (SCO) 591

1978 1. Alister Allan (SCO) 1194
2. Bill Watkins (WAL) 1191
3. Stewart Watterson (IOM) 1187

PRONE

1982 1. Alan Smith (AUS) 1184
2. Malcolm Cooper (ENG) 1184
3. Bill Watkins (WAL) 1177

THREE POSITIONS

1982 1. Alister Allan (SCO) 1146
2. Malcolm Cooper (ENG) 1145
3. Guy Lorion (CAN) 1144

SMALL BORE RIFLE - THREE POSITIONS - TEAM

1982 1. Malcolm Cooper & Barry Dagger (ENG) 2301
2. Guy Lorian & Jean-Francois Senecal (CAN) 2279
3. Alister Allan & Bill MacNeil (SCO) 2277

SMALL BORE RIFLE - PRONE - TEAM

1982 1. Malcolm Cooper & Mike Sullivan (ENG) 1187
2. Colin Harris & Bill Watkins (WAL) 1183
3. Patrick Vamplew & Ernest Sopsich (CAN) 1180

FULL BORE RIFLE
(.303 rifle 1966, 7.62 rifle from 1974)

1966 1. Lord (John) Swansea (WAL) 394
2. Robert Stewart (PNG) 381
3. Tom Sutherland (NZ) 381

1974 1. Maurice Gordon (NZ) 387.26
2. Colin McEachran (SCO) 386.27
3. James Spaight (ENG) 383.35

1978 1. Desmond Vamplew (CAN) 391
2. James Spaight (ENG) 388
3. Patrick Vamplew (CAN) 387

1982 1. Arthur Clarke (SCO) 387
2. Lord (John) Swansea (WAL) 385
3. Charles Trotter (GUE) 384

FULL BORE RIFLE - TEAM

1982 1. Keith Affleck & Geoffrey Ayling (AUS) 572
2. John Bloomfield & Dick Rosling (ENG) 570
3. Hazel Mackintosh & David Calvert (NI) 563

FREE PISTOL
(.22 single shot)

1966 1. Charles Sexton (ENG) 544
2. Jules Sobrian (CAN) 538
3. Garfield McMahon (CAN) 536

1974 1. Jules Sobrian (CAN) 549
2. Norman Harrison (AUS) 549
3. Laslo Antal (ENG) 543

1978 1. Yvon Trempe (CAN) 543
2. Edward Jans (CAN) 540
3. Bertram Manhim (TRI) 536

1982 1. Thomas Guinn (CAN) 553
2. Geoffrey Robinson (ENG) 543
3. Phillip Adams (AUS) 540

FREE PISTOL - TEAM

1982 1. Phillip Adams & John Tremelling (AUS) 1077
2. Barrie Wickens & Rex Hamilton (NZ) 1075
3. Geoffrey Robinson & Frank Wyatt (ENG) 1074

CENTRE FIRE PISTOL

1966 1. James Lee (CAN) 576
2. Anthony Clark (ENG) 575
3. Julio Machado (JAM) 571

1982 1. John Cooke (ENG) 580
2. James Cairns (SCO) 579
3. Noel Ryan (AUS) 577

CENTRE FIRE PISTOL - TEAM

1982 1. Noel Ryan & Alexander Taransjy (AUS) 1151
2. Mohinder Lal & Ashok Pandit (IND) 1138
3. John Cooke & John Gough (ENG) 1131

RAPID FIRE PISTOL
(.22 semi automatic)

1966 1. Anthony Clark (ENG) 585
2. Michael Papps (AUS) 578
3. Jules Sobrian (CAN) 572

1974 1. William Hare (CAN) 586
2. Jules Sobrian (CAN) 583
3. Bruce McMillan (NZ) 581

1978 1. Jules Sobrian (CAN) 587
2. John Cooke (ENG) 581
3. Jeff Farrell (AUS) 581

1982 1. Solomon Lee (HK) 583
2. Jimmy Timmerman (CAN) 583
3. John Cooke (ENG) 582

RAPID FIRE PISTOL - TEAM

1982 1. Peter Heuke & Alexander Taransky (AUS) 1160
2. James Cairns & Hugh Hunter (SCO) 1152
3. Sharad Cahuran & R.K. Vij (IND) 1151

OLYMPIC TRAP
(Clay Pigeon)

1974 1. John Primrose (CAN) 196
2. Brian Bailey (ENG) 193
3. Philip Lewis (WAL) 191

1978 1. John Primrose (CAN) 186
2. George Leary (CAN) 185
3. Terry Rumbel (AUS) 183

1982 1. Peter Boden (ENG) 191
2. Terry Rumbel (AUS) 190
3. Peter Croft (ENG) 190

OLYMPIC TRAP - TEAM

1982 1. Jim Ellis & Terry Rumbel (AUS) 190
2. Peter Croft & Peter Boden (ENG) 186
3. James Young & Martin Girvan (SCO) 183

SKEET

1974 1. Harry Willsie (CAN) 194
2. Joe Neville (ENG) 191
3. Robin Bailey (AUS) 189

1978 1. Lawrence Woolley (NZ) 193
2. Paul Bentley (ENG) 191
3. Joe Neville (ENG) 190

1982 1. John Woolley (NZ) 197
2. Ian Hale (AUS) 196
3. Wally Sykes (ENG) 195

SKEET - TEAM

1982 1. Brian Gabriel & Fred Altmann (CAN) 191
2. Jim Sheffield & Wally Sykes (ENG) 190
3. Alex Crikis & Ian Hale (AUS) 190

AIR PISTOL

1982 1. George Darling (ENG) 576
2. Phillip Adams (AUS) 573
3. Thomas Guinn (CAN) 571

AIR PISTOL - TEAM

1982 1. Phillip Adams & Gregory Colbert (AUS) 1128
2. Geoffrey Robinson & George Darling (ENG) 1126
3. Jimmy Timmermann & Thomas Guinn (CAN) 1125

AIR RIFLE

1982 1. Jean-Francois Senecal (CAN) 574
2. Matthew Guille (GUE) 572
3. Malcolm Cooper (ENG) 570

AIR RIFLE - TEAM

1982 1. Alister Allan & Bill McNeil (SCO) 1137
2. Malcolm Cooper & Barry Dagger (ENG) 1126
3. Norbert John & Anton Wurfel (AUS) 1123

Shooting

Malcolm Cooper, world record holder and Olympic champion at the small bore rifle

Shooting is the one sport at the Games at which men and women compete together in direct competition. The first woman to win a gold medal was Mrs Yvonne Gowland in the 1974 small bore rifle event, when she beat predominantly male opposition. To date only one other woman has won a medal, Hazel Mackintosh of Northern Ireland in the 1982 full bore rifle.

Shooting was first included at the Games in Kingston in 1966, when there were five events, all individual competitions. England and Canada won two golds each with the fifth going to Lord Swansea, appropriately of Wales. The English winner of the free pistol title, Charles Sexton, was 59 years 328 days old, a record for the shooting events, although the 1982 full bore rifle champion, Arthur Clarke of Scotland, was also in his sixtieth year. Lord Swansea set a record in 1982 as he gained a silver medal after a 16-year gap.

After the sport was not held in 1970, the programme was increased to six events in 1974 and 1978, and there was then a massive expansion in 1982 to twenty individual and team competitions. This programme is being repeated in 1986. The greatest number of gold medals won by one marksman is three by Alister Allan of Scotland in 1978-82 and Englishman Malcolm Cooper won a record six medals at one Games in 1982, two gold, three silver and a bronze. He went on in 1984 to become the first Commonwealth gold medallist to win an Olympic title. In the days when there were fewer events Trinidad-born Dr. Jules Sobrian, representing Canada, collected two gold, three silver and a bronze, progressing from bronze to silver to gold in the rapid-fire pistol in 1966, 1974 and 1978. The Vamplew brothers from Canada won medals in the same event, the 1978 full bore rifle, gold for Desmond and bronze for Patrick.

Malcolm Cooper with his wife Sheila - both could be strong contenders in 1986.

SHOOTING - MEDAL TABLE BY NATIONS

Nation	G	S	B	Total
England	7	14	9	30
Canada	13	6	7	26
Australia	8	5	8	21
Scotland	4	3	3	10
New Zealand	3	2	2	7
Wales	1	4	2	7
Guernsey	-	1	1	2
India	-	1	1	2
Hong Kong	1	-	-	1
Papua-New Guinea	-	1	-	1
Isle of Man	-	-	1	1
Jamaica	-	-	1	1
Northern Ireland	-	-	1	1
Trinidad & Tobago	-	-	1	1

Now you can relax in Scandinavian style without leaving home.

PLAYHOUSE made from the finest Swedish pine.
Size 8′ x 5′.

GRILLHOUSE made from the finest Swedish pine.
Size 11′ x 9′.

SVENSKA LOG HOUSE

SVENSKA LEISUREHOUSE

James Donaldson & Sons Ltd. started as Timber Importers and Sawmillers in 1860. The business is still family-owned and has expanded considerably over the last ten years, we have been looking for some time now for a product appealing to both the trade and general public which will widen our product base and in the *Svenska Collection*, we have found it.

The *Svenska Collection* incorporating the finest Swedish materials and craftsmanship, ranges from hanging flower baskets to four apartment holiday homes including the products illustrated here.

The *Svenska Collection* has been tried and tested with great success on the Continent for several years and it gives us great pleasure to introduce this exciting range to Scotland for the first time. We are the sole U.K. distributors for the *Svenska Collection*.

James Donaldson & Sons Ltd.

Sole UK distributors for the Svenska Collection.

James Donaldson & Sons Limited
'The Svenska Collection'
Wemyss Sawmills, Leven, Fife KY8 4PS

Name ____________________

Address ____________________

____

____

I would like to receive a free colour brochure and price list

SWIMMING MEDALLISTS

100 METRES FREESTYLE

100 yards (91.44m) 1930-4, 110 yards (100.58m) 1938-66

1930 1. Munro Bourne (CAN) 56.0
2. Norman Brooks (ENG) 56.1
3. Bert Gibson (CAN
1934 1. George Burleigh (CAN) 55.0
2. George Larsen (CAN) 55.6
3. Noel Crump (NZL) 56.2
1938 1. Bob Pirie (CAN) 59.6
2. Terry Collard (SAF) 1:00.8
3. Bill Fleming (AUS) 1:01.0
1950 1. Peter Salmon (CAN) 1:00.4
2. Frank O'Neill (AUS) 1:00.6
3. Peter Kendall (ENG) 1:01.8
1954 1. Jon Henricks (AUS) 56.5
2. Cyrus Weld (AUS) 58.5
3. Rex Aubrey (AUS) 58.7
1958 1. John Devitt (AUS) 56.6
2. Gary Chapman (AUS) 56.6
3. Geoff Shipton (AUS) 57.0
1962 1. Richard Pound (CAN) 55.8
2. Bobby McGregor (SCO) 56.1
3. David Dickson (AUS) 56.1
1966 1. Mike Wenden (AUS) 54.0
2. Bobby McGregor (SCO) 54.2
3. David Dickson (AUS) 54.6
1970 1. Mike Wenden (AUS) 53.06
2. Greg Rogers (AUS) 54.26
3. William Devenish (AUS) 54.28
1974 1. Mike Wenden (AUS) 52.73
2. Bruce Robertson (CAN) 53.78
3. Brian Phillips (CAN) 54.11
1978 1. Mark Morgan (AUS) 52.70
2. Bill Sawchuk (CAN) 52.81
3. Gary MacDonald (CAN) 52.90
1982 1. Neil Brooks (AUS) 51.14
2. Greg Fasala (AUS) 51.28
3. Michael Delany (AUS) 51.57

200 METRES FREESTYLE

1970 1. Mike Wenden (AUS) 1:56.69
2. Ralph Hutton (CAN) 1:58.45
3. Greg Rogers (AUS) 1:58.63
1974 1. Steve Badger (AUS) 1:56.72
2. Bruce Robertson (CAN) 1:57.21
3. Mike Wenden (AUS) 1:57.83
1978 1. Ron McKeon (AUS) 1:52.06
2. Graeme Brewer (AUS) 1:52.86
3. Mark Morgan (AUS) 1:53.16
1982 1. Andrew Astbury (ENG) 1:51.52
2. Peter Szmidt (CAN) 1:51.65
3. Ron McKeon (AUS) 1:51.71

400 METRES FREESTYLE

400 yards (365.76m) 1930, 440 yards (402.34m) 1934-66

1930 1. Noel Ryan (AUS) 4:39.8
2. Gordon Bridson (NZL) 4:45.8
3. George Burleigh (CAN)
1934 1. Noel Ryan (AUS) 5:03.0
2. Norman Wainwright (ENG) 5:07.8
3. Bob Pirie (CAN) 5:14.8
1938 1. Bob Pirie (CAN) 4:54.6
2. Bob Leivers (ENG) 4:55.4
3. Robin Biddulph (AUS) 4:55.5
1950 1. Garrick Agnew (AUS) 4:49.4
2. Graham Johnston (SAF) 4:51.3
3. Buddy Lucas (NZL) 5:02.5
1954 1. Gary Chapman (AUS) 4:39.8
2. Jack Wardrop (SCO) 4:41.5
3. Graham Johnston (SAF) 4:43.3
1958 1. John Konrads (AUS) 4:25.9
2. Ian Black (SCO) 4:28.5
3. Gary Winram (AUS) 4:32.4
1962 1. Murray Rose (AUS) 4:20.0
2. Alan Wood (AUS) 4:22.5
3. Robert Windle (AUS) 4:23.1
1966 1. Robert Windle (AUS) 4:15.0
2. John Bennett (AUS) 4:15.9
3. Ralph Hutton (CAN) 4:16.1
1970 1. Graham White (AUS) 4:08.48
2. Ralph Hutton (CAN) 4:08.77
3. Greg Brough (AUS) 4:12.16
1974 1. John Kulasalu (AUS) 4:01.44
2. Brad Cooper (AUS) 4:02.12
3. Steve Badger (AUS) 4:04.07
1978 1. Ron McKeon (AUS) 3:54.43
2. Simon Gray (ENG) 3:56.87
3. Max Metzker (AUS) 3:58.83
1982 1. Andrew Astbury (ENG) 3:53.29
2. Peter Szmidt (CAN) 3:53.74
3. John Davey (ENG) 3:55.52

1500 METRES FREESTYLE

1500 yards (1371.6m) 1930-4, 1650 yards (1508.76m) 1938-66

1930 1. Noel Ryan (AUS) 18:55.4
2. Gordon Bridson (NZL) 19:41.0
3. George Burleigh (CAN)
1934 1. Noel Ryan (AUS) 18:25.4
2. Bob Pirie (CAN) 18:28.4
3. Norman Wainwright (ENG) 18:55.2
1938 1. Bob Leivers (ENG) 19:46.4
2. Bob Pirie (CAN) 19:59.2
3. Norman Wainwright (ENG) 20:17.4
1950 1. Graham Johnston (SAF) 19:55.7
2. James Portelance (CAN) 20:08.3
3. Buddy Lucas (NZL) 20:10.1
1954 1. Graham Johnston (SAF) 19:01.4
2. Peter Duncan (SAF) 19:22.1
3. Gary Chapman (AUS) 19:28.4
1958 1. John Konrads (AUS) 17:45.4
2. Gary Winram (AUS) 18:17.2
3. Murray McLachlan (SAF) 18:19.2
1962 1. Murray Rose (AUS) 17:18.1
2. Robert Windle (AUS) 17:44.5
3. Alan Wood (AUS) 17:55.6
1966 1. Ron Jackson (AUS) 17:25.9
2. Sandy Gilchrist (CAN) 17:33.9
3. Ralph Hutton (CAN) 17:38.9
1970 1. Graham Windeatt (AUS) 16:23.82
2. Max Travasci (AUS) 16:34.46
3. Mark Treffers (NZL) 16:44.69
1974 1. Steve Holland (AUS) 15:34.73
2. Mark Treffers (NZL) 15:59.82
3. Steve Badger (AUS) 16:22.23
1978 1. Max Metzker (AUS) 15:31.92
2. Simon Gray (ENG) 15:39.39
3. Andrew Astbury (ENG) 15:42.89
1982 1. Max Metzker (AUS) 15:23.94
2. Tim Ford (AUS) 15:27.00
3. Andrew Astbury (ENG) 15:34.41

4 x 100 METRES FREESTYLE RELAY

4 x 110 yards 1962-6

1962 1. Australia 3:43.9
2. Canada 3:48.3
3. England 3:51.3
1966 1. Australia 3:35.6
2. Canada 3:42.3
3. England 3:43.7
1970 1. Australia 3:36.02
2. Canada 3:37.65
3. England 3:41.24
1974 1. Canada 3:33.79
2. Australia 3:34.26
3. England 3:38.22
1978 1. Canada 3:27.94
2. Australia 3:28.62
3. England 3:30.10
1982 1. Australia 3:24.17
2. England 3:26.98
3. Canada 3:27.74

4 x 200 METRES FREESTYLE RELAY

4 x 200 yards 1930-34, 4 x 220 yards 1938-66

1930 1. Canada 8:42.4
2. England 8:42.8
Only two teams competed
1934 1. Canada 8:40.6
2. England 8:52.8
3. Scotland 9:23.4
1938 1. England 9:19.0
2. Canada 9:20.2
3. Australia 9:32.9
1950 1. New Zealand 9:27.7
2. Australia 9:34.5

Swimming

The pools used at the first two Commonwealth Games were 25 yards (1930) and 50 yards (1934) long, and the distances based on that multiple. In Sydney in 1938 the pool was 55 yards and so the competitive distances became multiples of this different pool size, i.e: 110, 220, 440 and 1,650 yards. In 1966 although metric distances had become almost universal, the rules of the Commonwealth Games Federation had not been changed for the almost outmoded Imperial equivalents. This forced the hosts, Jamaica, who already had a metric (50m) pool to extend the length to 55 yards at considerable expense. Since 1970, metric distances (100, 200, 400, 800 and 1500 metres) have been the rule.

June Croft, freestyle sprints champion of the 1982 Games, set records in both the 100m and 200m events.

The most swimming gold medals won is nine by Australian sprinter Mike Wenden in three Games from 1966 to 1974. He took a further three silver medals and a bronze for a grand total of 13 medals to equal the record for any sport held by the fencer Ivan Lund. Wenden uniquely won one event, the 100m freestyle, at three Games, and would have beaten Lund's total had not the Australian medley relay in 1966 been disqualified for a flying take-over. The most by a woman is six gold and two silver by Dawn Fraser, also of Australia, in 1958 and 1962. The most gold medals won at a single Games is six by the Canadian Graham Smith at Edmonton in 1978. Other prolific medallists were the Canadians Elaine Tanner and Ralph Hutton in 1966. The 15-year-old Tanner, nicknamed 'Mighty Mouse' as she was only 5ft 2in, won four gold and three silver medals and broke two world records, and Hutton, known as the 'Iron Man', won one relay gold, five silver and two bronze medals in the course of 13 races, totalling 13 miles in all, in six days. These eight medals are a record for any sportsman at one Games. He added a further four silvers in 1970.

The youngest Commonwealth champion in any sport is Jenny Turrall (AUS), who won the 1974 women's 400m freestyle at 13 years 262 days. The youngest men's swimming champion is Steve Holland, also of Australia, winner of the 1500m freestyle in 1974 when aged 15 years 245 days. On the way to that title Holland broke the world record for 800 metres. Probably the oldest champion was Roy Romain who was

4 x 200 Metres Freestyle Relay continued

3. England 9:36.8
1954 1. Australia 8:47.6
2. Canada 8:56.0
3. South Africa 8:56.3
1958 1. Australia 8:33.4
2. Scotland 8:54.2
3. Canada 9:01.8
1962 1. Australia 8:13.4
2. Canada 8:42.4
3. England 8:46.0
1966 1. Australia 7:59.5
2. Canada 8:15.0
3. England 8:24.0
1970 1. Australia 7:50.77
2. Canada 8:00.69
3. England 8:10.60
1974 1. Australia 7:50.13
2. England 7:52.90
3. Canada 7:53.38
1978 1. Australia 7:34.83
2. Canada 7:36.58
3. England 7:42.02
1982 1. Australia 7:28.81
2. England 7:30.00
3. Scotland 7:39.86

100 METRES BACKSTROKE

100 yards (91.44m) 1930-4, 110 yards (100.58m) 1938-66

1930 1. John Trippet (ENG) 1:05.4
2. Willie Francis (SCO) 1:05.8
3. John Besford (ENG) 1:07.0
1934 1. Willie Francis (SCO) 1:05.2
2. John Besford (ENG) 1:05.6
3. Ben Gazell (CAN) 1:06.6
1938 1. Percy Oliver (AUS) 1:07.9
2. Gordon Kerr (CAN) 1:09.0
3. Michael Taylor (ENG) 1:09.3
1950 1. Jackie Wiid (SAF) 1:07.7
2. John Brockway (WAL) 1:08.0
3. Bert Kinnear (SCO) 1:10.9
1954 1. John Brockway (WAL) 1:06.5
2. Lincoln Hurring (NZL) 1:06.9
3. Cyrus Weld (AUS) 1:08.6
1958 1. John Monckton (AUS) 1:01.7
2. John Hayres (AUS) 1:03.5
3. Robert Wheaton (CAN) 1:06.5
1962 1. Graham Sykes (ENG) 1:04.5
2. Julian Carroll (AUS) 1:05.4
3. Wayne Vincent (AUS) 1:06.2
1966 1. Peter Reynolds (AUS) 1:02.4
2. Ralph Hutton (CAN) 1:02.7
3. Neil Jackson (ENG) 1:03.3
1970 1. Bill Kennedy (CAN) 1:01.65
2. Mike Richards (WAL) 1:01.69
3. Erik Fish (CAN) 1:02.02
1974 1. Mark Tonelli (AUS) 59.65
2. Steve Pickell (CAN) 59.88
3. Brad Cooper (AUS) 1:00.17
1978 1. Glenn Patching (AUS) 57.90
2. Gary Abraham (ENG) 58.48
3. Jay Tapp (CAN) 59.05
1982 1. Michael West (CAN) 57.12
2. Cameron Henning (CAN) 57.82
3. Wade Flemons (CAN) 58.38

200 METRES BACKSTROKE

220 yards (201.17m) 1962-6

1962 1. Julian Carroll (AUS) 2:20.9
2. Tony Fingleton (AUS) 2:21.0
3. Alan Robertson (NZL) 2:23.0
1966 1. Peter Reynolds (AUS) 2:12.0
2. Ralph Hutton (CAN) 2:13.5
3. Karl Byrom (AUS) 2:18.8
1970 1. Mike Richards (WAL) 2:14.53
2. Ray Terrell (ENG) 2:15.48
3. Neil Rogers (AUS) 2:15.63
1974 1. Brad Cooper (AUS) 2:06.31
2. Mark Tonelli (AUS) 2:09.47
3. Robert Williams (AUS) 2:09.83
1978 1. Gary Hurring (NZL) 2:04.37
2. Glenn Patching (AUS) 2:05.76
3. Paul Moorfoot (AUS) 2:05.99
1982 1. Cameron Henning (CAN) 2:02.58
2. David Orbell (AUS) 2:03.93
3. Michael West (CAN) 2:04.36

100 METRES BREASTSTROKE

110 yards (100.58m) 1962-6

1962 1. Ian O'Brien (AUS) 1:11.4
2. William Burton (AUS) 1:13.9
3. Steve Rabinovich (CAN) 1:14.1
1966 1. Ian O'Brien (AUS) 1:08.2
2. Hamilton Graham (NZL) 1:12.9
3. Malcolm Tucker (ENG) 1:13.9
1970 1. Bill Mahony (CAN) 1:09.0
2. Peter Cross (CAN) 1:09.4
3. Paul Jarvis (AUS) 1:10.0
1974 1. David Leigh (ENG) 1:06.52
2. David Wilkie (SCO) 1:07.37
3. Paul Naisby (ENG) 1:08.52
1978 1. Graham Smith (CAN) 1:03.81
2. Duncan Goodhew (ENG) 1:04.24
3. Paul Naisby (ENG) 1:06.36
1982 1. Adrian Moorhouse (ENG) 1:02.93
2. Victor Davis (CAN) 1:03.18
3. Peter Evans (AUS) 1:03.48

200 METRES BREASTSTROKE

200 yards (182.88m) 1930-4, 220 yards (201.17m) 1938-66

1930 1. Jack Aubin (CAN) 2:38.4
2. Stanley Bell (ENG) 2:39.6
3. Reginald Flint (ENG) 2:44.8
1934 1. Norman Hamilton (SCO) 2:41.4
2. William McCatty (JAM) 2:42.4
3. William Puddy (CAN) 2:42.8
1938 1. John Davies (ENG) 2:51.9
2. Walter Spence (GUY) 3:00.5
3. James Prentice (CAN) 3:01.8
1950 1. David Hawkins (AUS) 2:54.1
2. Roy Romain (ENG) 2:54.2
3. Ronald Sharpe (AUS) 2:56.0
1954 1. John Doms (NZL) 2:52.6
2. Peter Jervis (ENG) 2:52.6
3. Alan Hime (ENG) 2:52.8
1958 1. Terry Gathercole (AUS) 2:41.6
2. Peter Rocchi (SAF) 2:44.9
3. Chris Walkden (ENG) 2:47.3
1962 1. Ian O'Brien (AUS) 2:38.2
2. William Burton (AUS) 2:42.1
3. Neil Nicholson (ENG) 2:42.6
1966 1. Ian O'Brien (AUS) 2:29.3
2. Hamilton Graham (NZL) 2:36.9
3. Bill Mahony (CAN) 2:38.9
1970 1. Bill Mahony (CAN) 2:30.29
2. Paul Jarvie (AUS) 2:30.70
3. David Wilkie (SCO) 2:32.87
1974 1. David Wilkie (SCO) 2:24.42
2. David Leigh (ENG) 2:24.75
3. Paul Naisby (ENG) 2:27.36
1978 1. Graham Smith (CAN) 2:20.86
2. Duncan Goodhew (ENG) 2:21.92
3. Lindsay Spencer (AUS) 2:22.49
1982 1. Victor Davis (CAN) 2:16.25
2. Glenn Beringen (AUS) 2:19.06
3. Adrian Moorhouse (ENG) 2:19.31

100 METRES BUTTERFLY

110 yards (100.59m) 1962-6

1962 1. Kevin Berry (AUS) 59.5
2. Neville Hayes (AUS) 1:02.3
3. Andy Meinhardt (CAN) 1:02.6
1966 1. Ron Jacks (CAN) 1:00.3
2. Graham Dunn (AUS) 1:00.9
3. Keith Bewley (ENG) 1:01.5
1970 1. Byron MacDonald (CAN) 58.44
2. Tom Arusoo (CAN) 58.98
3. Ron Jacks (CAN) 59.01
1974 1. Neil Rogers (AUS) 56.58
2. Byron MacDonald (CAN) 56.83
3. Bruce Robertson (CAN) 56.84
1978 1. Dan Thompson (CAN) 55.04
2. John Mills (ENG) 56.22
3. Bill Sawchuck (CAN) 56.37
1982 1. Dan Thompson (CAN) 54.71
2. Phil Hubble (ENG) 55.52
3. Tom Ponting (CAN) 55.64

200 METRES BUTTERFLY

220 yards (201.17m) 1958-66

1958 1. Ian Black (SCO) 2:22.6
2. Graham Symonds (ENG) 2:25.5
3. Brian Wilkinson (AUS) 2:31.0

David Wilkie

31 in 1950 when he was a member of England's 3 x 110 yards medley relay team. He also won a silver medal for 220 yards breaststroke that year, when he was as old as the combined ages of the other medallists. The oldest medallist was Walter Spence of British Guiana (now Guyana), who was aged 36 in 1938 when he was second in the 200 yards breaststroke.

Australian swimmers have achieved the greatest success, most dramatically with their unique achievement for a substantial team in 1966 when every member of it won a medal. Also in 1958 their swimmers won every event with the single exception of the men's 220 yards butterfly which went to Scotland's Ian Black.

There have been several notable family successes. Freddie Milton won a silver medal for England in the 4 x 200m freestyle relay in 1930, at which Games he met Irene Pirie of Canada, who also won a relay silver medal. In 1934 she won a complete medal set of gold, silver and bronze. They married in 1935 and their son Tony swam for Britain at the Olympics although not at the Commonwealth Games. Irene's brother Bob won three gold, four silver and a bronze in 1954 and 1958. Lincoln Hurring of New Zealand won two silver medals in 1954, when his future wife Jean Stewart won a silver

Commonwealth champion and world record holder Alex Baumann of Canada (centre) set for Olympic gold at 400m individual medley in 1984.

200 Metres Butterfly continued

1962 1. Kevin Berry (AUS) 2:10.8
2. Neville Hayes (AUS) 2:16.3
3. Brett Hill (AUS) 2:18.7
1966 1. David Gerrard (NZL) 2:12.7
2. Brett Hill (AUS) 2:12.8
3. Tom Arusoo (CAN) 2:14.2
1970 1. Tom Arusoo (CAN) 2:08.97
2. Martyn Woodroffe (WAL) 2:09.14
3. James Findlay (AUS) 2:09.41
1974 1. Brian Brinkley (ENG) 2:04.51
2. Ross Seymour (AUS) 2:06.64
3. John Coutts (NZL) 2:07.03
1978 1. George Nagy (CAN) 2:01.99
2. Claus Bredschneider (CAN) 2:02.49
3. Phil Hubble (ENG) 2:02.53
1982 1. Phil Hubble (ENG) 2:00.98
2. Paul Rowe (AUS) 2:01.18
3. Jon Sieben (AUS) 2:01.24

200 METRES INDIVIDUAL MEDLEY

1970 1. George Smith (CAN) 2:13.72
2. Ken Campbell (CAN) 2:16.57
3. Martyn Woodroffe (WAL) 2:16.64
1974 1. David Wilkie (SCO) 2:10.11
2. Brian Brinkley (ENG) 2:12.73
3. Gary MacDonald (CAN) 2:12.98
1978 1. Graham Smith (CAN) 2:05.25
2. Bill Sawchuk (CAN) 2:05.61
3. Peter Dawson (AUS) 2:09.05
1982 1. Alex Baumann (CAN) 2:02.25
2. Robin Brew (SCO) 2:05.83
3. Jeffrey Sheehan (CAN) 2:07.14

400 METRES INDIVIDUAL MEDLEY

440 yards (402.34m) 1962-6

1962 1. Alex Alexander (AUS) 5:15.3
2. John Oravainen (AUS) 5:16.3
3. John Kelso (CAN) 5:16.5
1966 1. Peter Reynolds (AUS) 4:50.8
2. Ralph Hutton (CAN) 4:51.8
3. Sandy Gilchrist (CAN) 4:58.7
1970 1. George Smith (CAN) 4:48.87
2. Ray Terrell (ENG) 4:49.85
3. James Findlay (AUS) 4:51.92
1974 1. Mark Treffers (NZL) 4:35.90
2. Brian Brinkley (ENG) 4:41.29
3. Ray Terrell (ENG) 4:42.94
1978 1. Graham Smith (CAN) 4:27.34
2. Simon Gray (ENG) 4:27.99
3. Bill Sawchuck (CAN) 4:27.99
1982 1. Alex Baumann (CAN) 4:23.53
2. Stephen Poulter (ENG) 4:27.09
3. John Davey (ENG) 4:27.91

4 x 100 METRES MEDLEY RELAY

3 x 100 yards 1934, 3 x 110 yards 1938-54, 4 x 110 yards 1958-66. Butterfly leg added from 1958.

1934 1. Canada 3:11.2
2. Scotland 3:15.2
3. England 3:16.0
1938 1. England 3:28.2
2. Canada 3.30.5
3. Australia 3:31.8
1950 1. England 3:26.6
2. Canada 3:29.4
3. New Zealand 3:30.1
1954 1. Australia 3:22.0
2. New Zealand 3:26.6
3. Scotland 3:27.3
1958 1. Australia 4:14.2
2. Canada 4:26.3
3. England 4:26.4
1962 1. Australia 4:12.4
2. England 4:19.9
3. Canada 4:19.9
1966 1. Canada 4:10.5
2. England 4:11.3
3. New Zealand 4:17.5
1970 1. Canada 4:01.10
2. Australia 4:04.55
3. Wales 4:08.05
1974 1. Canada 3:52.93
2. Australia 3:55.76
3. England 4:00.48
1978 1. Canada 3:49.76
2. England 3:50.22
3. Australia 3:53.16
1982 1. Australia 3:47.34
2. England 3:48.25
3. Scotland 3:55.45

WATER POLO

1950 1. Australia
2. New Zealand

WOMEN

100 METRES FREESTYLE

100 yards (91.44m) 1930-4, 110 yards (100.58m) 1938-66

1930 1. Joyce Cooper (ENG) 1:07.0
2. Ellen King (SCO) 1:07.4
3. Valerie Davies (WAL)
1934 1. Phyllis Dewar (CAN) 1:03.5
2. Irene Pirie (CAN) 1:03.6
3. Jean McDowall (SCO) 1:05.8
1938 1. Evelyn de Lacy (AUS) 1:10.1
2. Dorothy Green (AUS) 1:11.1
3. Dorothy Lyon (CAN) 1:12.1
1950 1. Marjorie McQuade (AUS) 1:09.0
2. Margaret Wellington (ENG) 1:09.6
3. Joan Harrison (SAF) 1:09.7
1954 1. Lorraine Crapp (AUS) 1:05.8
2. Virginia Grant (CAN) 1:06.3
3. Joan Harrison (SAF) 1:08.2
1958 1. Dawn Fraser (AUS) 1:01.4
2. Lorraine Crapp (AUS) 1:03.8
3. Alva Colquhoun (AUS) 1:04.0
1962 1. Dawn Fraser (AUS) 59.5
2. Robyn Thorn (AUS) 1:03.8
3. Mary Stewart (CAN) 1:04.4
1966 1. Marion Lay (CAN) 1:02.3
2. Lynette Bell (AUS) 1:03.2
3. Jan Murphy (AUS) 1:03.4
1970 1. Angela Coughlan (CAN) 1:01.22
2. Lynne Watson (AUS) 1:01.45
3. Jenny Watts (AUS) 1:01.81
1974 1. Sonya Gray (AUS) 59.13
2. Gail Amundrud (CAN) 59.36
3. Judy Wright (CAN) 59.46
1978 1. Carol Klimpel (CAN) 57.78
2. Rosemary Brown (AUS) 58.30
3. Wendy Quirk (CAN) 58.41
1982 1. June Croft (ENG) 56.97
2. Angela Russell (AUS) 57.39
3. Lisa Curry (AUS) 57.68

200 METRES FREESTYLE

1970 1. Karen Moras (AUS) 2:09.78
2. Angela Coughlan (CAN) 2:10.83
3. Alex Jackson (IOM) 2:13.52
1974 1. Sonya Gray (AUS) 2:04.27
2. Jenny Turrall (AUS) 2:06.90
3. Gail Amundrud (CAN) 2:07.03
1978 1. Rebecca Perrott (NZL) 2:00.63
2. Tracey Wickham (AUS) 2:01.50
3. Michelle Ford (AUS) 2:01.64
1982 1. June Croft (ENG) 1:59.74
2. Tracey Wickham (AUS) 2:00.60
3. Susie Baumer (AUS) 2:02.29

400 METRES FREESTYLE

400 yards (365.76m) 1930, 440 yards (402.34m) 1934-66

1930 1. Joyce Cooper (ENG) 5:25.4
2. Valerie Davies (WAL) 5:28.0
3. Cissie Stewart (SCO)
1934 1. Phyllis Dewar (CAN) 5:45.6
2. Jennie Maakal (SAF) 5:53.0
3. Irene Pirie (CAN) 5:54.4
1938 1. Dorothy Green (AUS) 5:39.7
2. Margaret Jeffrey (ENG) 5:40.2
3. Mona Leydon (NZL) 5:42.0
1950 1. Joan Harrison (SAF) 5:26.4
2. Margaret Wellington (ENG) 5:33.7
3. Denise Norton (AUS) 5:33.8
1954 1. Lorraine Crapp (AUS) 5:11.4
2. Gladys Priestley (CAN) 5:19.6
3. Margaret Girvan (SCO) 5:21.4
1958 1. Ilsa Konrads (AUS) 4:49.4
2. Dawn Fraser (AUS) 5:00.8
3. Lorraine Crapp (AUS) 5:06.7
1962 1. Dawn Fraser (AUS) 4:51.4
2. Ilsa Konrads (AUS) 4:55.0
3. Elizabeth Long (ENG) 5:00.4
1966 1. Kathy Wainwright (AUS) 4:38.8
2. Jenny Thorn (AUS) 4:44.5
3. Kim Herford (AUS) 4:47.2

Jubilation for Australia as their 4 x 100 metres freestyle relay team wins and breaks the Commonwealth record at Brisbane in 1982.

and bronze. Jean's brother Jack was twice a bronze medallist at springboard diving and Jean and Lincoln's son Gary added to the family medal haul by winning the 200m backstroke in 1978.

The outstanding family, however, must be the Smiths from Canada, five brothers and sisters, Graham, George, Susan, Sandra and Becky, who between them collected nine gold, seven silver and two bronze medals from 1970 to 1978. The only brother and sister combination to win gold medals at the same Games were John and Ilsa Konrads in 1958. Born in Latvia, but swimming for their adopted homeland Australia, John, a former polio victim, won the 440 yards and 1650 yards freestyle titles and gained a third gold in the freestyle relay, while Ilsa won the women's 440 yards title.

World championships for swimming were instituted in 1973. Since then just two men have won Olympic, Commonwealth and World titles, both in the same event, the 200 metres breaststroke. David Wilkie (SCO) won world titles in 1973 and 1975, Commonwealth in 1974 and Olympic in 1976. Victor Davis (CAN) won World and Commonwealth in 1982 and Olympic in 1984. No female swimmer has won this treble but Judy Grinham and Anita Lonsbrough of England each held Olympic, Commonwealth and European titles at the same time before the World Championships were started.

Lisa Curry won the 100m butterfly gold, but here tries the backstroke on the way to another gold at the medley.

400 Metres Freestyle continued

1970 1. Karen Moras (AUS) 4:27.38
2. Denise Langford (AUS) 4:31.42
3. Robyn Risson (AUS) 4:39.75
1974 1. Jenny Turrall (AUS) 4:22.09
2. Wendy Quirk (CAN) 4:22.96
3. Jaynie Parkhouse (NZL) 4:23.09
1978 1. Tracey Wickham (AUS) 4:08.45
2. Michelle Ford (AUS) 4:10.25
3. Rebecca Perrott (NZL) 4:16.70
1982 1. Tracey Wickham (AUS) 4:08.82
2. Jackie Willmott (ENG) 4:13.04
3. June Croft (ENG) 4:13.13

800 METRES FREESTYLE

1970 1. Karen Moras (AUS) 9:02.45
2. Helen Gray (AUS) 9:27.48
3. Robyn Risson (AUS) 9:37.89
1974 1. Jaynie Parkhouse (NZL) 8:58.49
2. Jenny Turrall (AUS) 8:58.53
3. Rosemary Milgate (AUS) 8:58.59
1978 1. Tracey Wickham (AUS) 8:24.62
2. Michelle Ford (AUS) 8:25.78
3. Rebecca Perrott (NZL) 8:44.87
1982 1. Tracey Wickham (AUS) 8:29.05
2. Michelle Ford (AUS) 8:33.74
3. Jackie Willmott (ENG) 8:36.66

4 x 100 METRES FREESTYLE

4 x 100 yards 1930-34, 4 x 110 yards 1938-66

1930 1. England 4:32.8
2. Canada 4:33.0
3. Scotland 4:37.0
1934 1. Canada 4:21.8
2. South Africa 4:34.0
3. England 4:34.4
1938 1. Canada 4:48.3
2. Australia 4:49.9
3. England 4:50.1
1950 1. Australia 4:44.9
2. New Zealand 4:48.7
3. England 4:56.0
1954 1. South Africa 4:33.9
2. Canada 4:37.0
3. England 4:41.8
1958 1. Australia 4:17.4
2. Canada 4:30.0
3. England 4:31.5
1962 1. Australia 4:11.0
2. Canada 4:21.1
3. England 4:21.3
1966 1. Canada 4:10.8
2. Australia 4:11.1
3. England 4:17.3
1970 1. Australia 4:06.41
2. Canada 4:12.16
3. England 4:14.90
1974 1. Canada 3:57.14
2. Australia 4:02.37
3. England 4:05.59
1978 1. Canada 3:50.28
2. England 3:53.27
3. Australia 3:54.11
1982 1. England 3:54.23
2. Scotland 4:01.46
3. New Zealand 4:07.41

100 METRES BACKSTROKE

100 yards (91.44m) 1930-4, 110 yards (100.58m) 1938-66

1930 1. Joyce Cooper (ENG) 1:15.0
2. Valerie Davies (WAL) 1:16.8
3. Phyllis Harding (ENG) 1:17.6
1934 1. Phyllis Harding (ENG) 1:13.8
2. Margot Hamilton (SCO) 1:15.0
3. Valerie Davies (WAL) 1:18.2
1938 1. Pat Norton (AUS) 1:19.5
2. Jeanne Greenland (WAL) 1:22.5
3. Margot Hamilton (SCO) 1:23.2
1950 1. Judy-Joy Davies (AUS) 1:18.6
2. Jean Stewart (NZL) 1:19.1
3. Helen Yate (ENG) 1:20.5
1954 1. Joan Harrison (SAF) 1:15.2
2. Pat Symons (ENG) 1:17.4
3. Jean Stewart (NZL) 1:17.5
1958 1. Judy Grinham (ENG) 1:11.9
2. Margaret Edwards (ENG) 1:12.6
3. Phillipa Gould (NZL) 1:13.7
1962 1. Linda Ludgrove (ENG) 1:11.1
2. Pam Sergeant (AUS) 1:11.5
3. Sylvia Lewis (ENG) 1:12.2
1966 1. Linda Ludgrove (ENG) 1:09.2
2. Elaine Tanner (CAN) 1:09.9
3. Janet Franklin (ENG) 1:11.8
1970 1. Lynne Watson (AUS) 1:07.10
2. Debra Cain (AUS) 1:07.73
3. Donna-Marie Gurr (CAN) 1:08.87
1974 1. Wendy Cook (CAN) 1:06.37
2. Donna-Marie Gurr (CAN) 1:06.55
3. Linda Young (AUS) 1:07.52
1978 1. Debra Forster (AUS) 1:03.97
2. Helene Boivin (CAN) 1:04.54
3. Cheryl Gibson (CAN) 1:04.68
1982 1. Lisa Forrest (AUS) 1:03.48
2. Georgina Parkes (AUS) 1:03.63
3. Audrey Moore (AUS) 1:03.91

200 METRES BACKSTROKE

220 yards (201.17m) 1962-6

1962 1. Linda Ludgrove (ENG) 2:35.2
2. Sylvia Lewis (ENG) 2:36.7
3. Pam Sergeant (AUS) 2:37.5
1966 1. Linda Ludgrove (ENG) 2:28.5
2. Elaine Turner (CAN) 2:29.7
3. Margaret MacRae (NZL) 2:34.7
1970 1. Lynne Watson (AUS) 2:22.86
2. Donna-Marie Gurr (CAN) 2:24.33
3. Debra Cain (AUS) 2:26.02
1974 1. Wendy Cook (CAN) 2:20.37
2. Sandra Yost (AUS) 2:22.07
3. Donna-Marie Gurr (CAN) 2:23.74
1978 1. Cheryl Gibson (CAN) 2:16.57
2. Lisa Forrest (AUS) 2:17.66
3. Glenda Robertson (AUS) 2:18.32
1982 1. Lisa Forrest (AUS) 2:13.36
2. Georgina Parkes (AUS) 2:13.95
3. Cheryl Gibson (CAN) 2:15.87

100 METRES BREASTSTROKE

110 yards (100.58m) 1962-6

1962 1. Anita Lonsbrough (ENG) 1:21.3
2. Vivien Haddon (NZL) 1:21.3
3. Dorinda Fraser (ENG) 1:21.7
1966 1. Diana Harris (ENG) 1:19.7
2. Jill Slattery (ENG) 1:19.8
3. Heather Saville (AUS) 1:21.6
1970 1. Beverley Whitfield (AUS) 1:17.40
2. Dorothy Harrison (ENG) 1:17.60
3. Chris Jarvis (ENG) 1:19.83
1974 1. Catherine Gaskell (ENG) 1:16.42
2. Marion Stuart (CAN) 1:16.61
3. Sandra Dickie (SCO) 1:17.17
1978 1. Robin Corsiglia (CAN) 1:13.56
2. Margaret Kelly (ENG) 1:13.69
3. Marian Stuart (CAN) 1:13.72
1982 1. Kathy Bald (CAN) 1:11.89
2. Anne Ottenbrite (CAN) 1:11.99
3. Suki Brownsdon (ENG) 1:13.76

200 METRES BREASTSTROKE

200 yards (182.88m) 1930-4, 220 yards (201.17m) 1938-66)

1930 1. Celia Wolstenholme (ENG) 2:54.8
2. Margery Hinton (ENG) 3:04.2
3. Ellen King (SCO)
1934 1. Claire Dennis (AUS) 2:50.2
2. Phyllis Haslam (CAN) 2:55.4
3. Margery Hinton (ENG) 2:58.6
1938 1. Doris Storey (ENG) 3:06.3
2. Carla Gerke (SAF) 3:12.1
3. Joan Langdon (CAN) 3:22.2
1950 1. Elenor Gordon (SCO) 3:01.7
2. Beatrice Lyons (AUS) 3:03.6
3. Elizabeth Church (ENG) 3:10.3
1954 1. Elenor Gordon (SCO) 2:59.2
2. Mary Morgan (SAF) 3:03.3
3. Margaret Grundy (ENG) 3:04.5
1958 1. Anita Lonsbrough (ENG) 2:53.5
2. Jackie Dyson (ENG) 2:58.2
3. Chris Gosden (ENG) 2:58.4
1962 1. Anita Lonsbrough (ENG) 2:51.7
2. Jackie Enfield (ENG) 2:54.7
3. Vivien Haddon (NZL) 2:56.3
1966 1. Jill Slattery (ENG) 2:50.3
2. Stella Mitchell (ENG) 2:50.3
3. Vivien Haddon (NZL) 2:53.9
1970 1. Beverley Whitfield (AUS) 2:44.12
2. Dorothy Harrison (ENG) 2:46.18
3. Amanda Radnage (ENG) 2:50.11

Left: The 100m freestyle medallists of 1966 (left to right) Scotland's champion sprinter Bobby McGregor took the silver, with Australians Mike Wenden the winner and David Dickson third.

Above: Victor Davis of Canada has been the world's top breaststroke swimmer of the 1980s, winning 200m gold and 100m silver at both 1982 Commonwealth and 1984 Olympic Games.

Left: Tracey Wickham retired after maintaining Australia's great women's swimming tradition, with gold medals at 400m and 800m freestyle in 1982.

Tale of two cities.

Take any city in the world and put it alongside Glasgow.

You'll discover that Glasgow is rich in assets that compare favourably with the best.

It's more than a tale or two. As any visitor to Glasgow will tell you, there's a lot to smile about.

The Burrell Collection Glasgow

New York/Glasgow

New York is one of the world's leading art centres with its many exquisite galleries and masterpieces.

On Glasgow, R W Apple Jnr., wrote in the New York Times "The Burrell Collection is one of the most remarkable assemblages of works of art ever brought together.

It's not surprising that The Burrell Collection is now Scotland's leading tourist attraction.

Theatre Royal Glasgow

Park Circus Glasgow

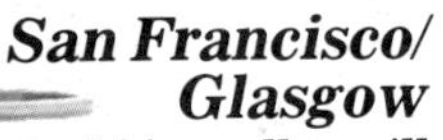

San Francisco/ Glasgow

The world traveller will know that San Francisco has much in common with Glasgow. Not least being its many superb eating places, and its not dissimilar architecture. The traveller will also know that Glasgow almost certainly has the finest Victorian architecture in Europe.

Sydney/Glasgow

The famous Sydney Opera House attracts the world's greatest performers. But so too, does the Theatre Royal in Glasgow.

It's not surprising that Glasgow is the home of Scottish Opera (and Scottish Ballet and the Citizen's Theatre Company!)

Kelvingrove Park Glasgow

Copenhagen/Glasgow

Copenhagen's Tivoli Gardens are truly magnificent. There's no doubt. There's also no doubt that there is only one other city in Europe that boasts as many parks and recreation grounds. Glasgow;(and fourteen golf courses!)

Glasgow's renaissance is now in full swing and is blooming with a new pride and vigour. And with the Garden Festival in 1988 is surely now the Flower of Scotland.

City of Glasgow

200 Metres Breaststroke continued

1974 1. Pat Beavan (WAL) 2:43.11
2. Beverley Whitfield (AUS) 2:43.58
3. Allison Smith (AUS) 2:45.08
1978 1. Lisa Borsholt (CAN) 2:37.70
2. Debbie Rudd (ENG) 2:38.07
3. Margaret Kelly (ENG) 2:38.63
1982 1. Anne Ottenbrite (CAN) 2:32.07
2. Kathy Bald (CAN) 2:36.06
3. Katherine Richardson (CAN) 2:36.45

100 METRES BUTTERFLY

110 yards (100.59m) 1958-66

1958 1. Beverley Bainbridge (AUS) 1:13.5
2. Tessa Staveley (NZL) 1:14.4
3. Margaret Iwasaki (CAN) 1:15.9
1962 1. Mary Stewart (CAN) 1:10.1
2. Anne Cotterill (CAN) 1:11.2
3. Linda McGill (AUS) 1:11.6
1966 1 Elaine Tanner (CAN) 1:06.8
2. Judy Gegan (ENG) 1:09.3
3. Ann Barner (ENG) 1:09.7
1970 1. Diane Lansley (ENG) 1:07.90
2. Susan Smith (CAN) 1:08.18
3. Allyson Mabb (AUS) 1:08.67
1974 1. Patti Stenhouse (CAN) 1:05.38
2. Kim Wickham (SCO) 1:05.96
3. Sandra Yost (AUS) 1:06.04
1978 1. Wendy Quirk (CAN) 1:01.92
2. Penny McCarthy (NZL) 1:02.27
3. Linda Hanel (AUS) 1:02.69
1982 1. Lisa Curry (AUS) 1:01.22
2. Janet Tibbits (AUS) 1:01.70
3. Michelle MacPherson (CAN) 1:01.93

200 METRES BUTTERFLY

220 yards (201.17m) 1966

1966 1. Elaine Turner (CAN) 2:29.9
2. Marilyn Corson (CAN) 2:34.8
3. Ann Barner (ENG) 2:35.0
1970 1. Maree Robinson (AUS) 2:24.67
2. Jane Comerford (AUS) 2:24.95
3. Allyson Mabb (AUS) 2:31.09
1974 1. Sandra Yost (AUS) 2:20.57
2. Patti Stenhouse (CAN) 2:20.66
3. Gail Neall (AUS) 2:21.66
1978 1. Michelle Ford (AUS) 2:11.29
2. Wendy Quirk (CAN) 2:13.65
3. Linda Hanel (AUS) 2:14.52
1982 1. Michelle Ford (AUS) 2:11.89
2. Janet Tibbits (AUS) 2:13.18
3. Ann Osgerby (ENG) 2:13.91

200 METRES INDIVIDUAL MEDLEY

1970 1. Denise Langford (AUS) 2:28.89
2. Shelagh Ratcliffe (ENG) 2:29.65
3. Diana Rickard (AUS) 2:30.80
1974 1. Leslie Cliff (CAN) 2:24.13
2. Becky Smith (CAN) 2:25.17
3. Susan Hunter (NZL) 2:26.18
1978 1. Sharron Davies (ENG) 2:18.37
2. Rebecca Perrott (NZL) 2:18.70
3. Becky Smith (CAN) 2:18.95
1982 1. Lisa Curry (AUS) 2:16.94
2. Cheryl Gibson (CAN) 2:19.91
3. Michele Pearson (AUS) 2:20.19

400 METRES INDIVIDUAL MEDLEY

440 yards (402.34) 1962-66

1962 1. Anita Lonsbrough (ENG) 5:38.6
2. Linda McGill (AUS) 5:46.1
3. Jennifer Corish (AUS) 5:53.0
1966 1. Elaine Tanner (CAN) 5:26.3
2. Jan Murphy (AUS) 5:28.1
3. Jane Hughes (CAN) 5:34.1
1970 1. Denise Langford (AUS) 5:10.74
2. Gail Neall (AUS) 5:15.82
3. Shelagh Ratcliffe (ENG) 5:17.89
1974 1. Leslie Cliff (CAN) 5:01.35
2. Becky Smith (CAN) 5:03.68
3. Susan Hunter (NZL) 5:07.20
1978 1. Sharron Davies (ENG) 4:52.44
2. Becky Smith (CAN) 4:57.83
3. Cheryl Gibson (CAN) 4:59.39
1982 1. Lisa Curry (AUS) 4:51.95
2. Michele Pearson (AUS) 4:53.73
3. Michelle MacPherson (CAN) 4:55.09

4 x 100 METRES MEDLEY RELAY

3 x 100 yards 1934, 3 x 110 yards 1938-54, 4 x 110 yards 1958-66. Butterfly leg added from 1958.

1934 1. Canada 3:42.0
2. England 3:43.0
3. Scotland 3:50.0
1938 1. England 3:57.7
2. South Africa 4:07.5
3. Australia 4:10.0
1950 1. Australia 3:53.8
2. England 3:56.6
3. Scotland 3:58.9
1954 1. Scotland 3:51.0
2. South Africa 3:52.7
3. Australia 3:55.6
1958 1. England 4:54.0
2. Australia 4:55.1
3. Canada 5:01.6
1962 1. Australia 4:45.9
2. England 4:47.9
3. Canada 4:48.1
1966 1. England 4:40.6
2. Canada 4:44.5
3. Australia 4:45.7
1970 1. Australia 4:30.66
2. England 4:38.94
3. Canada 4:39.65
1974 1. Canada 4:24.77
2. Australia 4:30.55
3. Scotland 4:31.68
1978 1. Canada 4:15.26
2. Australia 4:16.75
3. England 4:19.87
1982 1. Canada 4:14.33
2. England 4:19.04
3. Scotland 4:25.75

DIVING MEDALLISTS

SPRINGBOARD DIVING

1930 1. Alfred Phillips (CAN) 147 points
2. Cyril Kennett (CAN) 138
3. Arthur Stott (CAN) 127
1934 1. J. Briscoe Ray (ENG) 117.12
2. Doug Tomalin (ENG) 110.50
3. Harry Class (CAN) 106.57
1938 1. Ron Masters (AUS) 126.36
2. Doug Tomalin (ENG) 124.78
3. George Athans (CAN) 117.90
1950 1. George Athans (CAN) 169.21
2. Peter Heatly (SCO) 168.80
3. Jack Stewart (NZL) 168.17
1954 1. Peter Heatly (SCO) 146.76
2. Tony Turner (ENG) 145.27
3. Jack Stewart (NZL) 144.98
1958 1. Keith Collin (ENG) 126.78
2. William Patrick (CAN) 124.61
3. David Tarsey (ENG) 118.81
1962 1. Brian Phelps (ENG) 154.14
2. Thomas Dinsley (CAN) 147.22
3. Ernest Meissner (CAN) 145.03
1966 1. Brian Phelps (ENG) 154.55
2. Donald Wagstaff (AUS) 150.17
3. Christopher Robb (AUS) 136.52
1970 1. Donald Wagstaff (AUS) 557.73
2. Ken Sully (CAN) 497.37
3. Ronald Friesen (CAN) 495.90
1974 1. Donald Wagstaff (AUS) 531.54
2. Scott Cranham (CAN) 509.61
3. Trevor Simpson (ENG) 489.69
1978 1. Chris Snode (ENG) 643.83
2. Scott Cranham (CAN) 595.53
3. Donald Wagstaff (AUS) 572.16
1982 1. Chris Snode (ENG) 631.38
2. Stepehn Foley (AUS) 592.08
3. Mark Graham (NZL) 551.46

HIGHBOARD DIVING

1930 1. Alfred Phillips (CAN) 90.6 points
2. Samuel Walker (CAN) 83.3
3. Terry Scott (ENG) 82.3
1934 1. Tommy Mather (ENG) 83.83
2. Doug Tomalin (ENG) 83.63
3. Louis Marchant (ENG) 70.64

Diving

The outstanding diver in Games history has been Australia's Don Wagstaff, who won four gold, two silver and a bronze in the four Games from 1966 to 1978. His 12 year span in the springboard event is also a record. The most successful woman has been Canada's Beverley Boys, with three gold, two silver and a bronze from 1966 to 1974. Her first medal, silver at springboard, was gained when she was just 15 years old. Even younger was England's Brian Phelps, who won a silver in 1958 three months after his fourteenth birthday. He went on to win four gold medals at the next two Games. At the other end of the age scale is Scotland's Peter Heatly, who was 46 days past his 34th birthday when he became the 1958 highboard champion. From 1950 to 1958 he won three gold medals, a silver and a bronze. He was Vice-Chairman of the organising committee for the 1970 Games in Edinburgh and in 1982 was elected Chairman of the governing body for the Games, the Commonwealth Games Federation.

In 1938 Lynda Adams of Canada won two silver medals and then retired. She made a comeback twelve years later as Mrs Hunt to take the bronze medal in the springboard event in Auckland in 1950.

Sylvie Bernier, Commonwealth silver in 1982, but Olympic gold in 1984.

Highboard Diving continued

1938 1. Doug Tomalin (ENG) 108.74
2. Ron Masters (AUS) 102.87
3. George Athans (CAN) 98.93
1950 1. Peter Heatly (SCO) 156.07
2. George Athans (CAN) 145.36
3. Frank Murphy (AUS) 129.40
1954 1. William Patrick (CAN) 142.70
2. Kevin Newel (AUS) 142.06
3. Peter Heatly (SCO) 141.32
1958 1. Peter Heatly (SCO) 147.79
2. Brian Phelps (ENG) 144.49
3. Ray Cann (ENG) 138.50
1962 1. Brian Phelps (ENG) 168.35
2. Graham Deuble (AUS) 151.00
3. Tony Kitcher (ENG) 150.81
1966 1. Brian Phelps (ENG) 164.57
2. Donald Wagstaff (AUS) 148.44
3. Christopher Robb (AUS) 141.68
1970 1. Donald Wagstaff (AUS) 485.73
2. Philip Drew (ENG) 429.24
3. Andrew Gill (ENG) 421.47
1974 1. Donald Wagstaff (AUS) 490.74
2. Andrew Jackamos (AUS) 472.47
3. Scott Cranham (CAN) 460.98
1978 1. Chris Snode (ENG) 538.98
2. Ken Armstrong (CAN) 534.99
3. Scott Cranham (CAN) 512.37
1982 1. Chris Snode (ENG) 588.54
2. Stephen Foley (AUS) 524.55
3. John Nash (CAN) 523.41

WOMEN

SPRINGBOARD DIVING

1930 1. Oonagh Whitsett (SAF) 90.1 points
2. Doris Ogilvie (CAN) 89.7
3. Mollie Bailey (CAN) 88.7
1934 1. Judy Moss (CAN) 62.27
2. Lesley Thompson (AUS) 60.49
3. Doris Ogilvie (CAN) 57.00
1938 1. Irene Donnett (AUS) 91.18
2. Lynda Adams (CAN) 88.27
3. Marie Sharkey (CAN) 81.66
1950 1. Edna Child (ENG) 126.58
2. Noeline MacLean (AUS) 124.59
3. Lynda Hunt (née Adams) (CAN) 115.38
1954 1. Ann Long (ENG) 128.26
2. Barbara McAulay (AUS) 127.74
3. Irene MacDonald (CAN) 126.19
1958 1. Charmian Welsh (ENG) 118.81
2. Irene MacDonald (CAN) 117.01
3. Elizabeth Ferris (ENG) 113.30
1962 1. Susan Knight (AUS) 134.72
2. Elizabeth Ferris (ENG) 132.74
3. Lorriane McArthur (AUS) 125.13
1966 1. Kathy Rowlatt (ENG) 147.10
2. Beverley Boys (CAN) 134.92
3. Susan Knight (AUS) 134.90
1970 1. Beverley Boys (CAN) 432.87
2. Elizabeth Carruthers (CAN) 391.20
3. Gaye Morley (AUS) 389.04
1974 1. Cindy Shatto (CAN) 430.88
2. Beverley Boys (CAN) 426.93
3. Teri York (CAN) 413.83
1978 1. Janet Nutter (CAN) 477.33
2. Beverley Boys (CAN) 469.65
3. Eniko Kiefer (CAN) 447.42
1982 1. Jenny Donnet (AUS) 484.65
2. Sylvie Bernier (CAN) 478.83
3. Valerie Beddoe (AUS) 446.63

HIGHBOARD DIVING

1930 1. Pearl Stoneham (CAN) 39.3 points
2. Helen McCormick (CAN) 38.3
Only two competitors
1934 1. Elizabeth Macready (ENG) 30.74
2. Lesley Thompson (AUS) 27.64
3. Cecily Cousens (ENG) 27.36
1938 1. Lurline Hook (AUS) 36.47
2. Lynda Adams (CAN) 36.39
3. Irene Donnett (AUS) 34.57
1950 1. Edna Child (ENG) 70.89
2. Gwen Fawcett (AUS) 65.64
3. Noeline MacLean (AUS) 59.93
1954 1. Barbara McAulay (AUS) 86.55
2. Eunice Millar (ENG) 79.86
3. Ann Long (ENG) 79.53
1958 1. Charmain Welsh (ENG) 77.23
2. Ann Long (ENG) 73.69
3. Molly Wieland (ENG) 65.82
1962 1. Susan Knight (AUS) 101.15
2. Margaret Austen (ENG) 98.93
3. Patricia Plowman (AUS) 91.79
1966 1. Joy Newman (ENG) 98.87
2. Robyn Bradshaw (AUS) 98.85
3. Beverley Boys (CAN) 97.21
1970 1. Beverley Boys (CAN) 352.95
2. Nancy Robertson (CAN) 350.49
3. Shelagh Burrow (ENG) 330.63
1974 1. Beverley Boys (CAN) 361.95
2. Beverley Williams (ENG) 352.14
3. Madeline Barnett (AUS) 339.30
1978 1. Linda Cuthbert (CAN) 397.44
2. Valerie McFarlane (AUS) 383.40
3. Janet Nutter (CAN) 374.67
1982 1. Valerie Beddoe (AUS) 404.16
2. Jennifer McArton (CAN) 390.21
3. Kathy Kelemen (CAN) 359.31

Four Commonwealth diving gold medals for Chris Snode. He won by a huge margin in 1982 to emphasise his superiority.

Left: Brian Phelps remains England's best remembered diver. He won the double at both 1962 and 1966 Games.

Above right: Brian Phelps with the other 1966 medallists, Australians Don Wagstaff and Christopher Robb. Wagstaff went on to emulate Phelps with four golds, while Beverley Boys (above left) won just one fewer.

SWIMMING AND DIVING - MEDAL TABLE BY NATIONS

Nation		Men			Women		Total
	G	S	B	G	S	B	
Australia	70	43	44	54	47	41	299
Canada	40	46	42	37	42	32	239
England	25	37	42	36	29	35	204
New Zealand	5	8	11	2	6	12	44
Scotland	8	10	7	3	4	11	43
South Africa	3	4	3	4	6	2	22
Wales	2	3	2	1	3	2	13
Guyana	-	1	-	-	-	-	1
Jamaica	-	1	-	-	-	-	1
Isle of Man	-	-	-	-	-	1	1

WEIGHTLIFTING MEDALLISTS

From 1950 to 1970 the totals are given for the three lifts - Press, Snatch and Jerk. The Press was then dropped from international weightlifting, so from 1974 the totals are for Snatch and Jerk. Note that from 1950 to 1966 the lifts were in pounds, which have here also been converted to kilograms. From 1970 the lifts have been measured in kilograms.

FLYWEIGHT - up to 52kg

1970 1. George Vasiliades (AUS) 290kg
2. Abdul Ghafoor (PAK) 287.5
3. John McNiven (SCO) 265
1974 1. Precious McKenzie (ENG) 215
2. Anil Mondal (IND) 200
3. John McNiven (SCO) 192.5
1978 1. E. Karunakaran (IND) 205
2. Charles Revolta (SCO) 197.5
3. Roger Crabtree (AUS) 190
1982 1. Nick Voukelatos (AUS) 207.5
2. Grunadan Kombiah (IND) 200
3. Lawrence Tom (NIG) 192.5

BANTAMWEIGHT - up to 56kg

1950 1. Tho Fook Hung (MAL) 655lb/297kg
2. Rosaire Smith (CAN) 615/279
3. Keith Caple (AUS) 600/272
1954 1. Maurice Megennis (ENG) 620/281
2. Frank Cope (ENG) 610/276.5
3. Keith Caple (AUS) 605/274
1958 1. Reginald Gaffley (SAF) 660/299
2. Ronald Brownbill (ENG) 630/285.5
3. Marcel Gosselin (CAN) 605/274
1962 1. Chua Phung Kim (SIN) 710/322
2. Allen Salter (CAN) 685/310.5
3. Martin Dias (BGU) 675/306
1966. 1. Precious McKenzie (ENG) 705/319.5
2. Martin Dias (GUY) 677.5/307
3. Chon Hon Chan (CAN) 672/304.5
1970 1. Precious McKenzie (ENG) 335
2. Tony Phillips (BAR) 317.5
3. Chye Hong Tung (SIN) 302.5
1974 1. Michael Adams (AUS) 222.5
2. Yves Carignan (CAN) 212.5
3. Shanmug Velliswamy (IND) 212.5
1978 1. Precious McKenzie (NZL) 220
2. Tamil Selvan (IND) 220
3. Jeffrey Bryce (WAL) 215
1982 1. Geoffrey Laws (ENG) 235
2. Bijar Kumar Satpathy (IND) 227.5
3. Lorenzo Orsini (AUS) 222.5

FEATHERWEIGHT - up to 60kg

1950 1. Koh Eng Tong (MAL) 685lb/310.5
2. Julian Creus (ENG) 670/304
3. Barrie Englebrecht (SAF) 640/290
1954 1. Rodney Wilkes (TRI) 690/313
2. Jules Sylvain (CAN) 655/297
3. Ron Jenkins (WAL) 615/279
1958 1. Tan Ser Cher (SIN) 685/310.5
2. Chung Kum Weng (MAL) 675/306
3. Rodney Wilkes (TRI) 670/304
1962 1. George Newton (ENG) 720/326.5
2. Ieuan Owen (WAL) 645/292.5
3. Kam Hong Cheong (MAL) 620/281
1966 1. Kum Chung (WAL) 743.5/337
2. Mohon Ghosh (IND) 738/334.5
3. Allen Salter (CAN) 716/324.5
1970 1. George Perrin (ENG) 342.5
2. Phung Kim Chua (SIN) 340
3. Alexander Navis (IND) 335
1974 1. George Vasiliades (AUS) 237.5
2. Gerald Hay (AUS) 235
3. Brian Duffy (NZ) 232.5
1978 1. Michel Mercier (CAN) 237.5
2. Ivan Katz (AUS) 235
3. Darrell Schultz (CAN) 230
1982 1. Dean Willey (ENG) 267.5
2. M.T. Selvan (IND) 245
3. Koon-Siong Chua (SIN) 242.5

LIGHTWEIGHT - up to 67.5kg

1950 1. James Halliday (ENG) 760lb/344.5kg
2. Thong Saw Pak (MAL) 735/333
3. Verdi Barberis (AUS) 735/333
1954 1. Verdi Barberis (AUS) 765/347
2. George Nicholls (BAR) 760/344.5
3. Jan Pieterse (SAF) 735/333
1958 1. Tan Howe Liang (SIN) 790/358
2. Harold Webber (SAF) 750/340
3. Ben Helfgott (ENG) 750/340
1962 1. Carlton Goring (ENG) 775/351.5
2. Alan Oshyer (AUS) 750/340
3. James Moir (SCO) 750/340
1966 1. Hugo Gittens (TRI) 809/367
2. George Newton (ENG) 782/354.5
3. Ieuan Owen (WAL) 771/349.5
1970 1. George Newton (ENG) 372.5
2. Ieuan Owen (WAL) 355
3. Bruce Cameron (NZ) 335
1974 1. George Newton (ENG) 260
2. Ieuan Owen (WAL) 255
3. Bruce Cameron (NZ) 252.5
1978 1. Bill Stellios (AUS) 272.5
2. Adrian Kebbe (AUS) 267.5
3. Philip Sue (NZ) 262.5
1982 1. David Morgan (WAL) 295
2. Bill Stellios (AUS) 285
3. Patrick Bassey (NIG) 277.5

MIDDLEWEIGHT - up to 75kg

1950 1. Gerard Gratton (CAN) 795lb/360.5kg
2. Bruce George (NZL) 740/335.5
3. Fred Griffin (AUS) 720/326.5
1954 1. James Halliday (ENG) 800/362.5
2. Lionel De Freitas (TRI) 755/342
3. Julius Park (GUY) 745/338
1958 1. Blair Blenman (BAR) 795/360.5
2. Winston McArthur (GUY) 795/360.5
3. Adrien Gilbert (CAN) 785/356
1962 1. Tan Howe Laing (SIN) 860/390
2. Pierre St Jean (CAN) 830/376
3. Horace Johnson (WAL) 820/372
1966 1. Pierre St Jean (CAN) 892.5/404.5
2. Horace Johnson (WAL) 843/382
3. Russell Perry (AUS) 821/372
1970 1. Russell Perry (AUS) 412.5
2. Tony Ebert (NZL) 402.5
3. Pierre St Jean (CAN) 400
1974 1. Tony Ebert (NZL) 275
2. Stanley Bailey (TRI) 275
3. Robert Wrench (WAL) 270
1978 1. Sam Castiglione (AUS) 300
2. Newton Burrowes (ENG) 290
3. Stephen Pinsent (ENG) 290
1982 1. Stephen Pinsent (ENG) 312.5
2. Tony Pignone (AUS) 305
3. Jacques Demers (CAN) 302.5

LIGHT-HEAVYWEIGHT - up to 82.5kg

1950 1. James Varaleau (CAN) 815lb/369.5kg
2. Issy Bloomberg (SAF) 815/369.5
3. Tan Kim Bee (MAL) 765/347
1954 1. Gerry Gratton (CAN) 890/403.5
2. Louis Greeff (SAF) 810/367
3. Bruce George (NZL) 780/353.5
1958 1. Phil Caira (SCO) 875/396.5
2. Sylvanus Blackman (BAR) 850/385.5
3. Jack Kestell (SAF) 850/385.5
1962 1. Phil Caira (SCO) 900/408
2. George Manners (ENG) 890/403.5
3. Peter Arthur (WAL) 865/392
1966 1. George Vakakis (AUS) 925.5/419.5
2. Sylvanus Blackman (ENG) 914.5/414.5
3. Michael Pearman (ENG) 903.5/409.5
1970 1. Nicolo Ciancio (AUS) 447.5
2. John Bolton (NZL) 445
3. Peter Arthur (WAL) 427.5
1974 1. Tony Ford (ENG) 302.5
2. Paul Wallwork (WSA) 300
3. Michael Pearman (ENG) 292.5

Weightlifting

The sport was first included in the Games at Auckland in 1950. At that time there were seven weight categories, but two more were added in 1970 and a further one in 1978.

Only one man has won Commonwealth and Olympic titles. In Brisbane in 1982 Dinko 'Dean' Lukin won the super-heavyweight title for Australia and then in Los Angeles two years later, in the absence of the great East European lifters he won the Olympic gold medal. Prior to the 1984 Games, when the Eastern Bloc's boycott seriously weakened the fields, three lifters progressed from Commonwealth gold to Olympic silver: Gerard Gratton (CAN) 1950 and 1952 respectively, Howe Liang Tan (SIN) 1958 and 1960, Louis Martin (ENG) 1962 and 1964. Rodney Wilkes (TRI) achieved this double in reverse order, 1950 and 1948.

Dean 'Dinko' Lukin, Australia's first Olympic weightlifting champion. He followed Commonwealth super-heavyweight success in 1982 with gold at Los Angeles in 1984.

Middle-heavyweight Louis Martin has been one of the few Commonwealth lifters in recent years to be able to match the Eastern Europeans. He represented Jamaica in 1958, when he was eliminated early in the competition, but a year later won his first world title. Representing England he won three Commonwealth titles from 1962 to 1970. Traditionally the weightlifting programme is staged in ascending order of weights, but when the Games were staged in Martin's native country of Jamaica in 1966 his category was moved to the end to provide an appropriate climax to the events.

The delightfully named Precious McKenzie is the only man to have won four gold medals, and is also the oldest champion. He received his name after surprisingly, but happily, surviving surgery when he was born in South Africa. While still very young he lost his father to a crocodile. Although he was the best lifter at his weight in 1958 another, white, South African was sent to the

Light-Heavyweight continued

1978 1. Robert Kabbas (AUS) 322.5
2. Charles Quagliata (AUS) 287.5
3. Gary Shadbolt (ENG) 277.5
1982 1. Newton Burrowes (ENG) 325
2. Guy Greavette (CAN) 320
3. Cosmos Idioh (NGR) 317.5

MIDDLE-HEAVYWEIGHT - up to 90kg

1954 1. Keevil Daly (CAN) 880lb/399kg
2. Lennox Kilgour (TRI) 865/392
3. Joseph Barnett (ENG) 830/376.5
1958 1. Manoel Santos (AUS) 890/403.5
2. Tan Kim Bee (MAL) 865/392
3. Leonard Treganowan (AUS) 835/378.5
1962 1. Louis Martin (ENG) 1035/469.5
2. Cosford White (CAN) 900/408
3. Jackie Samuel (TRI) 880/399
1966 1. Louis Martin (ENG) 1019/462
2. George Manners (ENG) 947/429.5
3. Dudley Lawson (JAM) 931/422
1970 1. Louis Martin (ENG) 457.5
2. Robert Santavy (CAN) 425
3. George Manners (SVI) 410
1974 1. Nicolo Ciancio (AUS) 330
2. Brian Marsden (NZL) 315
3. Steven Wyatt (AUS) 310
1978 1. Gary Langford (ENG) 335
2. Terry Hadlow (CAN) 330
3. Brian Marsden (NZL) 312.5
1982 1. Robert Kabbas (AUS) 337.5
2. Peter Pinsent (ENG) 335
3. Mick Sabljak (AUS) 325

SUB-HEAVYWEIGHT - up to 100kg

1978 1. John Burns (WAL) 340
2. Steve Wyatt (AUS) 325
3. Robert Santavy (CAN) 315
1982 1. Oliver Orok (NGR) 350
2. Gary Langford (ENG) 350
3. Kevin Roy (CAN) 340

HEAVYWEIGHT - up to 110kg

1950 1. Harold Cleghorn (NZL) 900lb/408kg
2. Ray Magee (AUS) 830/376
Only two competed
1954 1. Doug Hepburn (CAN) 1040/471.5
2. Dave Baillie (CAN) 1000/453.5
3. Harold Cleghorn (NZL) 930/421.5
1958 1. Ken McDonald (ENG) 1005/455.5
2. Dave Baillie (CAN) 985/446.5
3. Arthur Shannos (AUS) 870/394.5
1962 1. Arthur Shannos (AUS) 1025/465
2. Donald Oliver (NZL) 1025/465
3. Brandon Bailey (TRI) 970/440
1966 1. Donald Oliver (NZL) 1096/497
2. Arthur Shannos (AUS) 1024/464.5
3. Brandon Bailey (TRI) 1019.5/462
1970 1. Russell Prior (CAN) 490
2. Dave Hancock (ENG) 470
3. Price Morris (CAN) 470
1974 1. Russell Prior (CAN) 352.5
2. John Bolton (NZL) 340
3. John Barrett (NZL) 320
1978 1. Russell Prior (CAN) 347.5
2. Wayne Smith (CAN) 337.5
3. Andy Drzwiecki (ENG) 335
1982 1. John Burns (WAL) 347.5
2. Joe Kabalan (AUS) 325
3. Mario LeBlanc (CAN) 315

SUPER-HEAVYWEIGHT - over 110kg

1970 1. Ray Rigby (AUS) 500kg
2. Terry Perdue (WAL) 500
3. Grant Anderson (SCO) 432.5
1974 1. Graham May (NZL) 342.5
2. Andy Kerr (ENG) 337.5
3. Terry Purdue (WAL) 330
1978 1. Jean-Marc Cardinal (CAN) 365
2. Bob Edmond (AUS) 322.5
3. John Hynd (SCO) 305
1982 1. Dean Lukin (AUS) 377.5
2. Bob Edmond (AUS) 347.5
3. Bassey Ironbar (NGR) 320

Associated Sports Photography

WEIGHTLIFTING - MEDAL TABLE BY NATIONS

Nation	G	S	B	Total
Australia	17	13	11	41
England	21	12	7	40
Canada	11	12	11	34
New Zealand	5	6	8	19
Wales	4	5	8	17
Trinidad & Tobago	2	3	4	9
India	1	6	2	9
Scotland	2	1	5	8
Singapore	4	1	2	7
Malaysia	2	3	2	7
South Africa	1	3	3	7
Nigeria	1	-	4	5
Barbados	1	3	-	4
Guyana	-	2	2	4
Pakistan	-	1	-	1
Western Samoa	-	1	-	1
Jamaica	-	-	1	1
St. Vincent	-	-	1	1

1978 lightweight champion Bill Stellios of Australia also took the silver in 1982.

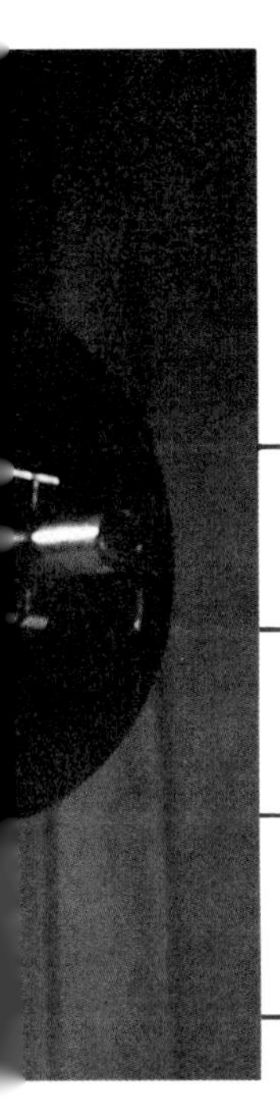

England's greatest lifters, and both triple gold medallists: middle-heavyweight Louis Martin (left) and bantamweight Precious McKenzie (below). McKenzie added a fourth gold at flyweight.

Games in Cardiff and indeed won the gold medal. Eventually Precious left and arrived in Britain shortly before the 1966 Games. Special efforts were made to rush through his citizenship so that he could acquire a British passport and he arrived in Kingston as a member of the English team. He won the gold medal, a feat he repeated at the next two Games. At the second, held in Christchurch, he was so attracted by New Zealand that he emigrated there and wore New Zealand colours when he won again in 1978. On that occasion the Queen and Prince Philip extended their visit to the weightlifting events by some two hours more than had been planned in order to be present when Precious made Games history, not only with his fourth title but also as the oldest champion at 42 years 59 days.

A previous visit by the Queen to Games weightlifting was nearly marred, for in 1974, only minutes before the royal party was due, Graham May, New Zealand's super-heavyweight, the eventual champion, passed out while holding the bar above his head, falling forward so that the enormous weight rolled into the first few rows of seats, just where the Queen was due to sit.

The youngest champion was probably David Morgan of Wales at 18 years 2 days when he won the lightweight title in 1982. At those Games English brothers Steve and Peter Pinsent won gold and silver respectively.

ONE COMPANY HAS THE ENERGY
TO RUN TO THE YEAR 2000-AND BEYOND.
BNFL
To reach the finish of its current export order book, British Nuclear Fuels will be producing energy up to the end of this century and on into the next.
With over 15,000 employees, the Company supplies nuclear fuel for all Britain's nuclear power stations, which together produce over 20% of the country's electricity.
As an international leader in the field of nuclear fuel manufacture, reprocessing and transportation, British Nuclear Fuels are making a significant contribution to meeting the worlds's energy needs.
British Nuclear Fuels plc,
Risley, Warrington,
Cheshire. WA3 6AS

WRESTLING MEDALLISTS

48kg - LIGHT-FLYWEIGHT

1970 1. Ved Prakash (IND)
2. Kenneth Shand (CAN)
3. Masih Sadiq (PAK) & Donald Urquhart (SCO)
1974 1. Mitchell Kawasaki (CAN)
2. Walter Koenig (AUS)
3. Radhey Shyam (IND)
1978 1. Ashok Kumar (IND)
2. George Gunouski (CAN)
3. Mark Dunbar (ENG)
1982 1. Ram Chander Sarang (IND)
2. Steven Reinsfield (NZL)
3. Maldwyn Cooper (CAN)

52kg - FLYWEIGHT

1950 1. Bert Harris (AUS)
2. Eric Matthews (NZL)
Only two wrestlers
1954 1. Louis Baise (SAF)
2. Fred Flannery (AUS)
3. Din Mohammad (PAK)
1958 1. Ian Epton (SAF)
2. Shujah-ud-Din (PAK)
3. Fred Flannery (CAN)
1962 1. Mohammad Niaz (PAK)
2. Peter Michienzi (CAN)
3. Warren Nisbet (NZL)
1966 1. Mohammad Nazir (PAK)
2. Shamrao Sable (IND)
3. Peter Michienzi (CAN)
1970 1. Sudesh Kumar (IND)
2. Mohammad Nazir (PAK)
3. David Stitt (CAN)
1974 1. Sudesh Kumar (IND)
2. Gordon Bertie (CAN)
3. John Navie (AUS)
1978 1. Ray Takahashi (CAN)
2. Sudesh Kumar (IND)
3. Ken Hoyt (AUS)
1982 1. Mahabir Singh (IND)
2. Ray Takahashi (CAN)
3. Ken Hoyt (AUS)

57kg - BANTAMWEIGHT

1930 1. James Trifunov (CAN)
2. Joseph Reid (ENG)
Only two wrestlers
1934 1. Edward Melrose (SCO)
2. Ted McKinley (CAN)
3. Joseph Reid (ENG)
1938 1. Ted Purcell (AUS)
2. Vernon Blake (CAN)
3. Raymond Cazaux (ENG)
1950 1. Douglas Mudgeway (NZL)
2. Jim Chapman (AUS)
Only two wrestlers
1954 1. Geoffrey Jameson (AUS)
2. Mohamad Amin (PAK)
3. Ian Epton (ZAM)
1958 1. Muhammad Akhter (PAK)
2. Geoffrey Jameson (AUS)
3. Daniel van der Walt (SAF)
1962 1. Siraj-ud-Din (PAK)
2. Walter Pilling (ENG)
3. James Turnbll (SCO)
1966 1. Bishamber Singh (IND)
2. Kevin McGrath (AUS)
3. Mohammad Saeed (PAK)
1970 1. Sardar Mohd (PAK)
2. Herbert Singerman (CAN)
3. Terence Robinson (ENG)
1974 1. Premnath (IND)
2. Amrik Singh Gill (ENG)
3. Kevin Burke (AUS)
1978 1. Satbir Singh (IND)
2. Michael Barry (CAN)
3. Amrik Singh Gill (ENG)
1982 1. Brian Aspen (ENG)
2. Ashok Kumar (IND)
3. Chris Maddock (NZL)

62kg - FEATHERWEIGHT

1930 1. Clifford Chilcott (CAN)
Only wrestler
1934 1. Robert McNab (CAN)
2. Joe Nelson (ENG)
3. Murdoch White (SCO)
1938 1. Roy Purchase (AUS)
2. Larry Clarke (CAN)
3. Joseph Genet (NZL)
1950 1. John Armitt (NZL)
2. Roland Milord (CAN)
3. Arnold Parsons (ENG)
1954 1. Abraham Geldenhuys (SAF)
2. Herbert Hall (ENG)
3. John Armitt (NZL)
1958 1. Abraham Geldenhuys (SAF)
2. Siraj-ud-Din (PAK)
3. Albert Aspen (ENG)
1962 1. Ala-ud-Din (PAK)
2. Matti Jutila (CAN)
3. Albert Aspen (ENG)
1966 1. Mohammad Akhtar (PAK)
2. Randhawa Singh (IND)
3. Albert Aspen (ENG)
1970 1. Mohammad Saeed (PAK)
2. Patrick Bolger (CAN)
3. Randhawa Singh (IND)
1974 1. Egon Beiler (CAN)
2. Shivaji Chingle (IND)
3. Raymond Brown (AUS)
1978 1. Egon Beiler (CAN)
2. Jagminder Singh (IND)
3. Brian Aspen (ENG)
1982 1. Bob Robinson (CAN)
2. Chris Brown (AUS)
3. Austine Atasie (NGR)

68kg - LIGHTWEIGHT

1930 1. Howard Thomas (CAN)
2. Harold Angus (ENG)
Only two wrestlers
1934 1. Richard Garrard (AUS)
2. G. North (ENG)
3. Howard Thomas (CAN)
1938 1. Richard Garrard (AUS)
2. Vernon Thomas (NZL)
3. Alfred Harding (SAF)
1950 1. Richard Garrard (AUS)
2. Morgan Plumb (CAN)
3. George Hobson (NZL)
1954 1. Godfrey Pienaar (SAF)
2. Ruby Leibovitch (CAN)
3. Richard Garrard (AUS)
1958 1. Muhammad Ashraf (PAK)
2. Alastair Duncan (SCO)
3. Anthony Ries (SAF)
1962 1. Muhammad Akhtar (PAK)
2. Sidney Marsh (AUS)
3. Kurt Boese (CAN)
1966 1. Mukhtiar Singh (IND)
2. Ray Lougheed (CAN)
3. Anthony Greig (NZL)
1970 1. Udey Chand (IND)
2. Mohammad Yaqub (PAK)
3. Ole Sorenson (CAN)
1974 1. Jagrup Singh (IND)
2. Joseph Gilligan (ENG)
3. Stephen Martin (CAN)
1978 1. Zsigmund Kelevitz (AUS)
2. Joseph Gilligan (ENG)
3. Jagdish Kumar (IND)
1982 1. Jagminder Singh (IND)
2. Zsigmund Kelevitz (AUS)
3. Lloyd Renken (CAN)

74kg - WELTERWEIGHT

1930 1. Reg Priestley (CAN)
2. Harry Johnson (ENG)
Only two wrestlers
1934 1. Joseph Schleimer (CAN)
2. William Fox (ENG)
3. Rashid Anwar (IND)
1938 1. Thomas Trevaskis (AUS)
2. Felix Standen (SAF)
3. Jeremiah Podjursky (NZL)
1950 1. Henry Hudson (CAN)
2. Jack Little (AUS)
3. Martin Jooste (SAF)
1954 1. Nicholas Laubscher (SAF)
2. Abdul Rashid (PAK)
3. Raymond Myland (ENG)
1958 1. Muhammad Bashir (PAK)
2. Lachmi Kant Pandey (IND)
3. Coenraad de Villiers (SAF)
1962 1. Muhammad Bashir (PAK)
2. Philip Oberlander (CAN)
3. Leonard Allen (ENG)
1966 1. Mohammad Bashir (PAK)
2. Richard Bryant (CAN)
3. Hukum Singh (IND)
1970 1. Mukhtiar Singh (IND)
2. Alfred Wurr (CAN)
3. Gordon Mackay (NZL)
1974 1. Raghunath Pawar (IND)
2. Anthony Shacklady (ENG)
3. Gordon Mackay (NZL)
1978 1. Rajinder Singh (IND)
2. Victor Zilberman (CAN)
3. Keith Haward (ENG)
1982 1. Rajinder Singh (IND)
2. Ken Reinsfield (NZL)
3. Brian Renken (CAN)

82kg - MIDDLEWEIGHT

1930 1. Mike Chepwick (CAN)
2. Stanley Bissell (ENG)
3. Max Thiel (SAF)
1934 1. Terry Evans (CAN)
2. Stanley Bissell (ENG)
3. Robert Harcus (SCO)
1938 1. Terry Evans (CAN)
2. Peter Sheasby (SAF)
3. Leslie Jeffers (ENG)
1950 1. Maurice Vachon (CAN)
2. Bruce Arthur (AUS)
3. Carel Reitz (SAF)
1954 1. Hermanus van Zyl (SAF)
2. James Christie (CAN)
3. Henry Kendall (ENG)
1958 1. Hermanus van Zyl (SAF)
2. George Farquhar (SCO)
3. Raymond Myland (ENG)
1962 1. Muhammad Faiz (PAK)
2. Michael Benarik (AUS)
3. Frederick Thomas (NZL)
1966 1. Muhammad Faiz (PAK)
2. Sebastien Donison (CAN)
3. Michael Benarik (AUS)
1970 1. Harish Rajindra (IND)
2. Nick Schori (CAN)
3. David Aspin (NZL) & Ron Grinstead (ENG)
1974 1. David Aspin (NZL)
2. Satpal Singh (IND)
3. Taras Hryb (CAN)
1978 1. Richard Deschatelets (CAN)
2. Walter Koenig (AUS)
3. Anthony Shacklady (ENG)
1982 1. Chris Rinke (CAN)
2. Walter Koenig (AUS)
3. Jai Parkash Kangar (IND)

90kg - LIGHT-HEAVYWEIGHT

1930 1. Bill McIntyre (CAN)
2. Edgar Bacon (ENG)
Only two wrestlers
1934 1. Mick Cubbin (SAF)
2. Bernard Rowe (ENG)
3. Alex Watt (CAN)

Wrestling

Sporting Pictures (UK) Ltd.

Noel Loban,Olympic light-heavyweight wrestling bronze medallist in 1984, will be a strong favourite for Commonwealth honours in Edinburgh.

Freestyle wrestling has been one of only four sports included at all Games. It was originally contested at seven weight categories, a class was added in 1954 and a further two in 1970.

More than a third of all gold medals won in wrestling have been won by men from India or Pakistan, before that nation left the Commonwealth. Indeed, two of the three men to win three gold medals were Pakistanis, Muhammad Bashir at welterweight 1958-66 and Muhammad Faiz at middleweight 1962-6 and light-heavyweight 1970. The third man to achieve this feat was one of the outstanding champions of the Games, Richard Garrard of Australia. He won his first two gold medals at lightweight in 1934 and 1938, but then had to wait until 1950 for his third, when he was 17 days past his 41st birthday. He was not finished, for he won a bronze medal in 1954. In his long wrestling career he lost only nine bouts out of a total of 525.

The youngest gold medallist was Ved Prakash of India who was stated to be not more than 14 when he won the light-flyweight title in 1970. He was thought to be as young as 12 by some of his team-mates and at first the authorities were close to barring him from competing due to his age. However his passport showed him as 14 years 7 months old. Only a little older had been the 15 year old New Zealander Eric Matthews, silver medallist in 1950.

90kg - Light Heavyweight continued

1938 1. Edward Scarf (AUS)
2. Sidney Greenspan (SAF)
3. Thomas Ward (SCO)

1950 1. Patrick Morton (SAF)
2. Arthur Sneddon (NZL)
3. Thomas Trevaskis (AUS)

1954 1. Jacob Theron (SAF)
2. Robert Steckle (CAN)
3. Daniel van Staden (ZAM)

1958 1. Jacob Theron (SAF)
2. Muhammad Ali (PAK)
3. Robert Steckle (CAN)

1962 1. Anthony Buck (ENG)
2. Muhammad Saeed (PAK)
3. James Armstrong (AUS)

1966 1. Robert Chamberot (CAN)
2. Wallace Booth (SCO)
3. Bishwanath Singh (IND)

1970 1. Muhammad Faiz (PAK)
2. Sajjan Singh (IND)
3. Claude Pilon (CAN)

1974 1. Terry Paice (CAN)
2. Netra Pal Singh (IND)
3. Maurice Allan (SCO)

1978 1. Stephen Danier (CAN)
2. Mick Pikos (AUS)
3. Kartar Singh (IND)

1982 1. Clark Davis (CAN)
2. Kartar Singh (IND)
3. Nigel Sargent (NZL)

100kg - HEAVYWEIGHT

1930 1. Earl McCready (CAN)
2. Alex Sanguine (ENG)
Only two wrestlers

1934 1. Jack Knight (AUS)
2. Pat Meehan (CAN)
3. Archie Dudgeon (SCO)

1938 1. Jack Knight (AUS)
2. James Dryden (NZL)
3. John Whelan (CAN)

1950 1. James Armstrong (AUS)
2. Patrick O'Connor (NZL)
3. Kenneth Richmond (ENG)

1954 1. Kenneth Richmond (ENG)
2. Keith Maltman (CAN)
Only two wrestlers

1958 1. Lila Ram (IND)
2. Jacobus Hanekom (SAF)
3. Ray Mitchell (AUS)

1962 1. Muhammad Niaz (PAK)
2. Ray Mitchell (AUS)
3. Dennis McNamara (ENG)

1966 1. Bhim Singh (IND)
2. Ikram Ilahi (PAK)
3. Dennis McNamara (ENG)

1970 1. Edward Millard (CAN)
2. Bishwanath Singh (IND)
3. Muhammad Riaz (PAK)

1974 1. Claude Pilon (CAN)
2. Dadu Chaugule (IND)
3. Ian Duncan (SCO)

1978 1. Wyatt Wishart (CAN)
2. Satpal Singh (IND)
3. Murray Avery (NZL)

1982 1. Richard Deschatelets (CAN)
2. Satpal Singh (IND)
3. Murray Avery (AUS)

OVER 100kg - SUPER HEAVYWEIGHT

1970 1. Ikram Ilahi (PAK)
2. Maruti Mane (IND)
3. Dennis McNamara (ENG)

1974 1. Bill Benko (CAN)
2. Bishwanath Singh (IND)
3. Gary Knight (NZL)

1978 1. Robert Gibbons (CAN)
2. Albert Patrick (SCO)
3. Ishwar Singh (IND)

1982 1. Wyatt Wishart (CAN)
2. Rajinder Singh (IND)
3. Albert Patrick (SCO)

No wrestler has won both Commonwealth and Olympic titles, the closest being Dick Garrard, who won the 1948 Olympic silver medal. Another Olympic medallist, Ken Richmond, bronze in 1952, won the 1954 Commonwealth heavyweight title and was even better known as the man who struck the gong in the introductory sequence to films made by the J. Arthur Rank organisation.

Another wrestler who achieved fame beyond his wrestling abilities was Archie Dudgeon of Scotland. He won a bronze medal in the 1934 heavyweight class. At a weight of 139kg (21½ stone) he was the heaviest known sportsman ever to compete at the Commonwealth Games and was nicknamed 'The Loch Ness Monster'.

Photo Library International

WRESTLING - MEDAL TABLE BY NATIONS

Nation	G	S	B	Total
Canada	31	26	15	72
India	20	18	9	47
England	3	17	22	42
Australia	13	15	11	39
Pakistan	18	9	4	31
New Zealand	3	7	14	24
South Africa	12	4	7	23
Scotland	1	4	9	14
Zambia	-	-	2	2
Nigeria	-	-	1	1

Kodak
KODAK. OFFICIAL SPONSORS OF BRITISH ATHLETICS
KODAK
1

1.

2.

3.

4.

1. Australian Gary Honey is a prime contender for the long jump title. He won the 1984 Olympic silver medal and is the defending Commonwealth champion.
2. Milt Ottey of Canada, the 1982 high jump champion, stands just 1.78m (5ft 10in) tall, but has cleared a bar 54cm above his own height.
3. Locked in conflict, wrestling has been on every Games programme.
4. Kirsty McDermott (Wales) won the Commonwealth title at 800m in 1982, but reached top world class at both 800m and 1500m in 1985.
5. David Corkill from Belfast, Northern Ireland's bowls hope.
6. Ben Johnson of Canada won the World Cup 100m in 1985 to establish himself as the Games sprint favourite.
7. Geoff Parsons (Scotland) improved his British high jump best to 2.30m indoors in 1986.
8. Judy Oakes has a fine big event record, including the 1982 Commonwealth shot title.

7.

5.

6.

8.

1. Graeme Fell, after marrying a Canadian, has switched allegiance to that country from England. He set a Canadian steeplechase record of 8:12.58, the fastest in the Commonwealth in 1985.
2. Grace Jackson, as her name implies, is a sublime 200m runner. The Jamaican was fifth at both 100m and 200m in the 1984 Olympics.
3. Helen Troke has improved fast to become England's top badminton player.
4. Speed of reaction and ice-cool nerves are needed in skeet shooting.
5. Number one for three successive years at the AAA 400m, Darren Clark (Australia) will face a world-class 400m line-up in Edinburgh.
6. The Australian high jumper Christine Stanton won the silver medal behind Debbie Brill in 1982. Mrs Stanton is also a former Commonwealth heptathlon record holder.
7. From raking the long jump pit in 1970, Allan Wells has pursued a brilliant Commonwealth Games career, with four golds, a silver and a bronze. Can he add more medals on his home track of Meadowbank Stadium?
8. The rowing events will take place in beautiful Strathclyde Park.

2.

1.

3.

4.

5.

7.

8.

6.

The brand new 1986/87 edition of the AA Members' Handbook is out now. The cover is grey.
But, with over 2,500 up-dated entries, the contents are far from it. For your free copy, just bring your current Personal Certificate along to any AA Centre or AA Roadside Centre. If you're not a Member, doesn't that make you green?

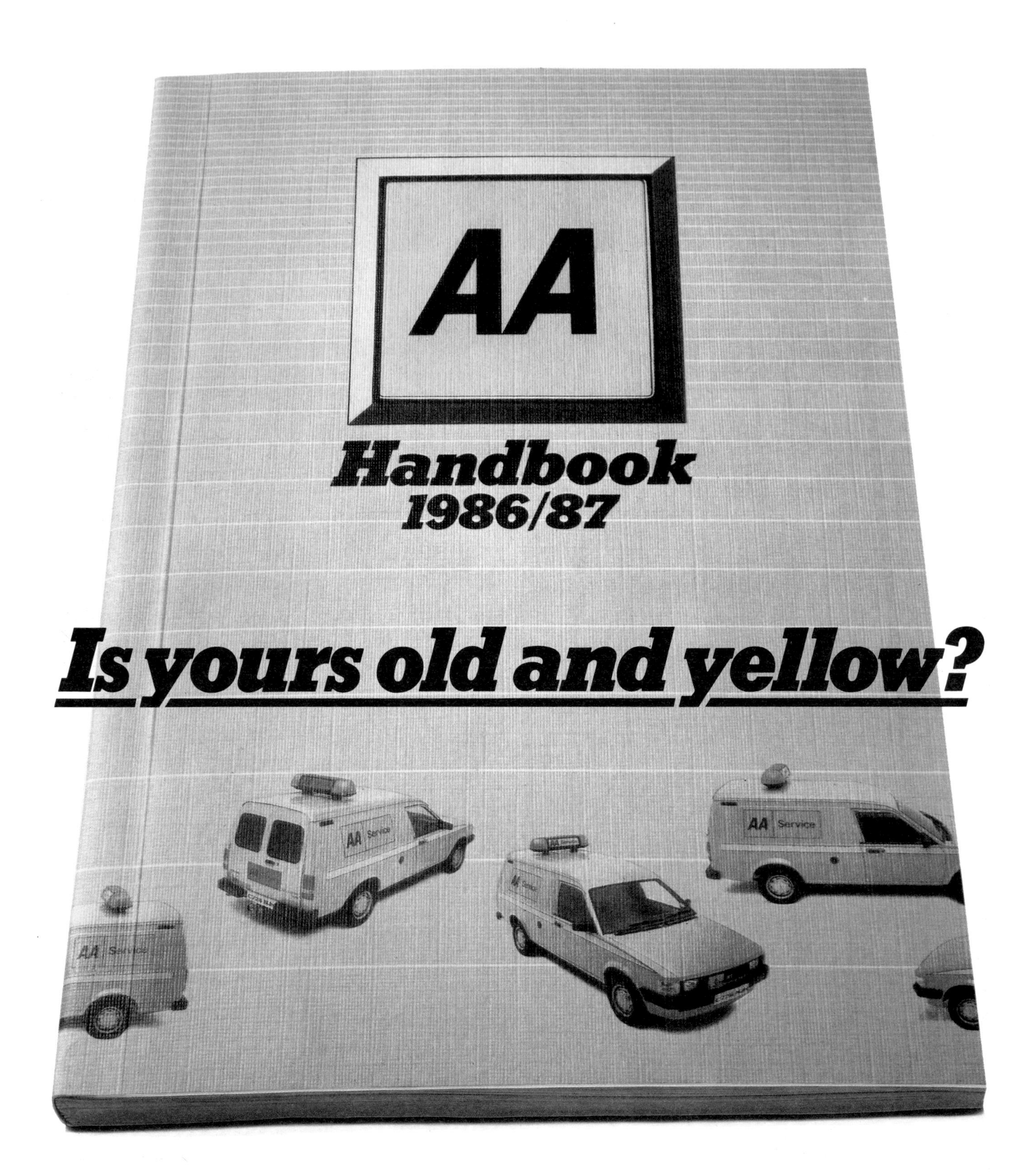

Anita Lonsbrough

on My Fair Lady

Looking back over my own swimming career,' which I must admit seems almost in another life, I always think of the Commonwealth Games because they do live up to their name of 'The Friendly Games'.

I had never dreamt of competing at such a high level and mixing with great names from all sports! Britain's number one swimmer at this time was Judy Grinham, the Olympic backstroke champion. In my memories Judy and my first Commonwealth Games are synonymous.

Prior to the Cardiff Games in 1958, Judy had seen 'My Fair Lady' and so led the sing song on the coach from the Commonwealth village at St. Athan to the Empire Pool for training sessions, and back. She would sit on the middle seat of the back row and lead us through all the songs. So now, every time I hear 'Oh! wouldn't it be lovely' or 'falls mainly on the plain' my mind drifts back to those happy times in Cardiff, and Judy.

Number One seemed to be my lucky number at the time. I was in the first event, first heat, lane one. Yes, you have guessed right - I was the first heat winner and the first swimmer to set a Games record!

Remembering anything about that swim is difficult, but I do recall Chris Gosden, who at the time was

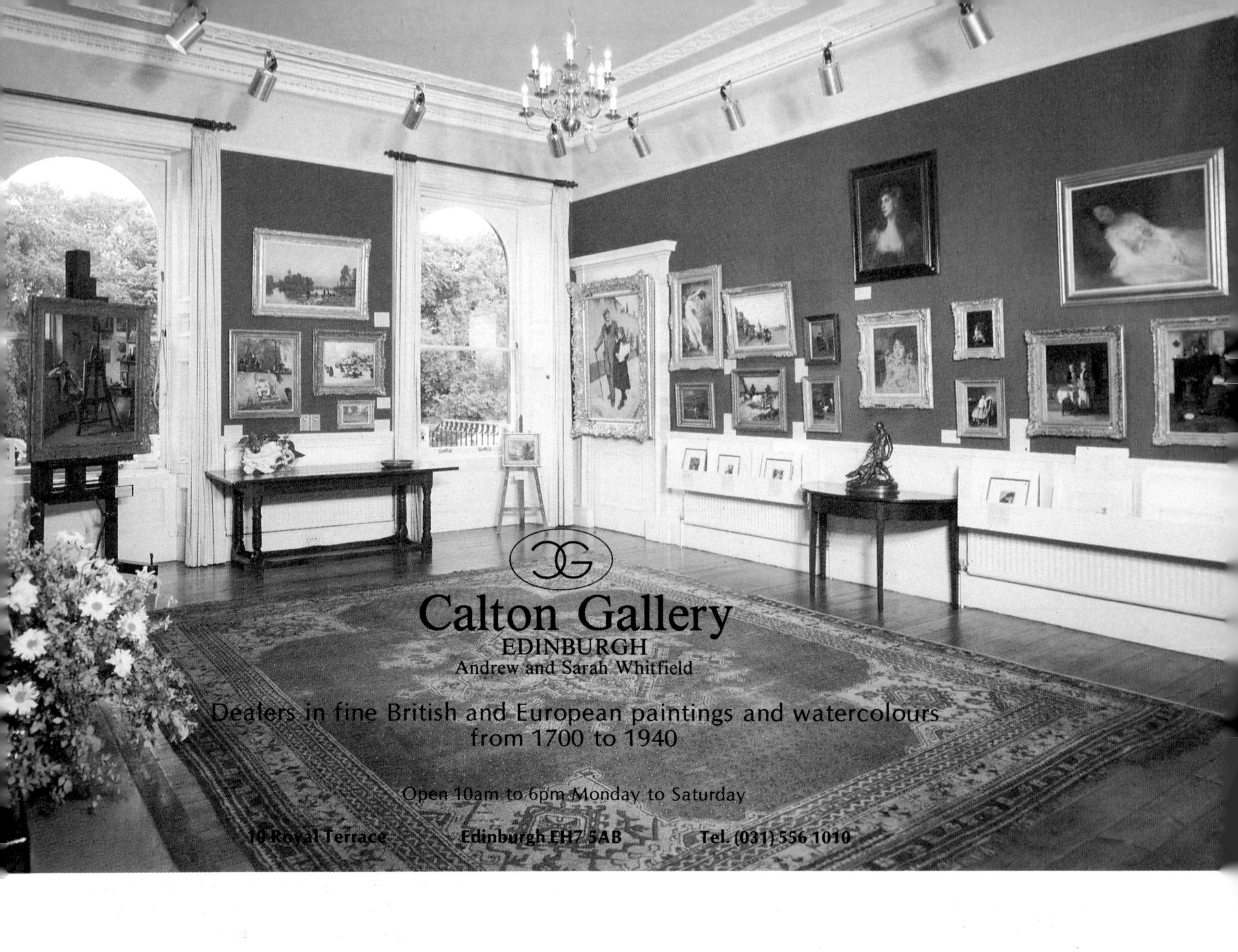
Calton Gallery
EDINBURGH
Andrew and Sarah Whitfield
Dealers in fine British and European paintings and watercolours
from 1700 to 1940
Open 10am to 6pm Monday to Saturday
10 Royal Terrace
Edinburgh EH7 5AB
Tel. (031) 556 1010

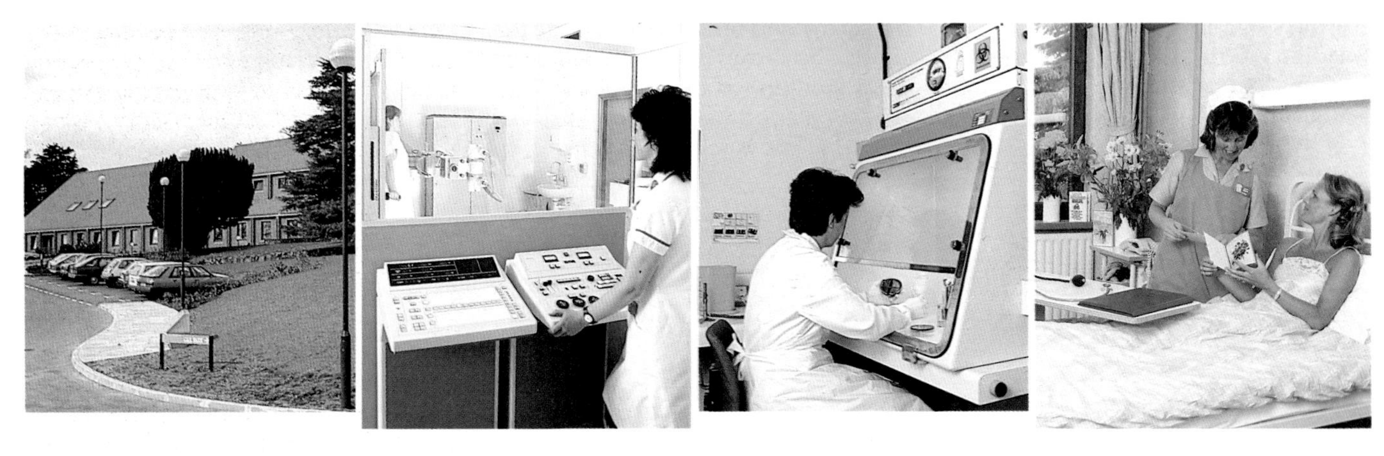

MURRAYFIELD
HOSPITAL
EDINBURGH

Dawn Fraser

Britain's number one breaststroke swimmer, introducing me to her mother and saying "This is my mum who is going to persuade you that I am going to win the final". My immediate thoughts were "We'll see about that".

Fortunately, this incident never affected our friendship; in fact Chris was one of my room-mates in Rome two years later. Unfortunately, Chris's hopes of winning the 220 yards breaststroke final never materialised, for I won the final and poor Chris was relegated to the bronze medal position. Another English girl, Jackie Dyson, took the silver.

This was not the end of the dream start to my swimming career, more was yet to come . . . all this and I had not even competed in our own national championships. After my success in the 220 yards I was selected to swim the breaststroke leg of England's medley relay and what a line up . . . Judy Grinham on backstroke, myself, Chris Gosden on butterfly and the young Di Wilkinson on freestyle. Everyone hoped and thought we could beat the mighty Australians but we were worried about their anchor swimmer, the great Dawn Fraser, Olympic champion and world record holder.

To be in with a chance we knew we had to put Di in with at least a three yard lead! Could we do this? Judy, winner of the gold in the 100m backstroke, we knew would put us in the lead, but could Chris and I increase that lead? It was going to be difficult!

All that day the four of us were inseparable. At the village, which was the RAF base, we had their regulation beds which were narrow to say the least. But that did not put the four of us off. We spent the whole afternoon in one bed, yes the four of us . . . two at one end the other two at the other end. Even this was not easy: Chris was 6ft tall, I am 5ft 11ins, Judy 5ft 8ins and Di just a little shorter. But there we sat and chatted all afternoon, never allowing each other to think of the task ahead.

We had tea of strawberries and cream. Di and I often laugh about this now, because for a long time afterwards her mother always gave her strawberries and cream before an important race.

The race is academic now but it went just as we hoped. Judy gave us the lead we wanted. Chris and I managed to put Di in well enough ahead of Dawn. Despite Dawn's split of the fastest time ever recorded by a women over the 110 yards she could not catch Di. Not only had we won the gold medal but we had also broken the world record.

In our excitement we all jumped in the water, congratulating each other. Our team manager, Alf Price, had been so convinced we would win that he had been out and bought us all charm bracelets. For me it was unbelievable, three months earlier I had been undecided as to which stroke to concentrate on. Should it be freestyle or breaststroke? Reluctantly I had chosen breaststroke and here I was a double gold medallist, with a share in a world record.

By the time the next Commonwealth Games came round I had gained a lot of swimming experience and had collected an Olympic gold medal, but still looked forward to the Commonwealth Games which this time were to be held in Perth, Western Australia. Each Games has it's own special memories. Perth will always live with me for its beautiful hot weather and friendly people.

Since retiring from competitive swimming I have had the pleasure of attending the last four Commonwealth Games as the swimming correspondent of the *Sunday Telegraph* and the last three with the BBC Radio commentary team. Even the journalists and broadcasters appear more friendly at these Games, or perhaps it is because the language barrier is not so acute.

Because this year's Games are in Edinburgh, more British competitors will get the chance to take part. For most it will be the taking part that they will remember for the rest of their lives but they will be happy memories that last a long, long time.

Ron Hill

My 1970 marathon

Winning the Commonwealth Games Marathon of 1970 was not the highlight of my marathon career, but it was the zenith. My winning time of 2:09.28 was the best of my life.

This marathon ended a remarkable (for me) progression of improvement and was the product of the crystallisation of all my training and peaking experience over many years.

The progression started a year earlier, almost to the day, when I won the Maxol (Manchester) Marathon, the trial race for the European Championships, in Athens, in September, in a personal best time of 2:13.42, defeating the then world record holder, Derek Clayton of Australia, by almost 2 minutes. Remarkably, my previous best had been set five years previously: 2:14.12 in the 'Polytechnic', Windsor to Chiswick, Marathon of 1964.

The European Championships Marathon in Athens in 1969 was emotionally my greatest victory, even though my winning time was only 2:16.48. At 32K I was 2 minutes behind the leader, Belgium's Gaston Roelants, but dramatically snatched the lead with only 1 kilometre remaining. My first ever 'Games medal', on the 'classic' course, Marathon to Athens, and with my wife and two sons, mother and father there to see my (and their!) triumph.

As a result of these two victories I was invited to run the famous Fukuoka Marathon in Japan. Victory was not mine there, that honour went to Canada's Jerome Drayton, who finished 41 seconds ahead of me, but my time of 2:11.54 had been achieved with what seemed relative ease.

As a result of the European win, another race had been arranged for me in April of 1970: the famous Boston Marathon, which had been going since 1897. No Briton had ever won it despite attempts by British champions Jim Peters and Brian Kilby, and the Road Runners Club of Great Britain opened a fund to raise money for my air fare. They succeeded.

This was to be a dream race for me. Jerome Drayton was entered and the American press billed it as a grudge contest following my defeat at his hands, or legs, in Fukuoka. I was happy to talk to the press but Drayton could not be contacted anywhere. He had gone to ground. He appeared shortly before the start, and immediately the gun fired, we blasted it, head to head, into cold rain and an adverse wind. By eleven miles, he was gone, out of the race. I had no idea what pace I was running, as the split times were given at odd distances such as 10.3 miles, 13.3 miles, 17.3 miles, but I held it together to the finish. Even then I had no idea of my finish time as there was no digital clock on the line as in modern day marathons, but later the news filtered through, as I was receiving my medal and laurel wreath, that I had done 2:10.30, knocking around 3 minutes off the previous record. To me it was amazing, especially on such an awful day.

This performance got me into the Edinburgh Commonwealth Games without having to run a trial, but even a run of this calibre did not give me automatic entry for England and the selectors said something like, "You make your own mind up whether you run or not, but if we were you we would be reasonably certain that three people will not beat your time in the trial race". It was a slight gamble, I did not run, and no-one beat my time.

My preparation for Edinburgh was ideal. After Boston I had four weeks 'rest': 61 miles (including the 26 of the marathon), 29, 32, 51 miles. Then commenced ten weeks of training: 100 miles, 120, 128, 128, 130, 140, 108 (a short week of this, as at the end of it I ran the 10000 metres for Great Britain against East Germany, on the cinders of the White City Stadium; I was 3rd in 28:40.0), 117½, then a 'taper down' week for the marathon race on Thursday, July 28th.

The race itself was almost a world championship, as the best marathon runners in the world at that time were all from the British Commonwealth. Derek Clayton (Australia), Jerome Drayton

(Canada), defending champion Jim Alder (Scotland), Bill Adcocks (England), Jack Foster (New Zealand), and of course myself.

The day was cool and damp, turning to warm and humid as the race progressed, and it was a totally uninhibited competition. As was the norm then, split times were given only every 5 miles, and at the first check point, passed in 23:31, there were only four left at the head of the field, Drayton, Philip Ndoo (Kenya), myself, and Clayton who was faltering. By 8 miles I was away on my own, passing 10 miles in 47:45.

I turned in 1:02.35 and headed for home trying to smile and giving the thumbs up sign as the other runners went through in the opposite direction. At 15 miles (72:18) everyone had passed me on their outward journey and I was alone and starting to get tired, 20 miles in 1:37.32 could have been a shock, but I told myself that I had run 1:36.28 for the same distance in 1968 and therefore should have something in hand. The finishing time did not interest me, just winning the gold medal. Doing a good job and getting the gold was the goal. No mistakes, fast times could come later.

There was a long climb over the last couple of miles to Meadowbank, but thankfully I made it and cruised round the final 400m, on the carpet-like track in 75 seconds to record 2:09.28. I had done the job well.

Sorrowfully, that remains my best time. A series of enforced trials for major games, despite that performance, led to injuries and below potential performances.

My interest in running was sparked off, at the beginning of the 50s, by a character in a boy's comic, the *Rover*, by the name of Alf Tupper, 'The Tough of the Track'. Well, some twenty years later, in 1970 Alf was still going, now in comic strip form and in a new magazine called the *Victor*. Alf ran the Commonwealth Marathon in Edinburgh, too, not for England, as due to injury he had been left out of the team, but as the sole representative of Tristan da Cunha! Fortified by a bag of fish and chips at the half way point, Alf passed two runners on the final lap in the stadium to take the title in a new British Record.

I wonder if I've got any ancestors from Tristan da Cunha?

Lynn Davies

looks back at his days at the Games

For Welsh Competitors the Commonwealth Games are a special occasion, giving us the opportunity to experience the same thrill and sense of Welsh identity in a major International Games as those lucky enough to wear the red rugby shirt of Wales.

I was fortunate enough to compete for Great Britain in three Olympic Games and four European Championships, win medals, and experienced great pride in wearing the British vest on those occasions. It was a marvellous feeling though to wear the red vest of Wales in three Commonwealth Games, and hear the Welsh National anthem played in the stadium as I stood on the winner's rostrum.

My first experience of the Games came in 1958 at Cardiff as a young spectator at the Empire and Commonwealth Games, as they were then known. I had travelled to the Arms Park on many occasions as a schoolboy to watch my Welsh rugby heroes, but I was there now to see great athletes like Herb Elliott, Dave Power, Tom Robinson and the only Welsh athletics medallist of the Games, John Merriman, who we cheered on to the silver medal in the 6 miles. But the biggest cheer was reserved for the great Ken Jones, who had represented Britain in the 1952 Olympics, Wales in the 1954 Empire Games, and of course as an outstanding international wing three quarter. Ken jogged around the bright red cinder track carrying the message which announced that the Queen had named her son Charles as Prince of Wales.

I met many athletes in the years to follow who had competed in Cardiff and it was good to hear them say how much they enjoyed the first Games hosted by Wales. Little did I realise in Cardiff that four years later I would be flying out to Perth, Western Australia, with the Welsh team to compete in my first Games. It was only the second occasion I had flown, the first being to the Belgrade European Championships a few months earlier. By the time we arrived in Perth, 36 hours after leaving Heathrow, I felt like an experienced traveller. We were exhausted and spent the first three days sleeping.

Indian Ocean

We were housed in brand new bungalows just five minutes from the Indian Ocean and my room-mate was the man I had admired four years ago in Cardiff, John Merriman, who helped me a lot with advice based on years of experience.

Perth was experiencing a freak heatwave at the time and the opening ceremony was held in temperatures well over 100°F. Our red flannel blazers looked great as we marched around the stadium but we were dying to take them off, it was so hot!

It was 112°F as the first rounds of the 100 yards were contested and I discovered what world class sprinting was all about when, despite a cracking start, I was way down on Harry Jerome of Canada in the first 15 yards.

In the long jump the silver medal was in my grasp until the final round when Mike Ahey of Ghana and New Zealander Dave Norris pushed me back to fourth place. I had lost the silver and bronze medals by half an inch and not even a new British record helped. I was bitterly disappointed.

The triple jump was even more traumatic. I had been confined to the sick bay in the village with tonsillitis and traveller's tummy! Deciding however that 12,000 miles was a long way to come just to lie in bed, I climbed out of the window, collected my kit, hitch-hiked to the stadium and warmed up for the qualifying rounds feeling terrible. My legs felt like jelly and collapsed on the hop phase of my first attempt. I finished up with a badly sprained ankle to add to my problems!

Perth was not my most successful Games but I have fond memories of friends made, Australian hospitality, and valuable lessons learned about international athletics.

Four years later we travelled to Kingston, Jamaica, the Games everyone wanted to make. I well remember the excitement amongst the team as we assembled at Heathrow Airport for the flight to the 'Island in the Sun'. We all looked

forward to a great couple of weeks on a Caribbean island, and we were not disappointed.

I was married a few days before going to the Games and although Meriel, my wife, travelled with me, we decided that a conventional honeymoon would be poor preparation for winning a gold medal. So whilst I lived in the village with the rest of the Welsh team she lived in a hotel in Morgan's Harbour, a superb resort and location for the filming of the famous James Bond film *Dr. No.*

This dedication and sacrifice paid off and I won my first Commonwealth gold medal in rather unusual circumstances. We had asked for the rock-hard cinder runway to be watered prior to competition. This was done, but for about three hours by the over-enthusiastic groundsman, and we couldn't believe our eyes when chunks of wet mud clung to our spikes as we practised the run up. We asked for a meeting with the officials, who decided to bring on a heavy roller. Two hours later competition commenced at 8.15 pm. Four hours later, as beer cans were being swept from empty terraces, we were taking our final round jumps on what by now resembled a ploughed field.

Luckily I registered a good distance early on in the second round, which held off a late challenge from John Moreby, who had emigrated to Bermuda from Britain two years earlier.

Lord Swansea won Wales' other gold medal in full bore shooting and his victory ceremony created another incident. He mounted the rostrum, resplendent in the red blazer of Wales, when the band struck up the Scottish anthem. He stepped down and requested the Welsh anthem. The band tried again, closer, but not quite - 'Land of Hope and Glory'. Lord Swansea stepped down again. Luckily Alan Williams, the broadcaster, had by this time sprinted across to the band, explained the situation and within ten minutes 'Land of My Fathers' was being accompanied by the singing of a small group of Welsh supporters as the Welsh flag fluttered proudly in the Jamaican night.

Happy days

Everyone who attended those Games in Jamaica remembers the marvellous hospitality, welcome and warmth of the people. They really were happy days and a great place to be.

Edinburgh in 1970 matched the Kingston Games for the warmth of welcome and hospitality, but not temperature, and I have vivid memories of African athletes jogging around the superb Meadowbank stadium clad in two tracksuits, wet suits and balaclavas! I also remember the food - it was incredible and would have done justice to a five star hotel: starters of huge prawn cocktails, melon, smoked salmon, followed by superb fish dishes and huge T-bone steaks. Team managers, worried that athletes might put on too much weight, would stand at the entrance to the dining room off-loading food from the trays.

It's great when the host nation wins a medal and Lachie Stewart duly obliged for Scotland when he took the 10000 metre gold medal on the first day. We were delighted for him and Scotland and it gave the Scots a great boost.

The long jump pit was situated just below the Royal Box, and much as I hate name dropping I still treasure a photograph of my winning jump being watched by the Royal Family. When the competition was over I was approached by one of the young officials who had been raking the pit. He was a long jumper and questioned me for about an hour on methods of training, diet, weights, technique and so on. It must have helped because he went on to become quite a good athlete. His name was Allan Wells.

Fond memories, unforgettable experiences and great times. I hope competitors in the 1986 Commonwealth Games will enjoy them as much as I enjoyed my three Games. Good luck to Edinburgh and to you all.

Ron Clarke

The lottery loser

Running in the Commonwealth Games is like entering a lottery. Some events can be as hard to win as the Olympics - others fall short of the highest international class.

Unfortunately, the distance events were as tough as the Olympics, for me anyway.

I well remember sitting around on the bicycle track in Kingston in 1966 waiting for the 6 miles to start and thinking at last I had found a Games event that was literally a shoo-in. The only dilemma that concerned me was when to put in a couple of hard laps and burn everybody off. The race started very late, but it was so humid that the lack of a warm-up whilst we waited around didn't disturb anyone. I wouldn't lead straight away . . . just jog along for a while.

As the early pace became so slow, my normal impatience took over and , in a flash of brilliance (or so I thought at that time), I changed plans and decided to throw in a couple of hard laps early, get away from everybody, and then run steadily on in.

And it worked, I ran some quicker ones, no one went with me, and I settled down all alone. Then, pitter, patter, pitter someone catches me. I look around and see little Naftali Temu. I remembered racing him in a 5000 metres earlier in the year in Berlin after he had been given a bit of a build-up. Then, and it was only six weeks or so previously, he had been no trouble so I wasn't too concerned about him joining me in the lead in Kingston - I would just run on steadily. Wrong. Never underestimate anyone. You would have thought I would have learnt that lesson two years earlier in Tokyo when another 'also ran', Billy Mills, streamed home with an inspired last lap. In Kingston Temu had an inspired last four laps as I succumbed to the humidity and tottered on in second position.

Two days later I had to race his Kenyan compatriot Kip Keino in the three miles and, after giving the Kenyan team an invaluable confidence booster with Temu's success, I wasn't likely to dent Keino's record, particularly as I always felt him to have more ability than I did when his spirit was normal. To beat him I had to catch him on a 'down' day.

So my memories of the Commonwealth Games were that disastrous race, my first experience four years earlier in Perth (1962), and my last hurrah in Edinburgh in 1970, when Lachie Stewart did a 'Temu' on me.

In lots of ways the Commonwealth Games are a more enjoyable competition than the Olympics. They're smaller, so athletes are usually treated a little better than merely pieces of meat making up an interesting logistics problem, as is their wont at the Olympics. I sometimes felt an ideal Olympics for most officials would be one when the performers could be locked up without food and water until it became time for their 'treat' - then they could be let out in small batches, preferably chained to each other so none would be lost en route, allowed to compete, then shipped home.

The Commonwealth Games have a lot fewer sports on their programme, a smaller village and a common heritage - that's the theory of it at least - and these factors make it a more personal and relaxed atmosphere.

Perth in 1962 was my first Games of any sort. The village was right on City Beach, the late November sunshine was perfect for sun-bathing and swimming on the squeaky, pure white sands which are a feature of Perth's miles and miles of beaches. Add to this background the people of Perth themselves, who would never let a tracksuited figure walk to any destination without offering them a lift and often a meal and a tour of the city as well. I remember spending the day before the Games started, water skiing on the Swan river with Trevor Vincent (eventual steeplechase winner) and a host of friends in beautiful 90°F sunshine.

My main event, the 3 miles (I also ran the six but, at that time, thought it far too far to do any good at it), had a cream field: Bruce Tulloh (England) had just won the European 5000

metres championship; Murray Halberg (New Zealand) was the world record holder (13:10.0); defending Commonwealth Games and current Olympic champion, Bruce Kidd (Canada) was a prodigious 19 year old who had already won the 6 miles and, earlier in the year, inflicted a rare defeat in Los Angeles on Murray Halberg, from which Murrary was still smarting; Alby Thomas (Australia), the former world record holder at 13:10.8; Kip Keino (Kenya), the new African champion; and Pat Clohessy (Australia), straight back from a successful four year stay in the United States where he became the first to win three successive NCAA three-mile championships.

My only confidence booster was a very close pre-Games tussle with Bruce Tulloh over 2 miles. What this did mean was that when I saw Bruce sprint past me down the back straight, it generated me into action and he dragged me past Bruce Kidd for a sub-55 second last lap and a very unexpected silver medal behind Halberg.

I thought that if it was that easy, and all Games villages were that enjoyable, I should get serious about running and so, next winter, I really started training in earnest.

It always seems a pity to me that some of the latter-day top runners have taken to ignoring the Commonwealths. I suppose they have other priorities but, if you can get top grade exciting competition, in the friendly relaxed spirit under which these Games continue to be staged, what more can you ask of your sport - except money!

1.

2.

1. Steve Cram on his way to Commonwealth gold at Brisbane in the 1982 1500 metres.
2. Arching out at the start of the men's backstroke swimming.
3. Debbie Brill warms up for the high jump; she won as a 17 year old in Edinburgh in 1970, and after a silver medal in 1978, won again in 1982.
4. Linford Christie burst to the fore in the 1986 indoor season, when he won the European Indoor 200m title. He could challenge at either 100m or 200m as well as with England's sprint relay team.
5. The massed ranks of the cyclists. The riders have to steer clear of collisions, while watching closely for breaks away from the pack.

3.

4.

5.

XIII Commonwealth Games

The Federation

and Executive Committee Members

The Commonwealth Games Federation

Patron
HM Queen Elizabeth II

President
HRH Prince Philip, Duke of Edinburgh, KG, KT

Life Vice Presidents
The Lord Porritt, GCMG, GCVO, CBE, FRCS
Sir Alexander Ross
K.S. Duncan, OBE

Chairman
P. Heatly, CBE, DL

Vice Chairmen
A. de O. Sales, CBE
S.M. Kamau

Honorary Secretary
D.M. Dixon

Honorary Treasurer
M.B. Phillips

Honorary Medical Adviser
Dr. J. Howel Jones

Honorary Legal Adviser
S.S. Rao

Elected Vice Presidents

Africa:	R.A. Kubaga
America:	N.J. Farrell
Asia:	Tan Sri Hamzah
	B.H. Abu Samah
Caribbean:	K. Henderson
Europe:	R.J. McColgan, MBE
Oceania:	B.J. Wightman

20 Essex Street, London WC2R 3AL, England
Telephone 01-240 1671 Telex 24213

The XIII Commonwealth Games Executive Committee

Chairman
K.W. Borthwick, CBE

Vice Chairmen
Councillor C. Waugh, JP
Councillor A. Wood

Chief Executive
Blair Grosset

General Secretary
G.A. Hunter, OBE

Divisional Chairmen

Administration:	Councillor C. Waugh, JP
Finance:	J.M. Souness
Venues:	O.J. Clarke
Visitors:	J.S. Mackenzie
Sports:	J.B. Hall
Support Services:	Sir John Orr, OBE
Media:	I. McColl, CBE
Ceremonial:	Brigadier M. Thomson
Communications:	R.G. Fraser
Legal:	J.D. Cochrane, WS

Games Headquarters,
Canning House, Canning Street, Edinburgh EH3 8TH
Telephone 031-248 1986

Contributors

The Editors

Peter Matthews is a sports editor of the *Guinness Book of Records* and one of the ITV commentary team on athletics. Before leaving in 1984 to pursue a freelance career as author and broadcaster, he was editorial director of *Guinness Superlatives Ltd.* For BBC Radio he covered the Commonwealth Games of 1978 and 1982, and 16 years ago in Edinburgh he was chief announcer at Meadowbank Stadium for the athletics. His *Athletics - the Records* was published by Guinness in 1986.

Stan Greenberg was sports editor of the *Guinness Book of Records* from 1976 to 1982 and is author of *The Guinness Book of Olympic Facts and Feats.* He has worked as the BBC Television athletics statistician for many years and at Edinburgh will be working for them for the fifth time at a Commonwealth Games.

David Wilkie won Commonwealth swimming gold medals for Scotland at 200m breaststroke and 200m medley in 1974. He went on to win the Olympic 200m breaststroke title in 1976. He writes and commentates on swimming, and is a director of a sports sponsorship consultancy.

Mary Peters had a long and most distinguished athletics career, highlighted by her Olympic pentathlon victory in 1972. She competed at five Commonwealth Games, winning three gold medals and a silver. She was BBC Sports Personality of the Year in 1972, and now runs the Mary Peters Health Club in Lisburn, Northern Ireland.

Ron Clarke won four Commonwealth silver medals and revolutionised distance running standards in the 1960s. His brilliant running thrilled a generation and he set a total of 18 world records. He is managing director of Cannons Sports Clubs in the UK.

Lynn Davies jumped into the record books as the first athlete to hold simultaneously Olympic (1964), European (1966) and Commonwealth (1966) athletics titles. He added a second Commonwealth long jump gold for Wales in 1970.

Ron Hill won the 1970 Commonwealth marathon in Edinburgh. He was European marathon champion in 1969 and represented Britain at three Olympic Games from 1964 to 1972. Still a very active runner, he ran his 100th marathon in 1985. He is managing director of Ron Hill Sports Ltd.

Anita Lonsbrough won five Commonwealth swimming gold medals, an Olympic gold medal, and a gold, two silver and two bronze medals at the European Championships. She was twice voted Sportswoman of the Year by both the Sports Writers' Association and the readers of the *Daily Express.* In 1962 she became the first woman to win the BBC Sports Personality of the Year, and was awarded the MBE in 1963. She is a freelance journalist, reporting on swimming for the *Sunday Telegraph* and she commentates on the sport for BBC Radio. Married to Hugh Porter, cycling contributor to this book.

Bowls

Patrick Sullivan is technical editor of *World Bowls Magazine* and is bowls correspondent to *The Guardian* and a contributor to *The Observer.* He is author of *Bowls - The Records,* published by Guinness in 1986 and is also a writer and broadcaster on jazz. He is printing supervisor at the University of Kent in Canterbury.

Boxing

Harry Carpenter is an internationally renowned expert on boxing and long-time sports presenter on BBC Television. A former Fleet Street journalist, he has covered all Olympic and Commonwealth Games since 1956.

Badminton and Weightlifting

Sandy Sutherland, who lives in Edinburgh, has been a freelance journalist since 1973 and has covered the last four Commonwealth Games. He writes on athletics, badminton and weightlifting for the *Scotsman* and the Edinburgh *Evening News.* He was twice Scottish champion at the shot put as well as Scottish junior mid-heavy weightlifting champion, and his wife Liz set British and Commonwealth records at 400m hurdles in 1977-8.

Cycling

Hugh Porter won the Commonwealth gold medal at pursuit cycling in 1966. He turned professional the following year and went on to win a record four world professional pursuit titles. He was awarded the MBE in 1973 for his services to sport. He will be working for BBC TV in Edinburgh.

Shooting

David Parish is a member of the rifle committee of the UIT, shooting's international governing body. He was president of the rifle jury at the 1984 Olympic Games and was four times British small bore rifle champion.

Judo and Wrestling

John Goodbody, a Fleet Street journalist for 20 years, has always been fascinated by combat sports and was himself a member of the British judo squad in 1970 when he also practised freestyle wrestling. He has reported 51 sports at international level, and on five Olympic Games.

Rowing

Richard Ayling has been editor of *Rowing Magazine* since 1976. He contributes regularly to the *Daily Express* and many rowing publications throughout the world. As a rower he represented Britain at the 1974 World Championships and was a member of the 1976 Olympic team. He is deeply involved in the sport as a coach, the current ARA director of coaching, and through his profession as a racing boatbuilder with the family company of Aylings Racing Boats at East Molesey.

Swimming and Diving

Pat Besford is the doyenne of swimming journalists, swimming correspondent of the *Daily Telegraph*, and edited the *Encyclopaedia of Swimming.* She is president of the swimming committee of the AIPS, the international sports journalists' association, and is press attache of the England Commonwealth Games and British Olympic Associations.